STUDIES

IN THE

SCRIPTURES

"The Path of the Just is as the Shining Light,
Which Shineth More and More
Unto the Perfect Day."

SERIES II

The Time is at Hand

1,209,000 Edition.

"Times of Refreshing Shall Come From the Presence of the Lord; and He Shall Send Jesus Christ, * * * Whom the Heavens Must Retain until
THE TIMES OF RESTITU-
TION OF ALL THINGS
Which God Hath Spoken by the Mouth of All His Holy Prophets Since the World Began." "Ye Brethren, Are Not in Darkness, That That Day Should Overtake You as a Thief."—Acts 3: 19-21; 1 Thes. 5 : 4.

INTERNATIONAL BIBLE STUDENTS ASSOCIATION
BROOKLYN, LONDON, MELBOURNE, BARMEN,
ELBERFELD, OREBRO, CHRISTIANIA.

1912

To the King of Kings and Lord of Lords

Studies in the Scriptures.

Christian people are becoming more and more awake to the fact that a great tidal wave of unbelief is sweeping over Christendom;—not the blasphemous atheism voiced by Thomas Paine and Robert Ingersoll, but the cultured kind represented in the scholarship of our day, which makes the danger all the more insidious.

Not only are the great Colleges and Seminaries undermining the faith of the better educated, but the Common School books, and especially those used in the High Schools, are similarly inculcating a distrust in the Bible, a contradiction of its teachings. For a college graduate of to-day to declare his faith in the inspiration of the Scriptures would bring upon him the scorn of his companions—a scorn which few would court, or could endure. At very best, a few will be found to claim that they believe that Jesus and his Apostles were sincere, though they blundered in quoting from the Old Testament as inspired.

Such a belief in Jesus and his Apostles is no belief at all; for if present-day "higher critics" are wise enough to know when and where our Lord and his Apostles erred in their quotations from the Old Testament, then these wise men of our day are our proper guides, —more inspired than Jesus and his Apostles.

Our Society, realizing the need, is seeking to do all in its power to stem the tide and lift up the Lord's "standard for *the people*." It has prepared six sets of Bible Studies (of which this volume is one) for Christian people of all denominations to use in lending a helping hand to all perplexed inquirers with whom they may, by God's providence, come in contact. These are supplied at bare cost, and can be had direct from the Society's warerooms or of its colporteurs, who are gradually reaching forth these helping hands far and near. These valuable "studies" are supplied at little more than two cents each;—15 of them well bound in a cloth case, embossed in gold, for 35 cents.

The thought is this: As a Christian man or woman you have children or relatives or neighbors or friends open to your influence—perhaps, indeed, asking your counsel—asking, "How do we know that there is a God?" or, "What proofs have we that the Bible is inspired?" It is no longer wise to call these silly questions, nor to ask, "Are you an infidel?"

However competent you might be to prepare answers to these and a score of other questions, you may not have the needed time and opportunity to do so. How convenient then to step to your book-case, take down the proper study on the subject, and to say to the inquirer, Sit down and read that short study, and the whole matter of your question will be fully and satisfactorily settled; and if your doubts ever again arise come over and read the same afresh.

Possibly you may be a member of an Epworth League or Christian Endeavor Society, or of a Baptist Young People's Union, and may be called on for an essay on some Scripture topic. How convenient to select one among these numerous studies (covering almost every topic) and to find therein the appropriate Scriptures cited. Ministers use them thus when composing special sermons and addresses.

Ministers who have large libraries touching every conceivable religious topic—many volumes costing $6 to $8 per volume—may not feel their need of these "Bible Studies," but to others they are almost indispensable. Indeed, in addition to the price feature, which brings them within the reach of everybody—six volumes of over 3,000 pages for $2.00—the usual price of one such volume—they are written in pure, but simple English, whereas the "scholarly works" are replete with technical terms and only for the few.

We invite Christian people of all denominations to join us in our work of extending these "helping hands" to the rising generation. A single friend or relative helped—rescued from doubt or unbelief—would repay the cost of these studies a thousand times.

CONTENTS.

STUDY I.

SPECIAL TIMES AND SEASONS DIVINELY APPOINTED.

STUDY II.

BIBLE CHRONOLOGY.

STUDY III.

THE FULFILMENT OF TIME-PROPHECY AT THE FIRST ADVENT OF CHRIST.

Dan. 9:23-27.

STUDY IV.

THE TIMES OF THE GENTILES.

STUDY V.

THE MANNER OF OUR LORD'S RETURN
AND APPEARING.

STUDY VI.

EARTH'S GREAT JUBILEE.

STUDY VII.

THE PARALLEL DISPENSATIONS.

STUDY VIII.

ELIAS SHALL FIRST COME.

STUDY IX.

THE MAN OF SIN—ANTICHRIST.

STUDY X.

THE TIME IS AT HAND.

STUDY I.

SPECIAL TIMES AND SEASONS DIVINELY APPOINTED.

The Times and Seasons of Divine Appointment.—Why Not More Plainly Stated.—In Due Time Revealed.—Earnest Desire to Know the Times and Seasons Commendable.—Mistakes of Adventists.—The Real Object of Time Prophecies.—Our Present Position.—The Object of Succeeding Chapters.

AS in "THE PLAN OF THE AGES" we endeavored to set forth the prominent outlines of the divine arrangement for human salvation from a purely Scriptural standpoint, so it is the purpose of this volume to show, on the same authority, that the various features of that plan have definitely appointed times and seasons for their accomplishment; that, so far as that plan has progressed, each succeeding feature of it has been accomplished exactly on time; and that *the time is now at hand* for its culmination in the blessing of all the families of the earth.—Gen. 28: 14; Gal. 3: 16.

During the long centuries of the Gospel age, the Church, as instructed by her Lord, has prayed, "Thy kingdom come; thy will be done on earth as it is done in heaven." But, like drowsy children, because the time was long, many have almost forgotten the import of the words that now seem to die upon their lips. To all such whose hearts are still loyal to the Lord, we call in the words of the Apostle

13

Paul, "It is high time to awake out of sleep; for now is our salvation nearer than when we believed. The night is far spent, the [Millennial] day is at hand." Yea, it is even at the doors. The kingdom of heaven is now at hand, not in its mere embryotic or incipient stage, as at our Lord's first advent (Matt. 3:2), but in the sense in which he declared it was yet to come (John 18:36, 37)—"in power and great glory."

Only those, however, who have made a careful study of the Plan of the Ages will be prepared to appreciate the teaching of this volume concerning the divinely appointed times and seasons for the development of the various features of that plan, and for its final consummation. It is hoped that none will undertake this study, therefore, before they have thoroughly comprehended the lessons of the preceding volume. Otherwise it will not be meat in due season to them. Truth is only meat in season when we are prepared to receive it. A child is not prepared to solve a mathematical problem until he has first been instructed in the use of figures and of language. So also with divine truth: it is built up step by step, and to gain an understanding of it we must ascend by the steps provided—carefully, of course, proving by the Scriptures every advance step we take, yet not fearful to take the steps as we thus find for them sure footing. Only those who have implicit faith in God, and to whom a "Thus saith the Lord" is the end of all doubt and controversy, can be led by the Spirit of God into advanced truth as it becomes due—led into things new, as well as confirmed in things old and proved true by the same authority.

Only such, God proposes so to lead. In the end of the age, which is the harvest time, much truth is due to be uncovered, which God did not make known in times past, even to his most faithful and devoted children. It was in *the time of the end* that the Prophet Habakkuk (2 : 3) declared that the vision, concerning the glorious consummation of God's plan, should speak and not lie; and that to some of God's children it should speak so plainly that they would be able, as directed, to make it plain on tables; that through their instrumentality others might be enabled to read it clearly: and then Daniel also (12 : 4, 9, 10) declared that knowledge should be increased, and that the wise (through faith) should understand the vision.

Our object here is not to prophesy out of the abundance of human imagination, nor in any sense to be wise above what is written in the sacred Scriptures. Therefore, discarding all human inventions, we keep close to the fountain of divine truth, endeavoring to read prophecy in the light of prophecy and its manifest fulfilment; and to make plain upon tables that which God said would be sealed up, and which therefore could not be understood before this time of the end, but of which he gave assurance that it should *then* be understood.

In this volume we offer a chain of testimony on the subject of God's appointed times and seasons, each link of which we consider Scripturally strong, while the whole of it when viewed together, in the relationship which one part bears to another, gives evidence of a plan so broad and comprehensive, a design so deep, and a harmony so perfect, as to clearly manifest to the studious and reverent inquirer that it is beyond the breadth and depth of human thought, and therefore cannot be of human origin.

We find that the end of the Gospel age, like the end of the Jewish age, is called a harvest (Matt. 9 : 37; 13 : 24, 30, 39); that like that also, it is a period of forty years; and that upon the harvests of the ages the rays of prophetic testimony are specially concentrated, particularly upon the harvest of this age, where even all the light of the Jewish age—because of its typical character—converges in a glorious focus. In this light we may now distinctly see the stately steppings of our God, not only in the long vista of the ages past, but also in the present outworkings of his plan. And not only so, but according to his promise to show us things to come (John 16 : 13), we see, with wonderful distinctness of vision, his wise policy for the blessing of all in the incoming Millennial age—even down to its glorious consummation in the restitution of all things. We find that many great and wonderful events center in this harvest : that in it occur the great time of trouble, the day of Jehovah ; the final and complete overthrow of Antichrist and the fall of Great Babylon ; the beginning of returning favor to the Jew ; the second advent of our Lord and the establishment of his kingdom ; and the resurrection and reward of the saints.

We find in prophecy the beginning and the ending of this harvest period clearly marked, as well as the events due to occur in it. And to call attention to and trace the various lines of prophetic time to the events in which they culminate is, in substance, the object of this volume. To receive its testimony, the reader will need to have an ear to hear (Rev. 2 : 7 ; Matt. 11 : 15), and must expect meekly to cast away many preconceived opinions as fast as he comes to see their lack of harmony with God's Word. To such as are thus minded, and who pursue the lessons of this volume with patience and care, and in the order of their arrangement, we doubt not it will be a great blessing. If its lessons are received into good and honest hearts, we trust it will be a power to separate them from the world and to ripen them as wheat for the garner. To thus quicken and ripen and separate the saints, as wheat from tares, in this time of harvest, is the object for which, we apprehend, these prophecies now unfolding were designed by our Lord.

Those permitted to view God's grand chart of the ages, which so clearly maps out the orderly arrangement, the deep design and the wonderful scope of the divine plan as set forth in the preceding volume, should be anxious to discover whatever God may be pleased to reveal concerning its times and seasons. Their interest in this subject should be many fold greater than that of any in the past ages who did not see the great blessings in reservation for all. Faithful children of God long to know when the King of Glory shall come in, and the prince of darkness be bound; when the children of the light shall shine forth as the sun, and the darkness be scattered; when the saints shall be received into full divine adoption, and the groaning creation released from the bondage of corruption; and when our heavenly Father's glorious character shall be fully revealed to an astonished world, causing all who love righteousness to bow their hearts in adoration and love and obedience.

To be devoid of such desires indicates a lack of interest in, and appreciation of, God's plans. The apostles, the prophets and the angels all desired and sought earnestly to know what *time* the spirit of God indicated through the prophets. And this interest on the part of his children is ever pleasing to God; for though he never heretofore gratified such desires to any considerable extent, because the due time had not yet come, he never once chided such interest. On the contrary, he called the inquiring Daniel greatly beloved, and answered his inquiry so far as was consistent with his plan.

Such inquiry, therefore, should not be regarded as an improper prying into the secrets of God. God would have us manifest that interest in his plans which would "search the Scriptures," and "take heed to the sure word of prophecy," and thus be in that proper, waiting attitude which will quickly discern the truth as it becomes *due.* Secret

2–B

things belong unto God, but things revealed belong unto us and our children forever. (Deut. 29 : 29.) Therefore, if we confine ourselves strictly to the Word of God, and avoid idle speculation, we are on safe ground. If God's plan and times and seasons are not recorded in the Scriptures, none can find them there; and God has surely had nothing recorded by his prophets and apostles which he desires to keep secret forever. In due time and order every recorded feature of the divine plan, and its time and season, is manifested to those watching; but the entire outline of the plan, together with the time features of it, was not due to be understood until the period designated "The time of the end." (Dan. 12 : 9, 10.) And let it be borne in mind that until such time as God purposes to reveal his secrets, neither learning nor piety can find them out. Although the prophecies have stood for centuries before the eyes of all, they *could not* be unlocked and their secrets read until the due time had come.

When some of the disciples came to our Lord inquiring concerning the time for the establishment of the Kingdom of God, before it was yet due to be revealed, he answered, "It is not for you to know the times or the seasons which the Father hath appointed by his own authority." Acts 1 : 7.) And on another occasion, concerning the same subject, he said, "Of that day and hour knoweth no man, no, not the angels who are in heaven, neither the Son, but the Father. Take ye heed, watch and pray; for ye know not when the time is. . . . And what I say unto you, I say unto all, *Watch.*"—Mark 13 : 32, 33, 37.

These words of our Lord cannot be understood to mean that none but the Father will *ever* know of his times and seasons; hence it no more proves that we cannot know those times and seasons *now*, than that our Lord cannot know them now. And the very fact that the entire outline of our Father's plan, and also his times and seasons, are now clearly discernible, is strong proof that we are now living in the time of the end of the present dominion of evil, and the dawn of the Millennial Day, when knowledge should be increased, and the wise should understand. (Dan. 12 : 4, 10.) If prophecy was never designed to be understood, there could have been no reasonable object in giving it.

These expressions of the Master indicate that God is not executing the various parts of his plan in a random, haphazard manner, but that he has *fixed* and definite times and seasons for every feature of his great work. And his infinite power and wisdom guarantee that there can be no miscarriage or delay.

The words also impress the thought that up to that time the Father had revealed the times and seasons connected with his plans to no one, not even to our Lord Jesus. So far from warranting the general supposition, that our Lord rebuked investigation and interest in the times and seasons, and by these words *forbade* such examination, the very reverse is true. His words clearly show that though the times and seasons were *not yet* given to them to know, they would be very important some time, and would then be revealed to those watching. In view of the fact that they would be unsealed some time, and that they would be very important *then*, he urges them to "*take heed*," and not to allow indifference to come over them, but to "*watch*" continually, that they might know when the due time should come.

Those who *watched* all down the age, though they did not see all they watched for, were nevertheless greatly blessed and kept separate from the world, by so doing; while those who will be living in the "*due time*" and shall obediently "*watch*," shall know, shall see, "shall understand," and not be in ignorance, in the midst of the wonderful events of the "harvest" of this age. He who at any time neglects to watch, loses a blessing upon which the Master laid great stress, and proves himself to be either blinded with prejudice by the god of this world, or overcharged with matters of this life and present interests, to the neglect of his vow of full consecration to the Lord, to seek chiefly the Kingdom and life to come.

The Apostles Peter and Paul call attention to this subject of the times and seasons. Peter declares (2 Pet. 1:16), that we are not following cunningly devised fables; that he saw in a figure the glory of the coming kingdom of Christ on the mount of transfiguration, when he beheld the glorious "*vision*" of Moses and Elijah and Jesus in glittering garments,—Moses representing the ancient worthies (Heb. 11: 38–40) who shall be the earthly representatives of the heavenly Kingdom, and Elijah representing the "overcomers" of this Gospel age—the scene as a whole foreshadowing the "glory to follow," after the sufferings for righteousness' sake shall have completed the election according to favor. Yet Peter, even while relating his vision, points to the prophetic testimony, saying, "We have a *more sure* word of prophecy, whereunto ye do well that ye take heed as unto a light that shineth in a dark place until the Day-dawn." (2 Pet. 1:19.) He well knew that all the prophecies could not be fully understood by any *then*, and thus urged a watching attitude on the part of the saints—not a watching of the sky, but a watching for the fulfilment of all that God had spoken by the holy prophets concerning the restitution, and the "*times* of restitution*,*" which form so large and important a part of their testimony. He assures us that prophecy will have freshly important truths for us, all the way along *until* Day-dawn.

The Apostle Paul declares, " Of the times and seasons, brethren, ye have no need that I write unto you; for yourselves know perfectly that the Day of the Lord so cometh as a thief in the night. [Quietly, stealthily it will come, and after it has come, many will not for some time know that they are in it.] When they shall say, Peace and safety, then sudden destruction cometh upon them [sudden or rapid, compared with the slow processes of the past six thousand years, as our day is called the fast day of steam and electricity—not sudden as lightning, but sudden] *as travail* upon a woman. But ye, brethren, are not in darkness, that that day should overtake you as a thief."—1 Thess. 5: 1–4.

The "brethren" all have the lamp, the sure word of prophecy mentioned by Peter, as a light in a dark place; and while they keep the proper attitude of brethren, as faithful, meek and humble students of the Word, they will at no time be in darkness: *they* will always have the truth supplied as meat in *due season.* At no time have those then living in full harmony with God been left in ignorance of necessary truth, to grope their way in the dark with the world. Abraham and Lot knew of the destruction of Sodom *beforehand*, God saying, "Shall I hide from Abraham that thing which I do?" (Gen. 18: 17.) Noah knew of the flood in time to build the ark, and was informed of the *very day* that he should go into it. At the first advent, too, Simeon and Anna, and the wise men of the East, knew to expect Messiah. In fact, the expectation was general then. (Luke 2: 25–38; Matt. 2: 2; Luke 3: 15.) And if God so dealt with the house of servants, shall he do less for the house of Sons? Our Lord and Head has said, "Henceforth I call you not servants, for the servant knoweth not what his Lord doeth; but I have called you friends, for all things *that I have heard of my Father I have made known unto you.*" Our Lord certainly shall know of the times and seasons in *due time*, since he is to accomplish the plan, and unless *he has changed*, he will make known the plans to those close to him and associated in his work—*his friends, his saints.*

Reason, then, teaches us that so surely as it is written, "The Lord will do nothing, but he revealeth his secret unto his servants the prophets" (Amos 3 : 7), and that most of what he revealed unto them was not for themselves, but for us, the Gospel Church (1 Pet. 1 : 12), so surely will the faithful not be left in darkness, unable to discern it, when the day of the Lord has come. It will not come upon *them* as a thief and a snare—unawares ; for they will be watching, and will have the promised light then due upon the subject.

The Apostle states why he makes the positive assertion that ye, brethren, will know of the times and seasons when due, and will not be in darkness, saying (verse 5), "Ye are all the children of light, and the children of the day." Such are begotten of the truth, and are to be developed by the truth more and more unto the perfect day—to which they belong.—James 1 : 18 ; John 17 : 17, 19.

Notice how carefully the pronouns *ye* and *you*, and *they* and *them*, of this and other Scriptures, distinguish the classes referred to—the saints from the world. The knowledge which the saints will have in the day of the Lord is contrasted with the ignorance, on the part of the world, of the significance and tendency of transpiring events—"*Ye* have no need that I write unto *you*." "When *they* shall say, Peace and safety, then sudden destruction cometh upon *them* . . . and *they* shall not escape. But *ye*, brethren, are not in darkness that that day should overtake *you* as a thief. *Ye* are all children of the light." "Take heed," says our Lord, "to yourselves, lest at any time *your* hearts be overcharged with surfeiting, and drunkenness, and cares of this life, and so that day come upon *you* unawares ; for as a snare it shall come on all *them* that dwell on the face of the whole earth. Watch *ye*, therefore [watch yourselves and also the word of prophecy], and pray always, that *ye* may be accounted worthy to escape all these things that shall come to pass, and to stand before the Son of man."—Luke 21 : 24–36.

It follows, then, that if a child of God, living in the day of the Lord, remain in darkness or ignorance as to the fact, he must be either surfeited with the things of this life and intoxicated with the spirit of the world, or else overcharged with the cares of this life, and in either case indifferently neglecting to watch with his lamp trimmed and burning and with oil in his vessel—*i. e.*, with the Word of God in heart and mind, and with the spirit of truth in himself.

Though much, connected with the times and seasons, as well as with the details of the plan, had been foretold by the prophets, they confessed their ignorance of the import of the prophecies to which they gave expression. (See Dan. 12 : 8; Ezek. 20 : 49; Matt. 13 : 17; 1 Pet. 1 : 20–12.) Stated in dark and symbolic language, and linked with events then future, to understand them then was impossible. Thus, though recorded aforetime, and made to bear witness to the divine foreknowledge and arrangement, they were for the learning of those living in the due time for their fulfilment, and not for those who uttered them. (Rom. 15 : 4.) They awaited the unfolding of various connected features of the divine plan and human history, which, by God's arrangement, should unlock them, and enrich the patient, searching children of God with "meat in due season" for an hour of trial and need in "the evil day"—the day of trouble with which this age closes, and in the midst of which also the new era and dispensation dawns.

A wonderful modern device, which serves well to illustrate the divine arrangement of time prophecy, is what is termed a Combination Time-Lock, used in some of the largest banks. Like other combination locks, the key or handle remains in the lock constantly. Certain peculiar movements of the handle, known only to one aware of the arrangement, are needful to open it, while the slightest deviation from the proper movements only complicates the matter and makes it the more difficult to open. The Combination *Time*-Lock adds the peculiar feature, that by a clock arrangement inside the bank vaults, the doors when closed at night are so locked that they cannot be opened by any one until a fixed hour the next morning; and then, only in response to the use of the right combination upon which the lock has been set.

Thus our Heavenly Father has closed up and sealed many features of his plan during the night with his great Time-Lock, which was so set as to prevent their being opened until " the time appointed "— in the morning of the great day of restitution. And then Jehovah's Anointed, " he that hath the key" and understands the combination upon which it has been set, "openeth, and no man shutteth." (Rev. 3: 7.) He opens unto us by giving us the necessary information as to how the key of prophecy is to be operated by those desiring to find the treasures of infinite wisdom. And we may unlock the treasures of divine wisdom now, because the morning hour has come—though it is early and not yet light to the world. But only by carefully heeding the instructions, and applying the key to the combination set by the great Designer, will its treasures open to us.

In fact, this illustration fits the entire plan of God in all its parts: Each feature of truth and each prophecy is but a part of the one grand combination, which may be opened now because it is morning—because the bolts of the great Time-Lock are withdrawn. And this grand combination, once opened, discloses fully and grandly the boundless treasures of divine wisdom, justice, love and power. He who opens will indeed know God as never before.

Let us, then, examine the Scriptures with a reverent spirit, that we may learn what God is pleased to show us with reference to his times and seasons. Since he has recently made the grand outlines of his plan so clear, we may reasonably expect that his time is due to lead us into a knowledge of its time features. The times and seasons were wisely hidden in the past, and the saints were thus saved from discouragement, because the time was long; but as the plan nears its glorious consummation, it is the privilege of the saints to know it, that they may lift up their heads and rejoice, knowing that their deliverance draweth nigh. (Luke 21 : 28.) The revealing of the time, in the "time of the end," will be as profitable and stimulating to the saints as its revealing before would have been unprofitable and discouraging.

Evidently our God is a God of order. Every thing that he does is in accordance with a definitely pre-arranged plan; and his appointed times and seasons are no insignificant or unimportant part of that plan. Notice that Jesus was born on time—"*In the fulness of time* God sent his only begotten Son." (Gal. 4: 4.) Not before, nor after, but just when the time was full. Our Lord's first preaching was on the subject of time,—"He came preaching, and saying, *The time is fulfilled.* . . . Repent and believe the good tidings." (Mark 1 : 15.) "*In due time* Christ died." (Rom. 5 : 6.) "He rose again the third day [at the appointed time] *according to the Scriptures.*" (1 Cor. 15 : 4.) During his ministry his enemies frequently sought to take him, but it is stated that they could not, "*because his hour was not yet come.*"—John 7 : 30.

The time-prophecies were not given to satisfy mere curiosity, but to enable the student of the Word to recognize the foretold events *when due.* For instance : Although prophecy marked the time and manner of the first advent, it was not understood until Christ had come; and then it helped those who carefully studied the Scriptures to recognize the man Jesus as the Christ, sent of God according to appointment and prophecy. And, just so, prophecies marking the time and manner of the second advent are due to be understood at about the time of that event, to aid us in recognizing his day when it has come—and its order of events and the duties of the hour. One cannot read the Old Testament Scriptures thoughtfully without noticing the prominence given to dates, and the great particularity with which some are marked, even to a day, though quite frequently they are attached to what may seem to be very insignificant events. But the close student will find that these various dates and chronological references are links in a wonderful chain of evidence which points out with great precision particularly two of the most notable and important events in the history of the world, viz. : the first and second advents of the world's Redeemer and Lord, and the important matters associated therewith.

The fact that the majority of Christians are indifferent to these things is no reason why those who love his appearing, and desire to be found approved of him, should drop into a similar condition of lukewarmness.

It should be borne in mind that fleshly Israel, except the "friends" of God, stumbled and *knew not the time* of their visitation (Luke 19: 44), and that the prophet has foretold the stumbling of *both* the houses of Israel—the nominal Jewish house, and the nominal Christian house. (Isa. 8: 14.) Only "*a remnant*" in the close or harvest of each dispensation is prepared to receive and appreciate the truths then due, and therefore to enter into the special privileges and blessings of the dawning dispensation. It therefore remains for each individual Christian, in the closing period of this age, to see to it that he is one of "the remnant," and not one of the lukewarm, listless, indifferent mass of the *nominal* Christian Church, which will surely stumble, as foretold by the Prophet, by the Lord and by the Apostles, and as foreshadowed by the course of fleshly Israel, which was declared to be its shadow or type.

But while time-prophecy will be of great advantage in its due time, showing various features of God's plan pertaining to the harvest, etc., it is also true that a knowledge of the manner of our Lord's coming and appearing is very necessary. To this, very careful attention, in its appropriate place, is requested. And back of all this knowledge must lie holiness and humility, which must pave the way for its reception by enabling the child of God to remove prejudice from his heart and to search diligently to know what has been revealed. So it was at the first advent: the earnest, consecrated, meek ones alone discerned the time and manner. The worldly and overcharged ones, the full ones, will not discern either the prophecies or the signs of the times fulfilling them, until the harvest is past and the summer of special favor is ended.

In the end or "harvest" of the Jewish age, the truly humble and earnest "Israelites indeed" were in a condition of expectancy which differed widely from that of the proud, worldly-minded and self-righteous about them; so that not only were they more ready to accept God's plan as he had arranged it, but they were more ready to hear and examine the truth when they came in contact with it. And our Lord, while dismissing the self-satisfied, fault-finding quibbles of the Pharisees with dark or evasive answers, took time and care in making truth clear and plain to the humble, earnest seekers. (Matt. 13: 10–17; 16: 1–4; Mark 7:1–23; Luke 18: 18–30; John 1: 45–51; Luke 24: 13–32 and 33–49; John 20: 24–28; 21: 1–12.) The proud and self-satisfied, and all who followed them, stumbled (Matt.

15 : 14), while the humble and truth-hungry inquired earnestly for the truth. (Matt. 13: 36; Mark 4: 10.) And the Lord expounded the dark sayings to such, and said, " Unto *you* it is given to know the mystery of the Kingdom of God, but to them that are without [not Israelites *indeed*], all these things are done in parables, that seeing they may see and not perceive, and hearing they may hear and not understand."

So, too, it is at the end of this age. Truth here, as there, separates the earnest and humble, and leads them forward into the knowledge now due to such, and strengthens and enlightens them, that they may not stumble with the mass of nominal Christians; while the lukewarm and self-satisfied reject the truths here due, because blinded by their own improper condition of heart. Hence they will be rejected by the Lord as unworthy of becoming his bride.—Eph. 4: 1; 1 Cor. 9: 27.

It is a serious error into which many fall, to suppose that a knowledge of God's doings and plans is of little importance, that the graces of Christian character are all that God requires, and that these are better conserved by ignorance. How differently the Scriptures present the matter! They counsel us, not only to cultivate the graces of the Christian character, but to preserve constantly that condition of heart which will enable us to discern the truth—especially that great truth of the Lord's presence when due—and when dispensational changes take place. A knowledge of dispensational truth is quite as important in the end of this age as it was in the end of the Jewish age. Those who did not discern the truth then due did not receive the favors then due. And just so in the end of this age: Those who cannot discern the truth now due, being blinded by unbelief and worldliness, cannot receive *special* favors now due. They are not overcomers, and hence are unfit to be the bride of

Christ, and to enter into the glorious inheritance of the saints as joint-heirs with him. Truth, in this age, under the adverse circumstances for its reception, becomes a test of our faithfulness to God, and therefore as a sickle separates the fit ones from those unfit—the wheat from the tares.

Odium attaches to the study of prophetic time by reason of past misapplications of it by "Second Adventists" and others, and the consequent failures to realize the events expected to occur at stated times. We see, however, that even this has been a part of God's plan to obscure the subject to all but the class for whom it was intended, by permitting contempt and ridicule to attach to it, thus hindering the worldly-wise and prudent from apprehending it. (Matt. 11 : 25.) This, we doubt not, was as much a part of the divine plan as the sending of Jesus into Nazareth, a despised place, "that he might be called a Nazarene" (Matt. 2 : 23), though he was really born in the honorable town of Bethlehem. As the worldly-wise and prudent of that day said, " Can any good thing come out of Nazareth?" so to-day, when prophetic time or anything relating to the Lord's second advent is mentioned, many cry "Adventist," as if to say, " Can any good thing come out of Adventism ?" —even though they admit that many prophecies containing time are not yet fulfilled, and that the second coming of the Lord is the most prominent topic of Scripture.

We have great sympathy for both the First Adventists (the Jews) and the Second Adventists, though only a few of either realized the truths they so nearly apprehended, yet failed to grasp, each being blinded by *false expectations*. Our Adventist friends have failed to recognize both the manner and the object of the Lord's return as taught in the Scriptures ; consequently they have not been expecting to "see him as he *is*," but as he *was*. They consider the object of his coming one which will fill the hearts of all except the saints with dismay and terror; that his object is to gather the elect, destroy all others of mankind, and burn up the world. Having such ideas, they used the time prophecies as a whip to scourge and drive the world to God. But the world coolly looked on, and said that these were unreasonable enthusiasts, and, if there is a God, he is certainly more reasonable and just than that. The scorn of the world grew more and more intense, as time after time they foretold a wreck of matter and a crush of worlds, and time after time their predictions failed—until now the very mention of prophetic time is received very generally with an incredulous smile, or with open contempt, even by Christians who well know that prophecy and chronology constitute a large proportion of God's revelation.

But blessed is he

> "Who bears unmoved the world's dark frown,
>   Nor heeds its scornful smile;
>   Whom seas of trouble cannot drown,
>   Nor Satan's arts beguile."

But God provided time-prophecies for no such purpose, nor will he attempt to convert the world in any such way as this; for he seeketh such to worship him as worship in spirit and in truth (John 4: 23), and not such as are frightened into his service. If he had designed to terrorize men into obedience, he could have devised some more successful method than the proclamation of *time*—as our Adventist friends have proved. Prophetic time was given, not to alarm the world—nor for the world in any sense—but to enlighten, strengthen, comfort, encourage and guide *the Church* in the troublous times in the end of the age. Therefore it is written, None of the wicked shall understand, but the wise only. To these, this becomes meat in due season, and it, with other meat, will strengthen those who use it, so that they will be "able to *stand in* the evil day"

—the day of trouble with which this age closes. It will enable them to understand the wonderful events transpiring around them, so that they will neither be consumed by fear and dread, nor swallowed up by the projects and false theories—science falsely so called—with which this day will abound. And, withal, they may be in the devouring fire [trouble], witnesses for God and his plan, and teachers of the people—pointers to the glorious outcome of Jehovah's plan, lifting up a standard for the people.—Isa. 62 : 10.

This is the object of time prophecy, and how important, how indispensable—that the man of God may be perfect, thoroughly furnished, at this time. Without these prophetic time-proofs, we might see the events of this Day of the Lord, and know not of it, or of our duties and privileges in it. Let none, then, of the truly consecrated undervalue these prophetic time-evidences, which were designed to guide our words and deeds in the early Dawn of the Millennial Day, before sunrise, while the world and the nominal church are yet asleep, ignorant and heedless of the dispensational changes now occurring. These prophetic time-proofs were largely God's means of drawing the attention of the writer more fully and carefully to other features of the divine plan. Attention given to these must result in lasting profit to the student, not only by informing him of "present truth," but also by giving force and vital reality to all Scriptural truths, by furnishing proof that all God's plans are working together in *time*, as well as in *kind*, to the development of his glorious purposes.

The failure of the predictions of Adventists, who attempted to fix a time for the burning of the world, etc., etc., has been more in regard to the character of the events expected than in the time. Like the Jews, they erred by looking for the *wrong thing* at the *right time*. This was the secondary cause of their failure to clearly apprehend the truth, but the primary cause of it was the fact that it was not yet time for a clearer unfolding. And yet it was time for the stirring up of the saints to look for the Lord's appearing—for a going forth to meet the Bridegroom, and a disappointment prior to his actual coming—all of which was indicated in our Lord's parable of the Ten Virgins, as will be shown at length hereafter. As shown in the preceding volume, the fire which is to devour the earth in the Day of the Lord is symbolic, not literal; and in succeeding chapters it will be shown that the applications of some time-prophecies which Adventists have discarded as failures were not failures, but correct, and that they clearly mark the symbolic fire of this time—already getting under way.

The Advent people, laboring under the difficulty of expecting a literal burning of the earth, attempted to force all the prophetic periods to one common day of termination —a twenty-four hour day at that—and thus they did violence to some prophecies to make them fit and end with others. But the clearer view of the divine plan now reveals the perfect harmony of the various time-prophecies, and there is no necessity for twisting or doing violence to any, to make it fit with the others. As in succeeding chapters we institute an examination of the leading prophecies, we do not form a theory and then endeavor to bend all the prophetic periods to it, but we carefully trace each period to its termination, and then weave together the theory or plan thus indicated by the great Revealer of secrets. It will be found that the order and harmony of God's plan are just as manifest in its times and seasons as in the glorious features of that plan traced in the preceding volume, and mapped out on the Chart of the Ages. And when the great clock of the ages strikes the hours indicated on the prophetic dial, the events foretold are as sure to follow as that God foretold them.

STUDY II.

BIBLE CHRONOLOGY.

CHRONOLOGY NECESSARY TO AN UNDERSTANDING OF PROPHECY.—INDISPENSABLE DATA FURNISHED IN THE BIBLE.—FROM THE CREATION OF ADAM TO A. D. 1873 WAS SIX THOUSAND YEARS.—A STATEMENT OF BIBLE CHRONOLOGY IN GREAT PERIODS.—ITS EXAMINATION IN DETAIL.—FROM CREATION TO THE DAY THE FLOOD WAS DRIED UP.—TO THE ABRAHAMIC COVENANT.—TO THE GIVING OF THE LAW.—TO THE DIVISION OF CANAAN AMONG THE TRIBES.—THE PERIOD OF THE JUDGES.—THE PERIOD OF THE KINGS.—THE PERIOD OF THE DESOLATION.— TO A. D. 1873.—WHEREIN THIS CHRONOLOGY DIFFERS FROM THAT OF BISHOP USHER, NOTED IN OUR ENGLISH BIBLES.—THE TRUE DATE OF OUR LORD'S BIRTH.

IN this chapter we present the Bible evidence which indicates that six thousand years from the creation of Adam were complete with A. D. 1872; and hence that, since 1872 A. D., we are chronologically entered upon the seventh thousand or the Millennium—the forepart of which, the "Day of the Lord," the "day of trouble," is to witness the breaking into pieces of the kingdoms of this world and the establishment of the Kingdom of God under the whole heavens.

Chronology is necessary, too, as a basis for the examination of the prophetic periods. We must ascertain first of all where we are on the stream of time; and to do this, we must have reliable dates for the calculation; hence we take up the subject of chronology first in order. And a complete chronology of human history must of necessity begin with the creation of man.

The length of time since the creation of man is variously estimated. Among those who accept the Bible record, there can be but little difference of opinion; but among those who reject it, the differences are enormous, varying all the way from ten thousand to hundreds of thousands of years. These suppositions are based upon facts which afford but slight ground for such extravagant and reckless conclusions. For instance, the finding of flint arrow-heads in the peat bogs of Switzerland and Ireland, at a considerable depth below the surface, is taken as a *proof* that their level was once the surface, and that the peat mosses gradually grew up around and above them; and the time necessary for such a growth is calculated from the present rate of growth per century, which is very slight. If their premises were true, of course it would prove that man had lived hundreds of thousands of years ago. But other geologists will show, and with good reason, that these peat bogs were once so soft that a flint arrow-head might easily sink to a great depth gradually, during a few centuries.

Another instance we quote:—"In making soundings in the slimy soil of the Nile valley two baked bricks were discovered, one at a depth of twenty, the other of twenty-four yards. If we estimate the thickness of the annual deposit formed by the river at eight inches a century, we must assign to the first of these bricks an age of 12,000 years and to the second that of 14,000. *By means of analogous calculations*, Burmeister [a celebrated geologist] supposes seventy-two thousand years to have elapsed since the first appearance of man upon the soil of Egypt; and Draper [another noted geologist] attributes to the European man who witnessed the last glacial epoch an antiquity of more than 250,000 years." *

Of course "*if we estimate*" just as these *great* men do, we should reach the same *great* conclusions. But some of us are unscientific enough to inquire, whether it is not more than probable that the slime deposits of the Nile river have been very irregular, as of other rivers, which sometimes shift

* Prof. N. Joly, in "Man Before Metals," page 183.

their beds and wash away their banks wonderfully in a single freshet. Again, we remember the Flood of Noah's day, not only particularly mentioned in the Bible, but preserved in the oldest traditions of the heathen nations, and we wonder how much slime and debris that caused, over and above the eight inches a century. We wonder, too, why it has not occurred to these *great* minds, as it naturally does to some not *too great*, that two bricks thrown into that "*slimy* soil," at a time when it was covered with water and very soft, would sink quite a distance by their own weight, being so much more dense than the slimy soil. As for the difference in depth of the two bricks, it would seem to an *unscientific* mind much more reasonable to suppose that the one fell into the slime edge-wise or end-wise, while the other, falling flat, would sink more slowly, than to suppose that men living two thousand years apart made two bricks exactly alike.

It is not many years since the skeleton of a man was found in a former bed of the Mississippi river, and some geologists began to calculate how many thousands of years *might* be indicated by the many feet of silt, slime, etc., covering the skeleton, and fancied they had a very valuable sample of pre-historic man. But finding later, several feet below the skeleton, parts of a "flat boat," such as was in use on the Mississippi less than fifty years ago, it completely upset the calculations, and relieved mankind of "another *proof*" that the world is hundreds of thousands of years older than the Bible teaches.

Leaving the discordant and wholly unreliable guessing of some geologists on this subject of chronology, we appeal to human history for information. And what do we find?— The history of the oldest of the Gentile nations can be traced back clearly and distinctly less than three thousand years. Back of that all is dark, uncertain, mythical, fabulous, and untrustworthy tradition. Roman history does not extend so far back, as it is only twenty-seven hundred years since Rome was founded, and then its first centuries are wrapped in uncertain tradition. Three thousand years back in the Babylonian, Syrian, and Egyptian histories brings us to a period where their records are fragmentary and involved in great obscurity. In the history of China, it brings us to the Tchou dynasty, where the events of Chinese history "*begin* to be more trustworthy." In Greece, noted for its scholarship in the past three thousand years, with whom above all nations we might expect to find accurate history, what do we find? We find its dates accurate for the last twenty-six hundred years, but no farther back. Back of that, we come to what is known as the "fabulous, mythical or pre-historic age" of Greece. The only reasonable and connected account of the first three thousand years of man on the earth is found in the Bible; and this fact is surely in harmony with its claim to divine origin, direction and preservation.

As with history, so with dates: the world has, aside from the Bible, no means of tracing its chronology farther back than B. C. 776. On this subject we quote Prof. Fisher, of Yale College. He says: "An exact method of establishing dates was slowly reached. The invention of eras was indispensable to this end. *The earliest definite time* for the dating of events was established in Babylon—the era of Nabonassar, 747 B. C. The Greeks (from about 300 B. C.) dated events from the first recorded victory at the Olympic games, 776 B. C. These games occurred every fourth year. Each Olympiad was thus a period of four years. The Romans, though not for some centuries after the founding of Rome, dated from *that* event; *i. e.*, from 753 B. C."

In further evidence that the many so-called histories of the remote past so abound with vagaries and mythical traditions as to make them valueless as to chronological data, and wholly unworthy of consideration, we quote as follows from the American Cyclopædia, under the caption, *Chronology* :—

"The history of ancient nations, unless we make an exception in the case of the Hebrews, goes back into mythical periods of thousands or millions of years ; and even after the records begin to assume a historical aspect, the discrepancies are very great. . . . The Assyrian, Babylonian and Egyptian inscriptions are in extinct languages, and in characters long obsolete. . . . Greek and Roman dates are generally well authenticated to the first Olympiad, B. C. 776, and the establishment of the Consulate, B. C. 510, previous to which they are mainly traditional or legendary. Herodotus is valuable only as to events of his own time, about 450 B. C., and those of a century or two earlier."

Clinton in his work on Grecian Chronology (page 283) says, "The history contained in the Hebrew Scriptures presents a remarkable and pleasing contrast to the early accounts of the Greeks. In the latter we trace with difficulty a few obscure facts preserved to us by the poets, who transmitted, with all the embellishments of poetry and fable, what they had received from oral tradition. In the annals of the Hebrew nation, we have authentic narratives written by contemporaries under the guidance of inspiration. What they have delivered to us comes accordingly under a double sanction. They were aided by divine inspiration, in recording facts upon which, as mere human witnesses, their evidence would be valid."

The Bible, our God-provided history of the first three thousand years, is the only work in the world which—beginning with Adam, the first man mentioned in history, monument or inscription, whose name, the time of his creation and death are recorded, and from whom his descendants can be traced by name and age in successive links for nearly four thousand years—furnishes us a clear and connected history down to a period where secular history is well authenticated. As we shall see, the Bible record extends to the first year of Cyrus, B. C. 536, a well established and generally accepted date. There the thread of Bible chronology is dropped—at a point where secular history is reliable. God has thus provided for his children a clear and connected record down to the present time. The Bible by its prophecies even supplements history, down to the consummation of "the restitution of all things," in the end of the seventh millennium, whence the new era of eternal blessedness will begin to date. The Bible is therefore the only record in the world which furnishes a view of human history as a whole. It carries us from the lost paradise of Genesis to the restored paradise of Revelation, tracing the pathway of humanity into eternity. Taken together, the history and prophecy of the Bible afford a panoramic view of the whole course of events from the creation and fall of man to his reconciliation and restitution. The Bible, therefore, is the chart of all history. Without it, as has been truly said, history would be "like rivers flowing from unknown sources to unknown seas;" but under its guidance we may trace these rivers to their springs, yea, and see their glorious ending in the ocean of eternity.

In the Bible alone, therefore, we may expect to find a record which will order aright the inharmonious periods and chronological irregularities which the annals of human history at first sight present—into harmony with each other and with the periods of nature.

In starting with the question, How long is it since man's creation? we should and do feel confident that he who gave the prophecies, and said that in the time of the end they should be understood, has provided in his Word the data necessary to enable us accurately to locate those prophecies. However, any who expect to find these matters so plainly stated as to be convincing to the mere surface reader, or the insincere skeptic, will be disappointed. God's times and seasons are given in such a way as to be convincing, at this time, only to those who, by acquaintance with God, are able to recognize his characteristic methods. The evidence is given " that *the man of God* may be thoroughly furnished." (2 Tim. 3 : 17.) These well know that in all the paths by which their Father leads they must walk by faith and not by sight. To all who are prepared to walk thus, we expect to be able to point out, at every step, solid statements of God's Word—a sure foundation for reasonable faith.

We will not here discuss the merits of the Septuagint and Hebrew versions of the Old Testament Scriptures, their difference in chronological data, etc., but will satisfy ourselves, and we trust the reader, with the statement that the former was a translation by Egyptians, while the latter is the original Hebrew record ; which facts, taken in connection with the almost superstitious veneration with which the Hebrews guarded every jot and tittle of those sacred writings, is strong evidence of the reliability of the Hebrew version. Its acceptance by scholars is quite general, and in this volume we follow its dates, etc.

Here we furnish the evidence that from the creation of Adam *to* A. D. 1873 was six thousand years. And though the Bible contains no direct statement that the seventh thousand will be the epoch of Christ's reign, the great Sabbath Day of restitution to the world, yet the venerable tradition is not without a reasonable foundation. The law given to Israel, the typical people, appointing that six days of labor and weariness should be followed by one of refreshment and rest from their own works, seems fitly to illustrate the six thousand years in which the whole creation labors and groans under the bondage of sin and death (Rom. 8 : 22) in a vain endeavor to extricate itself, and the grand Millennial Day in which the weary and heavy laden may come to Christ Jesus, the shepherd and bishop of their souls, and through him find rest, refreshment and restitution—in which, through the merits of his precious blood, they may find repentance and remission of sins. On the typical seventh day he inquired of the impotent man, "Wilt thou be made whole?" and in answer to his faith and obedience gave him strength to take up his bed and walk. (See John 5 : 6–9; also Matt. 12 : 10, 13 ; John 7 : 23; Luke 13 : 11–16; 14: 1–5.) So, during the antitypical Sabbath, the Millennium, it will be declared to all the world that "*whosoever will*" may have life and health eternal if he will take the steps of faith and obedience.

We must not overlook the fact already noted (Vol. I., Chap. VIII.), that the term *day* is indefinite, and signifies merely a period of time, whether of long or of short duration. The Apostle Peter intimated that the seventh thousand-year period of the world's history would be the seventh day in God's reckoning, saying, "Beloved, be not ignorant of this one thing, that one day is with the Lord as a thousand years, and a thousand years as one day. . . . The day of the Lord will come," etc.—2 Pet. 3 : 8, 10.

If, then, the seventh thousand-year period of earth's history be an epoch specially noted as the period of Christ's reign, we shall, by showing that it began in A. D. 1873, be proving that we are *already in it.* This calls to mind what we have already noted in the preceding volume, that the Scriptures indicate that the dawn of the Millennium, or Day of the Lord, will be dark and stormy, and full of trouble upon the world and upon the nominal church, though its earliest dawning light will be full of comfort and cheer to the saints, who draw their comfort and peace from the hope set before them in the gospel, which, as an anchor, enters beyond the time of trouble, and fastens in the precious promises of the Millennial sunrise and glory :—they see, beyond the time of trouble, the glorious reign and blessings promised.

The general condition of the world to-day, and the rapid development since 1873 of Socialism, Nihilism and Communism, whose avowed object is the overturning of the powers that be, and the redistribution of the wealth of the world, are certainly not out of harmony with what we should expect, however much, in some respects, these things may be deprecated by those who love law and order and peace. Only those who see that the coming anarchy and trouble are God's agencies for the establishment of a yet more complete law and order, and a more lasting peace, will be relieved from overwhelming fear as they pass through it.

Nor is this pointing out of the seventh epoch, or Millennium, the only value of chronology ; for while we shall present several lines of prophecy entirely independent of chronology, it is the measure by which several lines of prophecy are established. The perfect agreement between these two classes of prophetic teaching, some dependent on, and some independent of, chronology, is very strong proof, not only of the correctness of those applications, but also of the correctness of the chronology which shows this harmony ; on the same principle that a key which will unlock a treasure-casket difficult to open is evidently the true key. The chronology given below harmonizes the various prophetic statements relating to Christ's Kingdom and its establishment, by showing their relative order and time. Chronology is the stem or handle by which all the prophetic time-proofs, as notches or wards of the key, are held together and operated.

A CONDENSED STATEMENT OF CHRONOLOGY TO THE YEAR A. M. 6000.

The following condensed statement of chronological periods may properly be termed Bible chronology, because the Bible record alone is followed down to the first year of Cyrus, B. C. 536, a date well authenticated and generally accepted by scholars. Here the thread of Bible chronology ends—a little beyond the period where secular history begins to be reliable. This, in itself, is a marked evidence of divine direction and oversight, in helping us only where we are unable to help ourselves.

FROM THE CREATION OF ADAM

To the end of the flood	1656 years.
Thence to the covenant with Abraham . .	427 "
Thence to the Exodus and the giving of the Law	430 "
Thence to the division of Canaan . .	46 "
The period of the Judges	450 "
The period of the Kings	513 "
The period of the desolation . . .	70 "
Thence to A. D. 1	536 "
Thence to A. D. 1873	1872 "
Total	6000 "

As we consider particularly each of these periods, let the reader figure it out for himself, and see how firm a foundation for our faith is laid in God's Word. Two breaks in the historic narrative of the Old Testament we shall find, yet when we discover that in the New Testament God has provided bridges to span these two chasms, it should increase our confidence that God so arranged the record as to hide his times and seasons, until his due time for revealing them had come—just as he has done with other truths already noticed.

We will now examine the foregoing periods separately, and in their order as named above, down to the reign of Cyrus. Have your Bible at hand and verify every quotation, that you may receive this as God's Word and not as man's.

CHRONOLOGY OF THE PERIOD FROM THE CREATION OF

ADAM TO THE DAY THE FLOOD WAS DRIED UP.

"Adam lived 130 years and begat a son and
    called his name Seth."—Gen. 5 : 3. . . 130 years.
"Seth lived 105 years and begat Enos."
—Gen. 5 : 6. . . . . . . 105 "
"Enos lived 90 years, and begat Cainan."
—Gen. 5 : 9. . . . . . . 90 "
"Cainan lived 70 years and begat Mahalaleel."
—Gen. 5 : 12. . . . . . 70 "
"Mahalaleel lived 65 years and begat Jared."
—Gen. 5 : 15. . . . . . 65 "
"Jared lived 162 years and begat Enoch."
—Gen 5 : 18. . . . . . 162 "
"Enoch lived 65 years and begat Methuselah."
—Gen. 5 : 21. . . . . . 65 "
"Methuselah lived 187 yrs. and begat Lamech."
—Gen. 5 : 25. . . . . . 187 "
"Lamech lived 182 years and begat a son and
    called his name Noah."—Gen. 5 : 28. . . 182 "
"Noah was 600 years old when the flood of
    waters was upon the earth."—Gen. 7 : 6. 600 "
Total from the creation of Adam *to the day* ——
    the flood was dried up.—Gen. 8 : 13. 1656 years.

Nothing more simple and exact to a day than this could be asked. Let us now examine the next period.

THE PERIOD FROM THE FLOOD TO THE COVENANT WITH
ABRAHAM, AT THE DEATH OF TERAH, HIS FATHER.

" Shem—begat Arphaxad 2 years after the flood." —Gen. 11 : 10.	2 years.
" Arphaxad lived 35 years and begat Salah." —Gen. 11 : 12.	35 "
" Salah lived 30 years and begat Eber." —Gen. 11 : 14.	30 "
" Eber lived 34 years and begat Peleg." —Gen. 11 : 16.	34 "
" Peleg lived 30 years and begat Reu." —Gen. 11 : 18.	30 "
" Reu lived 32 years and begat Serug." —Gen. 11 : 20.	32 "
" Serug lived 30 years and begat Nahor." —Gen. 11 : 22.	30 "
" Nahor lived 29 years and begat Terah." —Gen. 11 : 24.	29 "
"The days of Terah were 205 yrs. and he died." —Gen. 11 : 32.	205 "

Total . . . . . 427 years.

This, too, is very simple and exact. But the next period is not so easily traced; for the direct line of chronology is broken, until after the exodus of Israel from Egypt. Hence we would be quite unable to proceed, were it not that Paul and Stephen, as the mouth-pieces of the Spirit, furnish the connecting link.

THE PERIOD FROM THE COVENANT WITH ABRAHAM
TO THE GIVING OF THE LAW.

Paul declares that the length of this period was four hundred and thirty years. (Gal. 3 : 17.) The covenant included the promise of the land of Canaan for an ever-lasting possession, and though several times re-affirmed, to Abraham, to Isaac and to Jacob, it was always the same covenant. (See Gen. 12 : 7, 8 ; 13 : 14–18 ; 26 : 3, 4 ; 35 : 9–12 ; 46 : 2–4 ; 50 : 24.) As shown by a comparison of Gen. 12 : 1–5, 7 and Acts 7 : 2–5, the covenant was made (according to previous promise) as soon as Abraham had fully complied with the conditions on which he was to receive it : that was, as soon as he had entered Canaan, which he did immediately after the decease of his father, who died in Haran, on the way to Canaan. Having the date of the covenant—just after Terah's death—thus established by Stephen's statement, and having Paul's statement, that the Law was four hundred and thirty years after the covenant, the break in the Old Testament chronology is thus bridged by the New. But let us read the account carefully, and mark the particularity with which the bridge is constructed :—

"Now the Lord *had* [previously, before he left Mesopotamia, or Ur of the Chaldees] said unto Abraham, Get thee out of thy country, and from thy kindred, and from thy father's house [brethren, etc.], unto a land that I will show thee ; and [if you do so] I will make of thee a great nation," etc. (Gen. 12 : 1, 2. Compare Acts 7 : 2.) This indicates that God had *proposed* the covenant to Abraham before Terah, his father, died, and before he came to dwell in Haran or Charran. But there was a stipulation which demanded Abraham's faith and obedience before the covenant should be actually made. This stipulation was that he must manifest faith in the promise that such a covenant would be made with him, by leaving his native country and kindred and going to the land to which he was directed. This Abraham did, and as his wife, his nephew Lot and his aged father shared his faith and desired to share his fortunes with him, they were permitted to do so,

and the four started for the land of promise. His father
Terah died on the way, in Haran, after which Abraham
passed over into Canaan, that there he might secure and
bind the covenant. As Stephen declared to Israel: "When
his father was dead, he removed him into this land wherein ye now dwell." "So Abraham departed [out of Haran]
as the Lord had spoken unto him." (Acts 7 : 4 ; Gen. 12 : 4.)
And the covenant was made just after he entered the land.
(See Gen. 12 : 5–7.) Thus we have the date of the covenant, and the beginning of the four hundred and thirty
years, fixed as immediately following Terah's death, and
the chain of chronology complete to the giving of the Law.
The first feature of the Law was the Passover, which was
instituted the same day that Israel left Egypt.—Exod.
12 : 41–43, 47, 50, 51.

In harmony with this we read: "Now the sojourning of
the children of Israel who dwelt in Egypt was four hundred
and thirty years ; and it came to pass at the end of the four
hundred and thirty years, *even the self-same day* it came
to pass, that all the hosts of the Lord went out from the
land of Egypt."—Exod. 12 : 40–42, 51.

Some may suppose that the statements of Moses and Paul
(Exod. 12 : 40–42 and Gal. 3 : 17) are not in harmony,
the one affirming that the sojourning of Israel was four
hundred and thirty years, and the other, that from the
covenant with Abraham to the giving of the Law was four
hundred and thirty years, reasoning that if only four hundred and thirty years elapsed between Abraham's coming
into Canaan and the giving of the Law, the sojourn of the
children of Israel in Egypt must have been much less.
But it should be observed that the statement is not that
Israel sojourned in Egypt four hundred and thirty years,
but that the whole length of the sojourning of that people
who for some time lived in Egypt lasted four hundred and

thirty years :—"Now the sojourning of the children of Israel who *dwelt* in Egypt was four hundred and thirty years." The sojourning referred to began when Abraham first came into Canaan. (Heb. 11 : 8, 9.) Israel sojourned in Abraham and in Isaac and in Jacob, even as Levi paid tithes to Melchizedec, while yet *in the loins of his father*. —Heb. 7 : 9, 10.

The covenant with Abraham took effect from the time that, leaving Haran or Charran, he set foot in Canaan, the land of promise. From that time, he and all Israel in him, yet unborn, became heirs of the things promised, and *sojourners*, or pilgrims, waiting on God for the fulfilment of the promise. This sojourning had lasted four hundred and thirty years, to a day, when Israel left Egypt, and received that first feature of the Law, the institution of the Passover. The statements of Moses and Paul, therefore, refer to precisely the same period, thus giving most positive evidence that from the covenant with Abraham to the giving of the Law was four hundred and thirty years. Paul gave special emphasis to the fact that the Passover must be regarded as the beginning of the Law (which Moses also shows, Exod. 12 : 42, 43, 47, 50), and Moses gave special emphasis to the exactness of the period, to a day.

Thus we have our third period clearly established. And when we mark the Lord's particularity to a day, in furnishing this link in the chain of chronology, it gives us strong confidence, especially when we consider that such particularity was probably of no special interest to the Church of the past, and was given for no other than the present use.

PERIOD FROM THE EXODUS TO THE DIVISION

OF CANAAN AMONG THE TRIBES.

Israel's forty years, or " day of temptation in the wilderness " (Deut. 8 : 2 ; Psa. 95 : 8–10 ; Heb. 3 : 8, 9), was

followed by six years of war in Canaan, and the dividing
of the land among the tribes. One year, one month and
five days elapsed from their going out of Egypt to their
leaving Sinai for Paran. (Num. 33: 3; 10: 11–13.) And
it was then, from Kadesh-barnea in the wilderness of Paran,
that the spies were sent. (Num. 13: 3–26; 32: 8–13.)
One of these, Caleb, when applying for his portion at the
division of the land (Joshua 11: 23; 10: 42), said, "Forty
years old was I when Moses the servant of the Lord sent
me from Kadesh-barnea to espy out the land, and I brought
him word again. . . . And now, behold, the Lord hath
kept me alive, as he said, *these forty and five years, even
since the Lord spake this word* . . . while Israel wandered
in the wilderness; and now, lo, I am *this day* fourscore
and five years old." (Joshua 14: 7, 10.) Thus it will be
seen that it was forty-five years from the spying of the land
to its division among the tribes, as affirmed by Joshua, and
a little over a year from the exodus to the sending of the
the spies, making forty-six full years and a fraction * from
the exodus to the division of the land. As the first forty
years of this period were passed in the wilderness, as shown
by many Scriptures, notably Acts 7: 36 and Heb. 3: 9, the
remaining six to the division of the land were spent in Canaan,
conquering and taking possession of the land of promise.

---

* We take account of only the complete years, more accurate account
being impossible. Sometimes, as above, the years are fractionally long.
And again some are short, as in the case of Zedekiah's reign. Zedekiah
is said to have reigned eleven years (1 Chron. 36: 11; Jer. 52: 1); yet,
from verses 3 to 7 of the latter chapter, it is clear that his actual reign
was ten years four months and nine days. We believe that these frac-
tional parts of years counterbalance themselves; and that the Lord has
thus overruled and arranged the matter is our confidence, supported by
the outcome and the results deducible from it, and the accuracy to a day,
even in large periods, already noticed. As illustrating God's care and
particularity in this matter, see Gen. 7: 11; 7: 13; Exod. 12: 40, 41.

THE PERIOD OF THE JUDGES.

We come now to the most difficult portion of chronology, the period from the division of the land to the anointing of Saul as king. It is usually termed the period of the Judges, though the Judges did not fill the office continuously. The record given in the books of Judges and 1 Samuel mentions nineteen periods, approximating a total of four hundred and fifty years; but they are disconnected, broken, lapped and tangled so much that we could arrive at no definite conclusion from them, and should be obliged to conclude as others have done, that nothing positive could be known on the subject, were it not that the New Testament supplies the deficiency. Paul states that after God divided their land to them by lot, "He gave unto them Judges about [during] the space of four hundred and fifty years, until Samuel the Prophet. Afterward they desired a king, and God gave unto them Saul."—Acts 13: 19–21.

The Greek word rendered *about* in the common version is *hos*, and has the significance of *during*, or *while*. The same writer uses the word in three other places where the common version translates it *while*, viz.: Acts 1: 10; 10:17; Luke 24: 32. This passage would be better translated, "He gave unto them Judges *during* the space of four hundred and fifty years." The Syriac reads thus—"And for four hundred and fifty years he gave them Judges, until Samuel the Prophet"—the last of the "Judges."

The statement of the length of this period of the Judges, by the Apostle, we accept as a specially designed solution of the problem. In only two instances—the four hundred and thirty years from the Covenant to the Law, and this period of the Judges—is there any reasonable uncertainty about the Old Testament chronology, and both are clearly stated in the New. Can we suppose that this merely hap-

4–B

pened so? It is more reasonable to suppose that God first hid the matter, by leaving the Old Testament record incomplete, and later supplied the deficiency in the New Testament, so that in due time, when attention should be called to it, those having sufficient interest to compare the accounts might find the missing links supplied in a manner calculated to teach dependence upon the Great Time-Keeper.

THE PERIOD OF THE KINGS.

Saul's reign was in or during the space of forty years following the last Judge, until David was anointed king, as shown above; and following him, the periods of the kings in the line of David are easily traced in Chronicles, thus:—

Saul's "space"	.	. Acts 13:21	.	40 years.
David reigned	.	1 Chron. 29:27	.	. 40 "
Solomon "	.	2 Chron. 9:30	.	40 "
Rehoboam "	.	" " 12:13	.	. 17 "
Abijah "	.	. " " 13:2	.	3 "
Asa "	.	" " 16:13	.	. 41 "
Jehoshaphat "	.	. " " 20:31	.	25 "
Jehoram "	.	" " 21:20	.	. 8 "
Ahaziah "	.	. " " 22:2	.	1 "
Athaliah "	.	" " 22:12	.	. 6 "
Jehoash "	.	. " " 24:1	.	40 "
Amaziah "	.	" " 25:1	.	. 29 "
Uzziah "	.	. " " 26:3	.	52 "
Jotham "	.	" " 27:1	.	. 16 "
Ahaz "	.	. " " 28:1	.	16 "
Hezekiah "	.	" " 29:1	.	. 29 "
Manasseh "	.	. " " 33:1	.	55 "
Amon "	.	" " 33:21	.	. 2 "
Josiah "	.	. " " 34:1	.	31 "
Jehoiakim "	.	" " 36:5	.	. 11 "
Zedekiah "	.	. " " 36:11	.	11 "

       Total . . . . . 513 years.

THE SEVENTY YEARS OF DESOLATION.

This brings us to the period of the desolation of the land, which lasted seventy years, and was ended by the restoration of its people from Babylon, in the first year of Cyrus, B. C. 536 (See 2 Chron. 36 : 20, 23), a date well established in secular history, and beyond which the line of Bible chronology does not extend.

PERIOD FROM THE RESTORATION TO A. D. 1873.

The period from the time of the restoration of the Jews from Babylon, at the close of the seventy years desolation of their land, in the first year of Cyrus, down to the date known as A. D. 1, is not covered by Bible history. But, as before stated, it is well established by secular history as a period of 536 years. Ptolemy, a learned Greek-Egyptian, a geometer and astronomer, has well established these figures. They are generally accepted by scholars, and known as Ptolemy's Canon.

Thus we have found a clear and connected line of chronology from creation to the beginning of the Christian era (A. D.)—in all, a period of four thousand one hundred and twenty-eight (4128) years, which, together with eighteen hundred and seventy-two years of the Christian era, make six thousand years from creation *to* the year 1873 A. D.

THIS AND USHER'S CHRONOLOGY COMPARED.

It will be interesting to some to know wherein the above chronology differs from that inserted in the margin of the common version of the Bible, known as Usher's Chronology. The difference between the two, down to the time of the seventy years of desolation, is one hundred and twenty-four (124) years. This difference is made up of four periods of 18, 4, 2 and 100 years—as follows :

Usher dates the seventy years desolation *eighteen years* earlier than shown above—*i. e.,* before the dethronement of Zedekiah, Judah's last king—because the king of Babylon took many of the people captive at that time. (2 Chron. 36:9, 10, 17, 21; 2 Kings 24:8–16.) He evidently makes the not uncommon mistake of regarding those seventy years as the period of *captivity*, whereas the Lord expressly declares them to be seventy years of *desolation* of the land, that the land should lie "desolate, without an inhabitant." Such was not the case prior to Zedekiah's dethronement. (2 Kings 24:14.) But the desolation which followed Zedekiah's overthrow was complete; for, though some of the poor of the land were left to be vine-dressers and husbandmen (2 Kings 25:12), shortly even these—"all people, both small and great"—fled to Egypt for fear of the Chaldees. (Verse 26.) There can be no doubt here; and therefore in reckoning the time to the *desolation of the land*, all periods up to the close of Zedekiah's reign should be counted in, as we have done.

The *four years* difference is in the reign of Jehoram. Usher gives it as a reign of four years, while the Bible says it was eight years.—2 Chron. 21:5; 2 Kings 8:17.

Of the *two years* difference, one year is found in the term of the reign of Ahaz, which Usher gives as fifteen, while the Bible says it was sixteen years. (2 Chron. 28:1; 2 Kings 16:2.) And the other is in the term of Jehoash, which Usher reckons as thirty-nine, while the Bible gives it as forty years.—2 Kings 12:1; 2 Chron. 24:1.

These differences can be accounted for only by supposing that Usher followed, or attempted to follow, Josephus, a Jewish historian whose chronological dates are now generally recognized as reckless and faulty. We rely on the Bible alone, believing that God is his own interpreter.

Aside from these twenty-four years difference in the period

of the Kings, there is another variance between the above
Bible chronology and that of Usher, namely, *one hundred years* in the period of the Judges. Here Usher is
misled by the evident error of 1 Kings 6 : 1, which says
that the fourth year of Solomon's reign was the four-hun-
dred-and-eightieth year from the coming out of Egypt. It
evidently should read the five-hundred-and-eightieth year,
and was possibly an error in transcribing; for if to Solomon's four years we add David's forty, and Saul's space
of forty, and the forty-six years from leaving Egypt to the
division of the land, we have one hundred and thirty years,
which deducted from four hundred and eighty would leave
only three hundred and fifty years for the period of the
Judges, instead of the *four* hundred and fifty years mentioned in the Book of Judges, and by Paul, as heretofore
shown. The Hebrew character "*daleth*" (4) very much
resembles the character "*hay*" (5), and it is supposed that
in this way the error has occurred, possibly the mistake of
a transcriber. I. Kings 6: 1, then, should read *five* hundred and eighty, and thus be in perfect harmony with
the other statements.

Thus the Word of God corrects the few slight errors
which have crept into it by any means. * And remember
that those breaks occur in the period bridged effectually by
the inspired testimony of the New Testament.

So, then, whereas Usher dates A. D. 1 as the year 4005
from the creation of Adam, it really was, as we have shown,
the year 4129, according to the Bible record, thus showing

---

* A similar discrepancy will be noticed in comparing 2 Chron. 36 : 9
with 2 Kings 24 : 8, the one giving eighteen years and the other, evidently
incorrect, giving eight years as the age of Jehoiachin, who reigned three
months, and did evil in the sight of the Lord, and was punished by captivity, etc. Such a mistake could easily occur, but God has so guarded
his Word that the few trivial errors of copyists are made very manifest,
and the full harmony of his Word gives ample foundation for faith.

the year 1872 A. D. to be the year of the world 6000, and 1873 A. D. the commencement of the seventh thousand-year period, the seventh millennium, or thousand-year day of earth's history.

Thus chronology as gathered from the Bible alone, from creation down to well authenticated secular history, is clear and strong, bearing evidence, too, of the peculiar methods of divine providence in its record, in its concealing and in its gradual unfolding in due time. And this, together with the reliable dates of the Christian era and the several centuries before it at hand, enables us to locate ourselves accurately on the stream of time. And we begin hopefully to lift up our heads and rejoice, as we realize that we are actually sweeping into the glorious age of the seventh millennium—even though we recognize that its beginning is to be dark and full of trouble, as foretold by the prophets, and that the storm-clouds are already gathering and growing darker.

THE DATE OF OUR LORD'S BIRTH.

In the sixth century the Church began to reckon time from the birth of our Lord, and fixed the date A. D. as it now stands; *viz.*, 536 years after the first year of Cyrus, king of Persia.* Whether they placed it correctly or not does not affect the chronology as just given, which shows that the six thousand years from the creation of Adam ended with A. D. 1872; because it is eighteen hundred and seventy-two years since the year designated A. D., and the first year of Cyrus was five hundred and thirty-six years before that year (A. D.), whether it was the year of our Lord's birth or not.

---

* The year A. D. was fixed upon as early as the sixth century by Dionysius Exiguus, and other scholars of that period, though it did not come into general use until two centuries later.

We cannot, perhaps, explain this better than by the time-worn illustration of a line with a star upon it—thus:

B. C.＿＿＿＿＿＿＿＿ * ＿＿＿＿＿＿＿＿A. D. Let the line represent the six thousand years of earth's history from the creation of Adam to 1873 A. D.; and let the star represent the turning point between B. C. and A. D. To move that point either way would not alter the length of the entire period, though it would alter the names of the years. To move the A. D. point backward one year would make the B. C. period one year less, and the A. D. period one year more, but the *sum* of the B. C. and A. D. years would still be the same; for the amount taken from the one is always an addition to the other. Nevertheless, let us briefly examine the date of our Lord's birth, as it will be found useful in our subsequent studies.

It has become customary among scholars to concede that our commonly accepted A. D. is incorrect to the amount of four years—that our Lord was born four years previous to the year designated A. D., *i. e.*, in the year B. C. 4. And this theory has been followed by the publishers of the common version of the Bible. We cannot agree that B. C. 4 was the true date of our Lord's birth. On the contrary, we find that he was born only one year and three months before our common era, A.D., viz., in October of B.C. 2.

The general reason with most of those who claim that A. D. should have been placed four years earlier to correctly mark the Savior's birth, is a desire to harmonize it with certain statements of the Jewish historian Josephus, relative to the length of the reign of Herod the Great. According to one of his statements, it would appear that Herod died three years before the year reckoned A. D. If this were true, it would certainly prove that our Lord was born in the year B. C. 4; for it was this Herod, that issued the decree for the slaying of the babes of Bethlehem, from whom the infant Jesus was delivered. (Matt. 2 : 14–16.)   But is this statement of Josephus reliable?   Is it true that Herod died four years before the year A. D.? No, we answer: Josephus alone is not sufficient authority for such a decision, as he is known and admitted to be inaccurate in his record of dates.

But this notion has prevailed : the date B. C. 4 has been generally accepted, and historical events and dates have been somewhat bent to fit and support this theory.   Among other supposed proofs that B. C. 4 was the proper date, was an eclipse of the moon, said by Josephus to have occurred a short time before the death of Herod.   All that is known of that eclipse is as follows : Herod had placed a large golden eagle over the gate of the Temple.   Two notable Jews, named Matthias and Judas, persuaded some young men to pull it down.   They did so, were arrested and executed. To make the matter clear, Josephus relates that there was at that time another Matthias, a high-priest, who was not concerned in the sedition.   He then adds : " But Herod deprived this Matthias of his high-priesthood, and burnt the other Matthias who had raised the sedition, with his companions, alive, and that very night there was an eclipse of the moon."   This is recorded as one of the last prominent acts of Herod, and is given a date which might correspond with B. C. 4 by Josephus, who marks the date by the eclipse mentioned.

But since at times as many as four eclipses of the moon occur in one year, it is evident that except under very peculiar circumstances the record of such an occurrence proves nothing.   Where the time of the night, the time of the year and the amount of obscuration are all given, as has been done in several instances, the record is of great value in fixing dates ; but in the case under consideration, there is nothing of the kind ; hence absolutely nothing is proved by the record, so far as chronology is concerned. Josephus does mention a fast, as having been kept before the event, but what fast, or how long before, is not stated.

As it happens, there was only one eclipse of the moon in B. C. 4, while in B. C. 1 there were three. The eclipse of B. C. 4 was only partial (six digits, or only one-half of the moon being obscured), while all three in B. C. 1 were total eclipses—the entire moon was obscured, and of course for a longer time, causing the event to be much more noticeable. Hence if the eclipse theory has any weight it certainly is not in favor of the earlier date, B. C. 4.

Unfortunately, the time of Herod's death is not given by a reliable historian. Josephus gives some important periods in his history and the dates of some events, but these dates are not trustworthy. Some of them would teach that Herod died B. C. 4, but others cannot be reconciled with that date. For instance, his death is said to have been at the age of seventy. He was made governor of Galilee B. C. 47, at which time Josephus says he was twenty-five years of age. (Ant. 149:2.) This would date his birth B. C. 72 (47 plus 25). His death at seventy would then be B. C. 2 instead of B. C. 4.

In this connection it may be well to note the conflict of opinion among learned men, relative to the exact date of Herod's death, that thus it may be apparent to all that there is no well founded reason for accepting B. C. 4 as the only date in harmony with Matt. 2:14–16. Faussetts' Bible Encyclopædia gives Herod's age when made governor at about twenty years. This would make his death, at seventy years, A. D. 2. Chambers' Cyclopædia and Smith's Bible Dictionary give his age at that time as fifteen years, which would place his death A. D. 7. Appleton's Cyclopædia, article Chronology, says: "Josephus also gives dates, but he is altogether too careless to be taken into account."

We now proceed to offer the Scriptural evidence relating to this subject, which more nearly agrees with the common era, and shows that our Lord's birth occurred only one year and three months prior to January, A. D. 1. It is as follows:—

Our Lord's ministry lasted three and a half years. The sixty-nine symbolic weeks of years (Dan. 9 : 24–27) reached to his baptism and anointing as Messiah, and there the last or seventieth week (seven years) of Israel's favor began. He was cut off [in death] in the *middle* of that seventieth week—three and a half years from the beginning of his ministry. He was crucified, we know, at the time of the Passover, about April 1st, whatever the year. The three and *a half* years of his ministry, which ended in April, must consequently have begun about October, whatever the year. And October of some year must have been the true month of his birth, because he *delayed not* to begin his ministry as soon as he was thirty, and could not, according to the Law (under which he was born and which he obeyed), begin before he was thirty. As we read, "Now when Jesus *began to be* about thirty years of age *he cometh*" etc.

John the Baptist was six months older than our Lord (Luke 1 : 26, 36), hence he was of age (thirty years, according to the Law—Num. 4 : 3 ; Luke 3 : 23, etc.) and began to preach six months before our Lord became of age and began his ministry. The date of the beginning of John's ministry is clearly stated to have been the "fifteenth year of the reign of Tiberius Cæsar," the third emperor of Rome. (Luke 3 : 1.) This is a clearly fixed date of which there can be no reasonable doubt. Tiberius became emperor at the death of Augustus Cæsar, in the year of Rome 767, which was the year A. D. 14.

But those misled by the inaccurate statements of Josephus relative to Herod, and who place the birth of Jesus at B. C. 4, in order to harmonize with him, run across a difficulty in this clearly stated date given by Luke, and endeavor to make it also harmonize with their B. C. 4 theory. To accomplish this end they make the claim that Tiberius began to exercise authority some three or four years before Augustus died, and before he was fully constituted emperor. They claim that possibly his rule might have been reckoned from that date.

But such suppositions will be found baseless, by any who will investigate the matter on the pages of history. It is true that Tiberius was exalted to a very important position by Augustus, but it was not *four* years before Augustus' death, as their theory would demand, but *ten* years before, in A. D. 4. But the power then conferred upon him was only such as had been enjoyed by others before his day. It was in no sense of the word imperial power, and in no sense of the word can his "*reign*" be said to have begun there: he was only the heir-apparent. Even in the most exaggerated use of language, his "*reign*" could not be said to have commenced before Augustus' death and his own investiture in office at the hands of the Roman Senate, A. D. 14.

History says, "The Emperor, whose declining age needed an associate, adopted Tiberius A. D. 4, *renewing* his tribunian power."—Article TIBERIUS, *Rees' Cyclopædia.*

"He [Augustus] determined accordingly to devolve upon him [Tiberius] a share in the government. * * This formal investiture placed him on the same footing as that enjoyed by the veteran Agrippa during his later years, and there can be no doubt that it was universally regarded as an introduction to the first place in the empire. * * The programme *for the succession* was significantly shadowed out: Tiberius had been ordered to assume his place at the head of the Senate, the people, and the army." * * The *adop-*

tion, which took place at the same time, is dated June 27 (A. U. C. 757)—A. D. 4.—*Merivale's History of the Romans* (Appleton's), Vol. IV., pp. 220, 221.

Thus there is conclusive proof that the first year of the reign of Tiberius Cæsar was not three or four years before Augustus died; and that the honors referred to as conferred during Augustus' reign were conferred ten, and not four, years before Augustus' death, and then were in no sense imperial honors.

We may, therefore, consider the date of Luke 3 : 1 not merely the only one furnished in the New Testament, but an unequivocal one. There can be no doubt about it in the minds of any who have investigated it. Tiberius began to reign in A. D. 14. The fifteenth year of his reign, would therefore be the year A. D. 29, in which year, Luke states (3 : 1-3), John began his ministry. Since our Lord's thirtieth birthday and the beginning of his ministry were in October, and since John's birthday and the beginning of his ministry were just six months earlier, it follows that John began his ministry in the spring, about April first—just as soon as he was of age; for God's plans are always carried out on exact time. So, then, John was thirty years old in A. D. 29, about April first, consequently he was born B. C. 2 *, about April first. And Jesus' birth, six months later, must have been B. C. 2, about October first.

Again, there is clear, strong evidence that Jesus was crucified on Friday, April 3rd, A. D. 33. The fact that his crucifixion occurred at the close of the fourteenth day of the month Nisan, and that this date rarely falls on Friday, but did so in the year A. D. 33, substantiates that date so thoroughly that even Usher, who adopted B. C. 4 as the

---

* For the benefit of readers not much accustomed to calculating dates, we call attention to the fact that in the beginning of the year A. D. 29, only 28 full years had elapsed : the twenty-ninth was only beginning.

date of Jesus' birth, was forced to admit that his crucifixion was A. D. 33. Compare Usher's dates in the margin of the common version Bible at Luke 2 : 21 and Matt. 2 : 1 with those at Matthew 27 and Luke 23. The date of the crucifixion being A. D. 33, it follows that if Jesus had been born B. C. 4, he would have been 36 years old when he died ; and his ministry from his thirtieth to his thirty-sixth year would have been six years. But it is clear that our Lord's ministry was three and a half years only. And this generally conceded fact is proved by Daniel's prophecy concerning Messiah's cutting off in the *middle* of the seventieth week of Israel's favor.

Thus, it is again proven that Jesus' birth was about one year and three months before our common era, A. D. 1; for, his ministry ending when he was thirty-three and a half years old, April 3d, A. D. 33, the date of his birth may be readily found by measuring backward to a date thirty-three and a half years prior to April 3d, A. D. 33. Thirty-two years and three months before April A. D. 33 would be January 3d, A. D. 1, and one year and three months further back would bring us to October 3d, B. C. 2, as the date of our Lord's birth at Bethlehem. The difference between lunar time, used by the Jews, and solar time, now in common use, would be a few days, so that we could not be certain that the exact day might not be in September about the 27th, but October 1st, B. C. 2, is *about* correct. Nine months back of that date would bring us to about Christmas time, B. C. 3, as the date at which our Lord laid aside the glory which he had with the Father before the world was [made] and the taking of or changing to human nature began. It seems probable that this was the origin of the celebration of December 25th as Christmas Day. Some writers on Church history claim, even, that Christmas Day was originally celebrated as the date of the annunciation by Ga-

briel to the virgin Mary. (Luke 1 : 26.)   Certain it is that
a midwinter date does not well agree with the declaration
of Scripture, that at the time of our Lord's birth the shepherds were in the fields with their flocks.

> " Lift up your heads, desponding pilgrims;
>   Give to the winds your needless fears;
> He who has died on Calvary's mountain
>   Soon is to reign a thousand years.
>
> " A thousand years! earth's coming glory—
>   'Tis the glad day so long foretold:
> 'Tis the bright morn of Zion's glory,
>   Prophets foresaw in times of old.
>
> " Tell the whole world these blessed tidings;
>   Speak of the time of rest that nears;
> Tell the oppressed of every nation,
>   Jubilee lasts a thousand years.
>
> " What if the clouds do for a moment
>   Hide the blue sky where morn appears?
> Soon the glad sun of promise given
>   Rises to shine a thousand years."
>   —*Bonar.*

STUDY III.

THE FULFILMENT OF TIME–PROPHECY AT THE FIRST ADVENT OF CHRIST.

Dan. 9 : 23-27.

THE SEVENTY WEEKS OF DANIEL'S PROPHECY.—EVENTS FORETOLD TO TRANSPIRE WITHIN THAT TIME.—THE TIME OF MESSIAH'S ADVENT INDICATED, AND A PRINCIPLE ESTABLISHED BY THE MANNER IN WHICH IT IS INDICATED.—A KEY TO OTHER TIME-PROPHECIES.—THE TIME OF MESSIAH'S CRUCIFIXION INDICATED. —THE SPECIAL FAVOR TO ISRAEL AS A NATION CUT SHORT IN RIGHTEOUS-NESS, BUT CONTINUED INDIVIDUALLY.—ANOINTING THE MOST HOLY.—TROUBLE POURED UPON THE DESOLATE ONE.

"UNDERSTAND the matter, and consider the vision. Seventy weeks are determined upon thy people and upon thy holy city, to finish the transgression, and to make an end of sins, and to make reconciliation for iniquity, and to bring in everlasting righteousness, and to seal up the vision and prophecy, and to anoint the most holy. Know therefore and understand, that from the going forth of the commandment to restore and to build Jerusalem, unto the Messiah the Prince, shall be seven weeks, and threescore and two weeks [7 and 60 and 2 = 69 weeks]: the street shall be built again, and the wall, even in troublous times.

"And after threescore and two weeks shall Messiah be cut off, but not for himself. (And the people of the prince that shall come [the Roman prince—Titus' army] shall destroy the city and the sanctuary; and the end thereof shall be with a flood, and unto the end of the war desolations are determined.) And he [Messiah] shall confirm the covenant with many for one week [the seventieth, or last week of the covenant of favor]. And in the midst of the week

63

he shall cause the sacrifice and the oblation to cease, and
for [or because of] the overspreading of abominations, he
[Messiah] shall make it desolate—even until the consummation [or completion] and that [which is] determined
[in God's plan] shall be poured upon the desolate " [peo-
ple—represented by Jerusalem].—Dan. 9: 23–27.

While this prophecy marks the beginning of the " harvest " of the Jewish age and our Lord's presence there as
the chief reaper, there are several prophecies which much
more clearly mark the beginning of the " harvest " of the
Gospel age, in which also our Lord is, at his second advent,
to be the chief reaper. The fulfilment of this prophecy
illustrates prophetic fulfilments in general, as well as establishes a point marked in another prophecy, yet to be shown.

While many prophecies combine to fix and confirm the
date of the second coming of Christ, this one alone marked
the date of the first advent. If its fulfilment is clearly
established, it will aid us in calculating and judging of those
relating to the second advent. For this reason we here
give place to this fulfilled prophecy, as well as because some
of the dates established in this will be needful to be understood in connection with prophecies relating to the second
advent, considered farther along.

Daniel had been shown many visions, as recorded in
chapters 2, 4, 7 and 8 of his prophecy, all of which showed
great prosperity and exaltation to heathen or gentile kingdoms; but his special interest was in Israel, and he had not
been informed concerning Israel's future. He knew, however, from Jeremiah's prophecy (Jer. 29: 10; 2 Chron.
36: 20–23), that the desolation of Judea would continue
seventy years; and knowing that period to be nearly complete (Dan. 9: 2), he prayed earnestly for the return of God's
favor to Israel (verses 17–19), and the foregoing was God's
answer to him through an angel.

The *marked off* ("cut off," or "determined") period of Israel's history here shown is "*seventy weeks*" from a given starting point—viz., from the going forth of a decree "to restore and to build Jerusalem." (Mark! not the Temple.) During the period great things were to be accomplished:— The city would be rebuilt under unfavorable circumstances (Neh. 4), in troublous times; sin would be finished by a reconciliation being made for iniquity; and righteousness (justification) would be established—not like that accomplished year by year with the blood of bulls and goats, but the true and "everlasting righteousness," brought about by the sacrifice of Christ. Daniel was also informed that he who would introduce the better sacrifice would thereby cause the typical sacrifices and oblations of the Law to *cease*.

In this period, Messiah, the long-looked-for Saviour of Israel, would come, and seven weeks and threescore and two weeks, or sixty-nine weeks, are stated as the measure of the time to Messiah's presence. And after that he would be cut off, but not for himself. There would therefore remain, after Messiah's coming, one week, the last, the seventieth of this promised favor; and in the midst or middle of that week it was foretold that he would cause the typical sacrifices to cease, by making "his soul an offering for sin."—Isa. 53: 10–12.

These seventy weeks, or four hundred and ninety days, represented four hundred and ninety years, each symbolic day representing a year. And being *so fulfilled* in this, the only time-prophecy directly relating to the first advent, it furnishes a key to some other prophecies which will hereafter be shown to have been thus hidden in symbolic numbers—*a day for a year*—until their due time had come for solution. This prophecy was so worded that Daniel and other Jews might, if they chose, think it incredible, and in time forget it; or it might be remembered by those who "*waited* for the consolation of Israel," and who might infer the time to be symbolic, as in the case of Ezekiel. (Chap. 4:6.) Certain it is that faithful ones knew to expect Messiah; and it is even written that all men were in expectation of him (Luke 3:15), even if they were not all able to receive him in the way he came.

It should be noticed that the sixty-nine symbolic weeks, or four hundred and eighty-three years, reach *unto Messiah the Prince*, and not to the birth of Jesus in Bethlehem. The Hebrew word *Messiah*, corresponding to the Greek word *Christ*, signifies *The Anointed*, and is a title rather than a name. Jesus was not the Anointed, the Messiah, the Christ, until after his baptism. Compare Acts 10:37, 38 and Matt. 3:16. He was anointed with the holy Spirit immediately on coming out of the water. This was when he had attained manhood's estate, which was at thirty years according to the Law, under which he was born, and to which he and every Jew was subject until he ended its dominion by fulfilling its conditions—"nailing it to his cross." Therefore the sixty-nine weeks of this prophecy reach to the time of his baptism and anointing, from which time, and not before, he was the Messiah, the Christ, the Anointed. Hence the sixty-nine weeks, or four hundred and eighty-three years, ended in the autumn of A. D. 29. And there that portion of the prophecy was fulfilled which says: "From the going forth of the commandment to restore and to build Jerusalem (Dan. 9:25), unto Messiah [the Anointed] the Prince, shall be seven weeks and three-score and two [sixty-nine] weeks." Beginning there, we find the seventieth week fulfilled like the rest—a year for a day.

Most writers on this subject have commenced to count this period from the seventh year of Artaxerxes, when a commission was given to Ezra (Ezra 7:7-14), supposed to be the enforcement of the decree of Cyrus. (Ezra 1:3;

5 : 13 ; 6 : 1–12.)   It should be noted, however, that Cyrus'
order was to build the house of the Lord—the Temple and
its court wall.   But there was another decree granted to
Nehemiah in the twentieth year of Artaxerxes *to rebuild
the walls of Jerusalem*, which at that time were still unre-
paired. (Neh. 2 : 3–8 ; 6 : 15 ; 7 : 1.)   And it is from this
decree "to restore and to build Jerusalem" that this
prophecy of Daniel should be dated.   The entire account
harmonizes with this, there being but one seeming objection,
in a prophecy concerning it by Isaiah, which had said of
Cyrus, not only, " He shall let go my captives," but also,
"He shall build my *city*." (Isa. 45 : 13.)   This apparent
objection we answer thus :   The word here translated *city*
is *ir*, and signifies a walled place.   We understand the
court walls of the Temple to be referred to here; and with
this the facts above referred to agree.   The same word *ir*
is rendered *court* in 2 Kings 20 : 4.

The date of Nehemiah's commission is ordinarily stated
to be B. C. 445.   But Dr. Hale's work on chronology
(pages 449 and 531) and Dr. Priestlie's treatise on the
" Harmony of the Evangelists " (pages 24–38) show this
common view to be nine years short, which would give
B. C. 454 as the true date of Nehemiah's commission ; and
with this date Daniel's prediction (Chapter 9 : 25), concerning the decree to restore and to build Jerusalem, agrees.

Since sixty-nine weeks (7 and 62), or four hundred and
eighty-three years, reach *unto* Messiah (the Anointed)
the Prince, therefore from this period of sixty-nine symbolic weeks, or four hundred and eighty-three (483) years,
we deduct four hundred and fifty-four (454) years B. C. as
the true date of the decree to restore and to build Jerusalem ; and the remainder—29 A. D.—should be the year in
which the Anointed (Messiah) would be manifested.   This
is in exact accord with what we have already shown, viz. :

that Jesus was baptized by John and received the anointing
of the Spirit A. D. 29, about October 3d, at which time
he was thirty years of age, according to the true date of
his birth as shown in the preceding chapter.

Our Lord's ministry covered *three and a half* years, ending with his crucifixion, at the time of the Passover, in the
spring of A. D. 33.   In this he exactly fulfilled the prophecy concerning the remaining or last week (seven years) of
promised favor, which says: "*After* (7 and 62) sixty-nine
weeks shall Messiah be cut off [*Douay translation,* "be slain"]
but not for himself " *—" in the *midst of the week* [remain-
ing—the 70th] he shall cause the sacrifice and oblation
to cease."

The sacrifices which were offered according to the Law
there ceased; not that animals, incense, etc., were not
offered thereafter by the priests, for they continued to be
offered year by year, but that they were not accepted by
Jehovah, and were in no sense sacrifices for sin.   The true
sacrifice having come, our Lord Jesus having "put away
sin by the sacrifice of himself" (Heb. 9 : 26), Jehovah could
no longer recognize other offerings as sacrifices, nor any
necessity for them.

There, at the cross, Messiah, who had been sacrificing
himself for three and a half years, finished the work (John
19 : 30) and thus "made an end of sin," made full and
complete reconciliation toward God for the iniquity of
men, thus bringing to all mankind an *everlasting* justification from sin, instead of the typical yearly justification, accomplished by the types for the typical people, Israel.   The
death of Messiah was also the "*seal*"—the guarantee of
the fulfilment—of all the visions and prophecies of coming

---

* This expression, "but not for himself," is variously rendered in
other translations, several of which are before us; but in our opinion this,
of our common version, is the clearest and best rendering.

blessings, and "times of restitution of all things, which
God hath spoken by the mouth of all his holy prophets
since the world began." (Acts 3 : 21.) Those promises,
both the Abrahamic Covenant and the New Covenant, were
secured, made sure, with "his own precious blood" (Luke
22 : 20 ; 1 Cor. 11 : 25), which speaketh better things for us
than the blood of bulls and goats—even everlasting justification and putting away of sin, to all those who receive
him. And in the remainder or latter half of this seventieth or last week of Jewish favor—the three and a half
years, beginning with Pentecost—his followers, "the most
holy" of that nation, were anointed with the holy spirit of
God, as Messiah had been at the close of the sixty-ninth week.

Thus were fulfilled the statements of verse 24 of this
prophecy : "Seventy weeks are determined [set apart] upon
THY PEOPLE, and upon thy holy city—(*a*) to finish the
transgression, and to make an end of sins, and to make
reconciliation for iniquity, and to bring in everlasting righteousness—(*b*) and to seal up the vision and prophecy—
(*c*) and to anoint the most holy." The prophecy did not
show that this entire work would be deferred until the last
"week," when Messiah would be present ; and doubtless
they understood it to imply great moral reform on *their
part* which would prepare them for Messiah; and the anointing under him of their nation as the "most holy" people,
to bless the world in general. They had not learned by
centuries of experience that *they* were powerless to put
away sin and make reconciliation for iniquity, and that it
would require a perfect ransom-sacrifice to accomplish this
great work of blotting out sin and justifying the condemned.

On the other hand, Daniel's prophecy, while showing
that Messiah would be cut off [die] in the midst of the
last week, did not show that the mass of his people would
be *unholy* and therefore cast off. as they were, in the midst

of that week. (Matt. 23:38.) Another prophet had said, He shall finish the work and *cut it short* in righteousness [justly]; and all was finished in the half-week (three and a half years) of Jesus' ministry, except the anointing of the most holy.

But what of the balance of the seventieth week, the three and a half years of it which extended beyond the cross? Did Jehovah promise to set aside seventy weeks of favor upon Israel, and really give them but sixty-nine and a half? At first glance it has this appearance, especially when we recall that it was just five days before his death "in the midst of the week" that Jesus wept over their city and gave them up, saying, "Your house is left unto you desolate." But not so: Jehovah knew the end from the beginning; and when he promised seventy weeks, he meant it. Hence we must look for favor upon that people for three and a half years after the crucifixion, notwithstanding they were then left desolate nationally.

That the Israelites as a nation were not fit to be the recipients of the chief or spiritual favor (nor of the earthly favor either) was demonstrated by their rejection of Messiah, as God had foreseen and foretold; hence it was profitless to them to continue their national testing beyond the midst of their seventieth week, and it was cut short there, when they were left " desolate "—rejected from favor. During the remaining portion (three and a half years) of their period, the favor was *increased*, though confined to the " remnant," the most holy, the purest or fittest, whom alone it could benefit. (Isa. 10:22, 23. Compare Rom. 9:28.) The increase of favor consisted in the fact that it gave to that remnant three and a half years of exclusive attention and ministration, under the increased advantages of the spirit dispensation, which, beginning with the disciples at Pentecost, reached probably all the ripe wheat of that nation, during that period of special favor. See Acts 2 : 41 and 4 : 4 for the results of the first few days.

It was for this reason that, though Jesus had tasted death for all, and the Gospel was to be proclaimed to all, yet his instructions to his disciples were, that they *begin at Jerusalem*. Nor were they to leave that special work, or offer the favor of the new dispensation to any others, until the three and a half years of *promised favor to Israel* were fulfilled—until God specially sent it to the Gentiles as well as to the Jews.—Acts 10.

The exact date of the conversion of Cornelius, chronologers can only guess at; and hence it is variously estimated as having occurred from A. D. 37 to 40; but in view of this marked prophecy which we are now considering, we doubt not that it was in the autumn of A. D. 36; for there the seventy weeks, or four hundred and ninety years, of favor upon Israel ended. Since their exclusive favor ended there, most appropriately should it be marked by sending the gospel to the Gentiles. Israelites were not deprived of the gospel after that, but were treated the same as the Gentiles, though prejudice no doubt placed the remainder in a less favorable position. The "most holy" being already chosen out, the gospel was no longer confined to them exclusively, but was open to every creature having an ear to hear.

After the seventy weeks came the distress and trouble mentioned in the latter clauses of verses 26 and 27. The Roman prince came, and did destroy the city and the Temple, and, like a flood, he left behind him terrible waste and destruction. And Messiah, whom they rejected, has permitted various evils to befall that people since, and will continue to permit them "until the consummation," until they shall have had enough, until he shall say, "Speak ye comfortably to Jerusalem, and cry unto her that her appointed time is accomplished that her iniquity is pardoned." (Isa. 40: 2.) Meantime that *that is determined* shall be poured upon that desolate one (or cast off people) till her cup be full of sorrow—until that day when they shall say, "Blessed is he that cometh in the name of the Lord." That day of Israel's deliverance is now dawning, thank God ; and though their desolation and distress are not yet at an end, each hour hastens the time when their prejudice-blinded minds shall see out of obscurity him whom they have pierced, and when they shall mourn for him as one mourneth for his only son.—Zech. 12: 10.

Since many, in reading the passage here examined, have fallen into great confusion and error through a failure to understand rightly the arrangement of the Prophet's words, confounding Messiah the Prince with the Roman prince, etc., we suggest a careful study of the passage as arranged at the beginning of this chapter, noting the parenthesis and the explanatory remarks in brackets.

STUDY IV.

THE TIMES OF THE GENTILES.

[Since the topic considered in this chapter is very closely related to
that of chapter xiii. of Vol. I., the reader will be greatly assisted by a
review of that chapter before commencing this.]

"JERUSALEM shall be trodden down of the Gentiles,
until the times of the Gentiles be fulfilled."—Luke
21 : 24.

The term "Times of the Gentiles" was applied by our
Lord to that interval of earth's history between the removal
of the typical Kingdom of God, the Kingdom of Israel
(Ezek. 21 : 25–27), and the introduction and establishment
of its antitype, the true Kingdom of God, when Christ
comes to be "glorified in his saints, and to be admired
in all them that believe in that day."

During this interval, the dominion of earth was to be exercised by Gentile governments; and Israel, both fleshly
and spiritual, have been and are to be subject to these powers until their time is expired. While God does not approve of nor commend these governments, he recognizes
their dominion. In other words, he has for wise ends permitted their dominion for an appointed time.

The dominion of earth was originally given to Adam,
to subdue and possess and rule it in righteousness. (Gen.

73

1:28.) Adam failed, and the dominion forfeited by sin was taken from him. Angels were next permitted to have the control. Instead, however, of lifting up the fallen race, some of them "kept not their first estate," but fell into transgression. After the flood, God declared to Abraham his purpose to bring the needed help for the sinful, dying race through his posterity, by raising up from among them a great deliverer, ruler and teacher, saying, " In thy seed shall all the families of the earth be blessed."

This was the earliest suggestion of a national, universal dominion over earth. And this suggestion, coming from God, implied a special fitness, a peculiar superiority of this ruler over and above all others, and that it would be to the advantage of all mankind to be subject to such a ruler. That this promise to Abraham filled the hearts and minds of his posterity, Israel, and was well known by their relatives, the Moabites and Edomites, there can be no doubt. That such a national hope would become known to other nations is probable ; and, if known, we cannot doubt that pride would beget in them the desire to be the chief nation, and to have universal dominion, as being in every way as able and as fit to rule, and teach, and thus bless the nations, as any of Abraham's posterity.

Israel's hope of attaining universal dominion, not by the choice of the nations to have it so, but by God's choice and power manifested in their favor, seems to have spread to other nations also. At all events, we find that these Gentile kings and peoples accepted their dominions as favors from the gods whom they worshiped. And the same thought still clings to every petty ruler and prince, as well as to the more powerful kings and emperors. No matter how weak mentally or physically, and no matter how vicious and unfit to rule either themselves or others, they possess to an almost insane degree the idea that God specially chose them and their families to rule over and "BLESS" (?) all the earth. This theory, accepted by the masses of the people, is blazoned forth on medals, coins and papers of state in the words, "King ——— by the grace of God."

Thus, while Israel were waiting and hoping for the promised dominion of earth, and often supposed they were just within reach of its realization, particularly under kings David and Solomon, the desire for universal empire became general among other nations. And when God was about to remove the crown from Israel until the true seed of promise should come to take the dominion, he determined to let the Gentile kingdoms take control and try the experiment of ruling the world, that thus the world might also learn the futility of its own efforts at self-government while in its present sinful condition. As he had given the dominion forfeited by Adam to the angels, to demonstrate their inability to rule and bless the world, so he now delivered that dominion over to the Gentiles, to let them try their various methods, unaided by him. These various *experiments* God permits, as so many valuable and necessary lessons, filling the intervening time until the Lord's Anointed, whose right it is, shall come and take the dominion and accomplish all his gracious purposes.

Since Israel after the flesh was typical of spiritual Israel, the Gospel Church, which is also called in this higher sense "a royal priesthood and holy nation" (1 Pet. 2: 9), and which in due time is to rule and bless all nations, so their kingdom was typical in some respects of the Kingdom of Christ. Consequently, when God's time came to turn over the dominion of earth to Gentile rule, it was appropriate that he should first remove the typical crown from Israel, and that the typical kingdom should no longer be recognized. This he did, declaring that they had *proven themselves unfit* for exaltation to universal dominion, having become corrupt, vain and idolatrous, in proportion as they had attained national distinction. This was in the days of King Zedekiah; and the divine decree was expressed in the words of the prophet: "Thus saith the Lord God, remove the diadem and take off the crown: this shall not be the same: exalt him that is low and abase him that is high. I will overturn, overturn, overturn it; and it shall be no more until he come whose right it is, and I will give it him."— Ezek. 21 : 24–27.

This overturning of the crown, or dominion, has been accomplished. It was first turned over to Babylon, then to Medo-Persia, then to Grecia, and then to Rome. The character of these empires, as recorded on the pages of history, we have found to agree perfectly with the prophetic descriptions, as portrayed in Nebuchadnezzar's vision of the great image and in Daniel's vision of the four beasts. This overturned condition of Israel's dominion was to continue until Christ, the rightful heir to the throne of Israel and all the earth, who purchased it with his own precious blood, would come and take control. His, as we have seen, will be the fifth universal empire of earth, the Kingdom of God under the whole heavens. But unlike the preceding four dominions which were permitted for an appointed time, and therefore recognized, though not approvingly, this one will be approved and established by God, as his representative in the earth. It will be God's Kingdom, the Kingdom of Jehovah's Anointed. It will be established gradually, during a great time of trouble with which the Gospel age will close, and in the midst of which present dominions shall be utterly consumed, passing away amid great confusion.

In this chapter we present the Bible evidence proving that the full end of the times of the Gentiles, *i. e.*, the full end of their lease of dominion, will be reached in A. D.

1914; and that that date will be the farthest limit of the rule of imperfect men.   And be it observed, that if this is shown to be a fact firmly established by the Scriptures, it will prove:—

Firstly, That at that date the Kingdom of God, for which our Lord taught us to pray, saying, "Thy Kingdom come," will obtain full, universal control, and that it will then be "set up," or firmly established, in the earth, on the ruins of present institutions.

Secondly, It will prove that he whose right it is thus to take the dominion will then be present as earth's new Ruler; and not only so, but it will also prove that he will be present for a considerable period before that date; because the overthrow of these Gentile governments is directly caused by his dashing them to pieces as a potter's vessel (Psa. 2:9; Rev. 2:27), and establishing in their stead his own righteous government.

Thirdly, It will prove that some time before the end of A. D. 1914 the last member of the divinely recognized Church of Christ, the "royal priesthood," "the body of Christ," will be glorified with the Head; because every member is to reign with Christ, being a joint-heir with him of the Kingdom, and it cannot be fully "set up" without every member.

Fourthly, It will prove that from that time forward Jerusalem shall no longer be trodden down of the Gentiles, but shall arise from the dust of divine disfavor, to honor; because the "Times of the Gentiles" will be fulfilled or completed.

Fifthly, It will prove that by that date, or sooner, Israel's blindness will begin to be turned away; because their "blindness in part" was to continue only "*until* the fulness of the Gentiles be come in" (Rom. 11:25), or, in other words, until the full number from among the Gentiles, who are to be members of the body or bride of Christ, would be fully selected.

Sixthly, It will prove that the great "time of trouble such

as never was since there was a nation,'' will reach its culmination in a world-wide reign of anarchy; and then men
will learn to be still, and to know that Jehovah is God
and that he will be exalted in the earth.   (Psa. 46:10.)
The condition of things spoken of in symbolic language
as raging waves of the sea, melting earth, falling mountains
and burning heavens will then pass away, and the ''new heavens and new earth'' with their peaceful blessings will begin
to be recognized by trouble-tossed humanity.   But the
Lord's Anointed and his rightful and righteous authority
will first be recognized by a company of God's children
while passing through the great tribulation—the class represented by *m* and *t* on the Chart of the Ages (see also
pages 235 to 239, VOL. I.); afterward, just at its close, by
fleshly Israel; and ultimately by mankind in general.

Seventhly, It will prove that *before that date* God's Kingdom, organized in power, will be in the earth and then
smite and crush the Gentile image (Dan. 2:34)—and fully
consume the power of these kings.   Its own power and
dominion will be established as fast as by its varied influences and agencies it crushes and scatters the ''powers that
be''—civil and ecclesiastical—iron and clay.

THE BEGINNING OF GENTILE TIMES, 606 B. C.

Our Lord's words, ''until the *times** of the Gentiles be
fulfilled,'' imply that the times of the Gentiles must have
a definitely appointed limit; because an unlimited, indefinite period could not be said to be fulfilled.   So, then,
Gentile rule had a beginning, will last for a *fixed time*, and
will end at the time appointed.

---

* The Greek word here rendered ''times'' is *kairos,* which signifies *a
fixed time.*   It is the same word translated ''times'' in the following passages: Mark 1:15; I Tim. 6:15; Rev. 12:14; Acts 3:19; 17:26.
The word ''seasons'' in Acts 1:7 is from the same Greek word.

The beginning of these Gentile Times is clearly located by the Scriptures. Hence, if they furnish us the length *also* of the fixed period, or lease of Gentile dominion, we can know positively just when it will terminate. The Bible does furnish this fixed period, which must be fulfilled; but it was furnished in such a way that it could not be understood when written, nor until the lapse of time and the events of history had shed their light upon it; and even then, only by those who were watching and who were not overcharged by the cares of the world.

The Bible evidence is clear and strong that the "Times of the Gentiles" is a period of 2520 years, from the year B. C. 606 to and including A. D. 1914. This lease of universal dominion to Gentile governments, as we have already seen, began with Nebuchadnezzar—not when his reign began, but when the typical kingdom of the Lord passed away, and the dominion of the whole world was left in the hands of the Gentiles. The date for the beginning of the Gentile Times is, therefore, definitely marked as at the time of the removal of the crown of God's typical kingdom, from Zedekiah, their last king.

According to the words of the prophet (Ezek. 21: 25–27), the crown was taken from Zedekiah; and Jerusalem was besieged by Nebuchadnezzar's army and laid in ruins, and so remained for seventy years—until the restoration in the first year of Cyrus. (2 Chron. 36: 21–23.) Though Jerusalem was then rebuilt, and the captives returned, Israel has never had another king from that to the present day. Though restored to their land and to personal liberty by Cyrus, they, as a nation, were subject successively to the Persians, Grecians and Romans. Under the yoke of the latter they were living when our Lord's first advent occurred, Pilate and Herod being deputies of Cæsar.

With these facts before us, we readily find the date for

the beginning of the Gentile Times of dominion; for the first year of the reign of Cyrus is a very clearly fixed date —both secular and religious histories with marked unanimity agreeing with Ptolemy's Canon, which places it B. C. 536. And if B. C. 536 was the year in which the seventy years of Jerusalem's desolation ended and the restoration of the Jews began, it follows that their kingdom was overthrown just seventy years before B. C. 536, *i. e.*, 536 plus 70, or B. C. 606. This gives us the date of the beginning of the Times of the Gentiles—B. C. 606.

Recognizing God's lease of power to these worldly or Gentile governments, we know, not only that they will fail, and be overthrown, and be succeeded by the Kingdom of Christ when their "times" expire, but also that God will not take the dominion from them, to give it to his Anointed, until that lease expires—"until the Times of the Gentiles be fulfilled." Consequently, we are guarded right here against the false idea into which Papacy has led the world —that the Kingdom of God was *set up* at Pentecost, and more fully established when, as it is claimed, the Roman empire was converted to Christianity (to Papacy), and it attained both temporal and spiritual empire in the world. We see from this prophecy of the Times of the Gentiles that this claim made by the church of Rome, and more or less endorsed by Protestants, is false. We see that those nations which both Papacy and Protestantism designate Christian Nations, and whose dominions they call Christendom (*i. e.* Christ's Kingdom), are not such. They are "kingdoms of this world," and until their "times" are fulfilled Christ's Kingdom cannot take the control, though it will be organizing and preparing to do so in the few years which close the Gentile Times, while these kingdoms will be trembling, disintegrating and falling into anarchy.

During the Gospel age, the Kingdom of Christ has existed

only in its incipient stage, in its humiliation, without power or privilege of reigning—without the crown, possessing only the scepter of promise: unrecognized by the world, and subject to the " powers that be "—the Gentile kingdoms.   And the heirs of the heavenly kingdom must so continue, until the time appointed for them to reign together with Christ.   During the time of trouble, closing this age, they will be exalted to power, but their *" reign "* of righteousness over the world can date only from A. D. 1914 —when the Times of the Gentiles have expired.   Therefore it is the duty of the Church to await patiently the appointed time for its triumph and glorious reign ; to keep separate from the kingdoms of this world as strangers, pilgrims and foreigners ; and, as heirs of the Kingdom to come, to let their hopes and ambitions center in it.   Christians should recognize the true character of these kingdoms, and, while they keep separate from them, should render to them due respect and obedience, because God has permitted them to rule. As Paul teaches, " Let every soul be subject unto the higher powers ; for there is no power but of God."—Rom. 13 : 1.

Nor can fleshly Israel come into their long promised inheritance until that time, though preparatory steps will previously be taken ; for God will not fully establish either the earthly or the spiritual phase of his Kingdom until this lease to the Gentiles expires.

The crown (dominion) was removed from God's people (both the spiritual and the fleshly seed) until the Times of the Gentiles shall end—at the glorious presence of Messiah, who will be not only "King of the Jews," but "King over all the earth, in that day."   Some may think that this removal of the crown from Israel was a violation of the promise, " The scepter shall not depart from Judah, nor a law-giver from between his feet, until Shiloh come." (Gen. 49 : 10.)   Note, however, a distinction between the *crown*

6–B

and the *scepter;* for, though the crown passed away in the days of Zedekiah, the scepter, as we shall see, did not depart until six hundred and thirty-nine years afterward—when our Lord Jesus, of the tribe of Judah and seed of David according to the flesh, being approved of God, became the rightful and only heir of the long-promised scepter of earth.

God's promise to Abraham, renewed to Isaac and to Jacob, was that from their posterity should come the great deliverer who should not only bless and exalt their family in the world, but who should "*bless* ALL the families of the earth." It looked for a time as though Moses, the great Law-giver and deliverer, was the one promised; but he prophetically declared to the people, "A Prophet *like unto me* shall the Lord your God raise up unto you of your brethren," thus indicating that he was but a type of him that was to come; and Moses died. Next, the promise, "The scepter shall not depart from Judah," narrowed down the expectation to that tribe. And all the other tribes in a measure clung to Judah in proportion as they had faith in God's promises, expecting a blessing in conjunction with Judah, in due time.

When King David arose from the promised tribe, his victories led to great expectations of an extended kingdom, whose influence would spread and embrace the world, and *subject* all nations to the Law. And when Solomon's world-renowned wisdom and greatness were at their height, it surely looked as though the crown of *universal dominion* was almost within their grasp. The Lord's promise to David, that of the *fruit of his loins* he would raise up one to sit on his throne forever, had narrowed down the promise in the tribe of Judah to *one family*, and that family already on the throne of Israel. And when the grand Temple of Solomon was erected, and its hundreds of singers and priests were an imposing spectacle; when Solomon's fame for wisdom and riches was world-wide; when kings sent him presents and desired his favor; and when the queen of Sheba came with gifts to see this most renowned and wonderful king the world had yet known, no wonder the Jewish bosom swelled with hope and pride as the long expected moment for the exaltation of the seed of Abraham, and the blessing of all nations through them, seemed just at hand.

Sore was their disappointment when, after Solomon's death, the kingdom was torn, and finally utterly overturned, and the people who had expected to rule and bless all nations as God's holy nation were carried captives to Babylon. "By the rivers of Babylon there we sat down, yea, we wept when we remembered Zion."—Psa. 137.

But though the crown was removed, *i. e.*, though the *power* to govern even themselves was taken from them, the *right* to rule (the scepter), conveyed originally in God's promise, was not removed. Though universal dominion was given to Nebuchadnezzar and his successors, as illustrated in the great image, and by the four great beasts, yet it was to continue only a limited period. The original promise to Israel must be fulfilled—the crown was removed, but the scepter remained until Shiloh came. This was even pointed out in the decree against Zedekiah: Take off the crown—I will overturn it, *till* he come whose *right it is*, and I will give it unto him.

While the covenant made with Abraham promised the ruling and blessing of the world through his seed, the covenant of the Law made with Israel, Abraham's children, limited and restricted that Abrahamic Covenant, so that only such as would fully and perfectly obey the Law could claim, or had any right to hope for, a share in the ruling and blessing promised in the Abrahamic Covenant. Seeing this fact led to the formation of the sect of the Pharisees, who claimed to fulfil every particular of the Law blamelessly, and "trusted in themselves that they were *righteous* and despised **others,**" calling others " publicans and sinners " and themselves **the** " children of Abraham," heirs of the promised **dominion** which was to bless the world.

The clear, forcible teaching of our Lord Jesus was in part directed against the errors of the Pharisees, who supposed that their careful performance of some of the outward ceremonies of the Law was a full compliance with its letter and spirit. Our Lord taught what all Christians now know, that the Law, when seen in its fulness, is so majestically perfect, and man so fallen and *imperfect*, and so beset with temptations from without as well as by weakness from within, that none of them could possibly keep that Law perfectly nor claim the Abrahamic blessing. Our Lord's censures of Pharisaism must not therefore be understood as objections to their endeavor to keep the Law blamelessly; nor did he blame them for failing to keep the Law fully, which no imperfect man can do. But he did blame them for hypocrisy, in deceiving themselves and others with a claimed perfection and holiness, which they as well as others could see was merely a cleansing of the outside, while their hearts were still impure and unconsecrated. He censured them for having a mere form of godliness, and a lip service, while their hearts were far from God. So, then, as our Lord and Paul declare, none of them really did or really *could* keep the Law perfectly (John 7 : 19 ; Rom. 3 : 20), though they might have come much nearer to a perfect observance of its requirements than they did.

Our Lord not only declared in words the full import of the Law to be, "Thou shalt love the Lord thy God with *all* thy heart, and with *all* thy mind, and with *all* thy soul, and with *all* thy strength, and thy neighbor as thyself," but he *illustrated* this in his full surrender of himself to the will and plan of God, in his avoidance of any plan and ambition of his own, and of all self-seeking—a most hearty doing of the will of God with *all* his heart, mind, soul and strength, and loving his neighbor as himself;—all this even unto *death*.

Thus by fulfilling its conditions—by obeying the Law perfectly, as none of the imperfect human family *could do*— our Lord Jesus *became heir of all the blessings promised in that Law Covenant made with Israel at Mount Sinai; and thus also he was proved to be* THE SEED OF ABRAHAM *to whom the entire Abrahamic promise now applied.* Our Lord thus secured to himself the *sceptre* (the promised right or authority of earth's dominion) which for centuries had been promised should be merited by and given to some one in the tribe of Judah and family of David. The great prize, for which Israel had been hoping and striving and longing for centuries, was won at last by the Lion (the strong one) of the tribe of Judah. Shiloh, the great *Peace-maker*, had come: he who not only made peace between God and man by the blood of his cross, when he redeemed mankind from the condemnation of death justly upon all, but he who also, when he takes his great power and reigns King of kings and Lord of lords, will overthrow all wrong and evil and sin, and establish peace upon a sure basis of holiness. He is the Prince of Peace.

When the sceptre (the *right*) under the covenant passed to our Lord Jesus, that Law Covenant *ended;* for how could God continue to *offer* to others, on any conditions, the prize which had already been won by Shiloh? Hence, as the Apostle declares, "Christ made an end of the Law [covenant], nailing it to his cross."—Col. 2 : 14.

Thus the "Prince of Peace" secured for his subjects both forgiveness of sins and restitution, and established an ever-lasting kingdom on the basis of righteousness, such as could in no other way have been brought about. Thus was fulfilled the prediction, "The scepter shall not depart from Judah, nor a law-giver from between his feet [loins], *until* Shiloh come." Then it did depart from Judah, being given to "the Lion [the strong one, the highly exalted spiritual creature, the Lord of glory] *from* the tribe of Judah," who now holds this scepter [or title to authority] as King of kings and Lord of lords.

Even after the seventy years captivity in Babylon, when some returned and built again the Temple and the walls of the city, it was such as had respect to the promise of God, and who "waited for the consolation of Israel." These gathered about the tribe of Judah, remembering God's promise that the Lawgiver, the Deliverer, the great Shiloh or peace-maker, should come in that tribe. But alas! when the peaceful one who made peace and reconciliation for iniquity by the blood of his cross came, they despised and rejected him, expecting not a great High Priest, but a great general.

Shiloh having received the scepter and "all power" at his resurrection, because of his obedience unto death, will indeed bless Israel first—but not fleshly Israel, for they are not all true Israelites who are called such according to the flesh. (Rom. 9 : 6.) Shiloh, the *heir*, is seeking and finding children of Abraham according to the spirit—such as share the Abrahamic disposition of faith and obedience, both from his natural posterity and from among the Gentiles—to be a people for his name. (Acts 15 : 14.) And *"after this"* [after the gathering of his elect Church is accomplished—in the harvest or end of the Gospel age, at the close of the Gentile Times] he will turn again his favor and will build again the ruins of Israel, and finally of all the families of the earth, upon a better basis than has ever entered into the heart of man to conceive. He who now holds the scepter— "whose right it is" to rule—will at the expiration of the Gentile Times receive the crown also; "and unto him shall the gathering of the people be." (Gen. 49 : 10.) The scepter, or title to "all power in heaven and in earth," was given unto him at his resurrection, but he awaits the Father's appointed time—the limit of the Gentile Times—before he will take his great power and begin his glorious reign.—See Rev. 11 : 17, 18.

Now bear in mind the date already found for the beginning of these Gentile Times—viz., B. C. 606—while we proceed to examine the evidence proving their length to be 2520 years, ending A. D. 1914.

We must not expect to find this information stated in so many words. Had it been so stated, it would have been known before it was due. It is given in such a way as to conceal it until "the time of the end."—Dan. 12 : 4, 10.

Our Lord's words, "Jerusalem shall be trodden down of the Gentiles until the Times of the Gentiles be fulfilled," not only suggest a limit and definite period of Gentile domination, but they also suggest the thought that though spiritual as well as fleshly Israel has been subject to these Gentile powers, yet these "*times*" are somehow connected with and measured upon the earthly city, Jerusalem, and the fleshly house of Israel. And the thought occurs—Can it be that God foretold concerning Israel's history something which will give us the exact measure of these "*times*" to which our Lord refers? It is even so.

Turning to Leviticus we find recorded blessings and cursings of an earthly and temporal character. If Israel would obey God faithfully, they would be blessed above other nations; if not, certain evils would befall them. The conclusion is stated thus: "And I will walk among you and be your God, and ye shall be my people; . . . but if ye will not hearken unto me, and will not do all these commandments, . . . I will set my face against you, and ye shall be slain before your enemies ; they that hate you shall reign over you." "And ye shall sow your seed in vain ; for your enemies shall eat it." "*And if ye will not yet for all this hearken unto me*, THEN I WILL PUNISH YOU SEVEN TIMES *more* [further] *for your sins*."—Lev. 26 : 17, 18, 24, 28.

This threat of "*seven times*" of punishment is mentioned three times.　The various punishments mentioned before the "*seven times*" refer to the several captivities to the Assyrians, Moabites, Midianites, Philistines, etc., etc., during all of which God's care continued over them.　His dealings were to them "line upon line, precept upon precept, here a little and there a little ;" yet he kept hold of them, and when they repented and cried unto him, he heard them and answered, and delivered them from their enemies. (Judges 3 : 9, 15.)　But these chastisements having failed, he applied the threatened seven times : the crown was permanently removed, and Israel, as well as the whole world, was subject to the beastly powers for *seven times*.　Thus it befell them according to God's warning—"If ye will not yet for all this [previous chastisements] hearken unto me, then I will punish you *seven times*."

The connection in which the "*seven times*" (more, further, or additional) are threatened indicates that they include a final and conclusive punishment upon that people *after* the other chastisements had repeatedly failed to reform them permanently.　The punishment of these "*seven times*" will have the designed effect of thoroughly humbling them before the Lord, and thus preparing them to receive his blessings.　These *seven times* therefore refer to *the length of time* during which the Gentiles should rule over them. And to this period of "seven times" our Lord undoubtedly referred when speaking of "the *Times* of the Gentiles."

The time when the lesser captivities and chastisements gave place to this final great national chastisement of "seven times" was, as already shown, when their last king Zedekiah was removed—since which there has been one long period of chastisement—the predicted "seven times" or 2520 years.

In the Bible a *"time"* is used in the sense of a year, whether the year be literal or symbolic; but at the time of the utterance of any prophecy, it could not be known whether the *time* referred to was literal or symbolic. The prophets searched diligently, but in vain, to learn what time, or *manner of time* (literal or symbolic), the Spirit did signify. (1 Pet. 1:11.) A *symbolic* year as used in prophecy is reckoned on the basis of a lunar year—twelve months of thirty days each, or three hundred and sixty days—each day representing a year. Consequently, a "time" or year, if symbolic, signifies three hundred and sixty (360) symbolic days, and "seven times" represent twenty-five hundred and twenty (7x360=2520) symbolic days, or 2520 literal years.

The question here presenting itself is, Were these "seven times" literal or symbolic? Did they refer to seven years, or twenty-five hundred and twenty years? We answer, they were symbolic times, 2520 years. They cannot be understood as seven literal years; for Israel had many captivities of longer duration—for instance, they served the king of Mesopotamia eight years (Judges 3:8), the king of Moab eighteen years (Judges 3:14), King Jabin twenty years (Judges 4:2, 3), the Philistines one period of forty years and another of eighteen years (Judges 10:7, 8; 13:1), besides their seventy years in Babylon. All these periods being far longer than "seven times" or years literal, yet the "seven times" being mentioned as the last, greatest and final punishment, proves that symbolic, not literal time is meant, though the Hebrew word translated *"seven times"* in Leviticus 26:18, 21, 24, 28, is the same word so translated in Daniel 4:16, 23, 25, 32, except that in Daniel the word *iddan* is added, whereas in Leviticus it is left to be understood.

And, peculiarly, too, it is repeated four times in each case. In Nebuchadnezzar's case they were literal years, but, as we shall yet see, both Nebuchadnezzar and his "seven times" were typical.

The "*seven times*" of Nebuchadnezzar's degradation (Dan. 4: 16, 23–26) *proved* to be seven literal years, when actually so fulfilled ; and so the humiliation of Israel and the world under the "powers that be" has *proved* to be seven symbolic times—twenty-five hundred and twenty literal years. This period now lacks but twenty-six years of being fulfilled, and agencies are at work on every hand pointing to a termination of Gentile dominion, and the bringing in of everlasting righteousness and all the blessings of the New Covenant to Israel and to all the groaning creation.

THE END OF ISRAEL'S SEVEN TIMES.

This long period ("seven times," or 2520 years) of Israel's punishment is the period of Gentile dominion—the "Times of the Gentiles." Since, as we have already shown, the "Gentile Times" began B. C. 606, and were to continue twenty-five hundred and twenty years, they will end A. D. 1914. (2520 — 606 = 1914.) Then the blessings recorded in the latter part of the same chapter (Lev. 26 : 44, 45) will be fulfilled. God will remember and fulfil to Israel the covenant made with their fathers.—Rom. 11 : 25–27.

This may be shown more clearly to some thus :—

Israel's "seven times" of chastisement =   2520 years.
They began when the lease of power was
given to the Gentiles, which, as we have
shown, was 606 B. C. Consequently, in
A. D. 1,   606 "
of their period had passed, and the re-   — ——
mainder would indicate the A. D. date, viz.,   1914

In proof that a day for a year is *Bible usage* in symbolic prophecy, we cite the following instances thus fulfilled:—
(*a*) The spies were caused to wander forty days searching Canaan, typical of Israel's forty years wandering in the wilderness. (Num. 14: 33, 34.) (*b*) When God would announce to Israel by Ezekiel a period of adversity, he had the prophet symbolize it, declaring, "I have appointed thee each day for a year." (Ezek. 4: 1–8.) (*c*) In that notable and already fulfilled prophecy of Daniel 9: 24–27, examined in the preceding chapter, in which the time to the anointing of our Lord is shown, and also the seven years of favor to Israel thereafter, in the midst of which Messiah was "cut off," symbolic time is used: Each day of the seventy symbolic weeks represented a year, and was so fulfilled. (*a*) Again, in Dan. 7: 25 and 12: 7, the period of Papacy's triumph is given as three and a half times, and this we know (and will show in this volume) was fulfilled in twelve hundred and sixty years ($360 \times 3\frac{1}{2} = 1260$). The same period is mentioned in the book of Revelation: In chapter 12: 14 it is called three and a half times ($360 \times 3\frac{1}{2} = 1260$); in chapter 13: 5 it is termed forty-two months ($30 \times 42 = 1260$); and in chapter 12: 6 it is called twelve hundred and sixty days. The fulfilment of these prophecies will be particularly examined hereafter. Suffice it now to note that the use by the Spirit of the word "time," elsewhere, agrees with the present use of that term—that in symbolic prophecy a "time" is a symbolic year of three hundred and sixty years; and the fact that three and a half times, applied as a measure to the triumph of the apostate Church, has been fulfilled in twelve hundred and sixty years, establishes the principle upon which the *seven times* of Gentile dominion are reckoned ($360 \times 7 = 2520$) and proves their end to be A. D. 1914; for if three and a half times are 1260 days (years), seven times will be a period just twice as long, namely, 2520 years.

Had Israel's "seven times" been fulfilled in literal time (seven years), the blessing guaranteed to them by God's unconditional covenant with their fathers would have followed. (See Lev. 26 : 45 ; Rom. 11 : 28.) But this was not the case. They have never yet enjoyed those promised blessings ; and that covenant will not be fulfilled, says Paul (Rom. 11 : 25, 26), until the elect Gospel Church, the body of Christ, has been perfected as their deliverer, through whom the covenant will be put into operation. "This shall be the covenant that I will make with the house of Israel after *those days* [*i. e.*, the *seven times* of punishment], saith the Lord : I will put my law in their inward parts, and write it in their hearts, and will be their God and they shall be my people. And they shall teach no more every man his neighbor, and every man his brother, saying, Know the Lord ; for they shall all know me from the least of them unto the greatest of them, saith the Lord ; for I will forgive their iniquity, and I will remember their sin no more." (Jer. 31:33, 34; Heb. 10:16, 17.) "In those days [the days of favor following the seven times of punishment] they shall say no more, The fathers have eaten a sour grape and the children's teeth are set on edge. But every one [who dies] shall die for his own iniquity ; every man that eateth the sour grape, his teeth shall be set on edge."—Jer. 31 : 29, 30.

The restoration at the end of the seventy years in Babylon was not a release from Gentile rule ; for they were a tributary people ever after that. That restoration served merely to keep together a people to whom Messiah should be presented. It was while Gentile rule was already holding Israel in subjection, and in view of that fact, that our Lord declared that they would continue to be trodden down until the Times of the Gentiles expired, or were fulfilled. The world is witness to the fact that Israel's punishment under the dominion of the Gentiles has been continuous since B. C. 606, that it still continues, and that there is no reason to expect their national re-organization sooner than A. D. 1914, the limit of their "seven times"—2520 years. But as this long period of their national chastisement draws near its close, we can see marked indications that the barren fig tree is about to put forth, showing that the winter time of evil is closing, and the Millennial summer approaching, which will fully restore them to their promised inheritance and national independence. The fact that there are now great preparations and expectations relative to the return of Israel to their own land is of itself strong circumstantial evidence corroborative of this Scripture teaching. As to the significance of such an event, see Vol. I., pages 286–298.

ANOTHER LINE OF TESTIMONY.

Another view of the Gentile Times is presented by Daniel --Chapter 4. Here man's original dominion over the whole earth, its removal, and the certainty of its restitution, to begin at the end of the Gentile Times, is forcibly illustrated in a dream given to Nebuchadnezzar, its interpretation by Daniel, and its fulfilment upon Nebuchadnezzar.

In his dream, Nebuchadnezzar "saw, and behold a tree in the midst of the earth, and the height thereof was great. The tree grew and was strong, and the height thereof reached unto heaven, and the sight thereof to the end of all the earth; the leaves thereof were fair, and the fruit thereof much, and in it was meat for all: and the beasts of the field had shadow under it, and the fowls of the heaven dwelt in the boughs thereof, and all flesh was fed of it. And, behold, a watcher and a holy one came down from heaven. He cried aloud and said thus, Hew down the tree and cut off his branches; shake off his leaves and scatter his fruit; let the beasts get away from under it, and the fowls from his branches.   Nevertheless, leave the stump of his roots in the earth, even with a band of iron and brass, in the tender grass of the field ; and let it be wet with the dew of heaven, and let his portion be with the beasts in the grass of the earth.   Let his heart be changed from man's and let a beast's heart be given unto him ; and let *seven times* pass over him.   This matter is by the decree of the watchers, and the demand by the word of the holy ones, to the intent that the living may know that the Most High ruleth in the kingdom of men, and giveth it to whomsoever he will, and setteth up over it the basest of men.''

This remarkable tree, in its glory and beauty, represented the first dominion of earth given to the human race in its representative and head, Adam, to whom God said, '' Be fruitful, and multiply, and fill the earth, and subdue it ; and *have dominion* over the fish of the sea, and over the fowl of the air, and over every living thing that moveth upon the earth.'' (Gen. 1 : 28.) The original glory of man and the power vested in him were indeed sublime, and were over the whole earth, to bless, and feed, and protect and shelter every living thing.   But when sin entered, the command came to hew down the tree, and the glory and beauty and power of mankind were taken away ; and the lower creation no more found shelter, protection and blessing under his influence.   Death hewed down the great tree, scattered his fruit and foliage, and left the lower creation without its lord and benefactor.

So far as man was concerned, all power to recover the lost dominion was hopelessly gone.   But it was not so from God's standpoint. The dominion originally sprang out of his plan, and was his gracious gift ; and though he had command-ed it to be hewn down, yet the root—God's purpose and plan of a restitution—continued, though bound with strong fetters so that it should not sprout until the divinely appointed time.

As in the dream the figure changes from the stump of a tree to a man degraded and brought to the companionship and likeness of beasts, with reason dethroned and all his glory departed, so we see man, the fallen, degraded lord of earth: his glory and dominion have departed. Ever since the sentence passed, the race has been having its portion with the beasts, and the human heart has become beastly and degraded. How striking the picture, when we consider the present and past half-civilized and savage condition of the great mass of the human race, and that even the small minority who aspire to overcome the downward tendency succeed only to a limited degree, and with great struggling and constant effort. The race must remain in its degradation, under the dominion of evil, until the lesson has been learned, that the Most High ruleth in the kingdom of men, and giveth it to whomsoever he will. And while men are in this degraded condition God permits some of the basest characters among them to rule over them, that their present bitter experience may prove in the future to be of lasting benefit.

True to Daniel's interpretation, we are told that "All this came upon the king, Nebuchadnezzar," and that in this insane, degraded, beastly condition he wandered among the beasts until *seven times* (seven literal years in his case) passed over him. Daniel's interpretation of the dream relates only to its fulfilment upon Nebuchadnezzar; but the fact that the dream, the interpretation and the fulfilment are all so carefully related here is evidence of an object in its narration. And its remarkable fitness as an illustration of the divine purpose in subjecting the whole race to the dominion of evil for its punishment and correction, that in due time God might restore and establish it in righteousness and everlasting life, warrants us in accepting it as an intended type.

The dream in its fulfilment upon Nebuchadnezzar is specially noteworthy when we remember that he was made the representative ruling *head* of human dominion (Dan. 2 : 38), and, as lord of earth, was addressed by the prophet in almost the same words which God at the first addressed to Adam—"The God of heaven hath given thee a kingdom, power, and strength, and glory. And wheresoever the children of men dwell, the beasts of the field and the fowl of heaven hath he given into thy hand, and hath made thee ruler over them all." (Dan. 2 : 37–38. Compare Gen. 1 : 28.) Afterward, because of sin, Nebuchadnezzar received the "seven times" of punishment, after which his reason began to return, and his restitution to dominion was accomplished. He was re-established in his kingdom, and majesty was added unto him after he had learned the needed lesson to which he referred in the following language :—

"At the end of the days I, Nebuchadnezzar, lifted up mine eyes unto heaven, and mine understanding returned unto me, and I blessed the Most High, and I praised and honored him that liveth forever, whose dominion is an everlasting dominion, and his kingdom is from generation to generation. And all the inhabitants of the earth are reputed as nothing; and he doeth according to his will in the army of heaven, and among the inhabitants of the earth ; and none can stay his hand or say unto him, What doest thou ? At the same time my reason returned unto me ; and for the glory of my kingdom, mine honor and brightness returned unto me . . . and I was established in my kingdom, and excellent majesty was added unto me. Now I, Nebuchadnezzar, praise and extol and honor the King of heaven, all whose works are truth, and his ways judgment : and those that walk in pride he is able to abase."

The degradation of Nebuchadnezzar was typical of human degradation under beastly governments during seven symbolic times or years—a year for a day, 2520 years—from his day onward. And be it observed that this corresponds exactly with the seven times foretold upon Israel, which, as we have just seen, end A. D. 1914. For it was under this Nebuchadnezzar that Israel was carried away captive to Babylon, when the crown of God's kingdom was removed, and the seven times began.

It is in perfect harmony with this that God, in representing these governments of the Gentiles, portrayed them to Daniel as so many wild beasts, while the kingdom of God at their close is represented as given to *one like unto a son of man.*

Unless it was thus to foreshadow the degradation and the duration of Gentile Times, we know of no reason for the recording of this scrap of the history of a heathen king. That his seven years of degradation fitly illustrated human debasement, is a fact; that God has promised a restitution of earth's dominion after humanity has learned certain great lessons, is also a fact; and that the *seven* symbolic Gentile Times (2520 years) end at the exact point when mankind will have learned its own degradation and present inability to rule the world to advantage, and will be ready for God's kingdom and dominion, is a third fact. And the fitness of the illustration forces the conviction that Nebuchadnezzar's seven years, while literally fulfilled on him personally, had a yet greater and broader significance as a figure of the seven symbolic times of Gentile dominion, which he represented.

The exact date of Nebuchadnezzar's degradation is not stated, and is of no consequence, because the period of his degradation typified the entire period of Gentile dominion, which began when the crown of the typical kingdom of God was removed from Zedekiah. It was beastly from its very start, and its times are numbered: its boundaries are set by Jehovah, and cannot be passed.

7–B

How refreshing the prospect brought to view at the close of these seven times! Neither Israel nor the world of mankind represented by that people will longer be trodden down, oppressed and misruled by beastly Gentile powers. The Kingdom of God and his Christ will then be established in the earth, and Israel and all the world will be blessed under his rightful and righteous authority. Then the root of promise and hope planted first in Eden (Gen. 3: 15), and borne across the flood and transplanted with Israel the typical people (Gen. 12: 1–3), will sprout and bloom again.

It began to sprout at our Lord's first advent, but the appointed season had not arrived for it to bloom and bring forth its blessed fruitage in the restitution of all things. But at the end of the Gentile Times the sure signs of spring will not be lacking, and rich will be the summer fruitage and glorious the autumnal harvest to be reaped and enjoyed in the eternal ages of glory to follow. Then the original lord of earth, with reason restored, will be fully re-instated, with added excellence and glory, as in the type, and will praise and extol and honor the King of heaven.

Already we begin to see reason returning to mankind: men are awakening to some sense of their degradation, and are on the lookout to improve their condition. They are thinking, planning and scheming for a better condition than that to which they have been submitting under the beastly powers. But before they come to recognize God and his dominion over all, they will experience one more terrible fit of madness, from which struggle they will awake weak, helpless, exhausted, but with reason so far restored as to recognize and bow to the authority of him who comes to re-establish the long lost, first dominion, on the permanent basis of experience and knowledge of both good and evil.

True, it is expecting great things to claim, as we do, that within the coming twenty-six years all present governments will be overthrown and dissolved; but we are living in a special and peculiar time, the "Day of Jehovah," in which matters culminate quickly; and it is written, "A short work will the Lord make upon the earth." (See Vol. I., chap. xv.) For the past eleven years these things have been preached and published substantially as set forth above; and in that brief time the development of influences and agencies for the undermining and overthrow of the strongest empires of earth has been wonderful. In that time Communism, Socialism and Nihilism sprang into vigorous existence, and already are causing great uneasiness among the rulers and high ones of earth, whose hearts are failing them for fear, and for looking after those things which are coming on the earth; for the present powers are being mightily shaken, and ultimately shall pass away with a great tumult.

In view of this strong Bible evidence concerning the Times of the Gentiles, we consider it an established truth that the final end of the kingdoms of this world, and the full establishment of the Kingdom of God, will be accomplished near the end of A.D. 1915. Then the prayer of the Church, ever since her Lord took his departure—"Thy Kingdom come"—will be answered; and under that wise and just administration, the whole earth will be filled with the glory of the Lord—with knowledge, and righteousness, and peace (Psa. 72:19; Isa. 6:3; Hab. 2:14); and the will of God shall be done *"on earth, as it is done in heaven."*

Daniel's statement, that God's Kingdom will be set up, not after these kingdoms of earth are dissolved, but in their days, while they still exist and have power, and that it is God's Kingdom which shall break in pieces and consume all these kingdoms (Dan. 2:44), is worthy of our special consideration. So it was with each of these beastly governments: it existed before it acquired universal dominion. Babylon existed long before it conquered Jerusalem and

obtained the dominion (Dan. 2: 37, 38); Medo-Persia existed before it conquered Babylon; and so with all kingdoms:
they must first have existed and have received superior
power before they could conquer others. So, too, with
God's Kingdom: it has existed in an embryo form for
eighteen centuries; but it, with the world at large, was
made subject to "the powers that be," "ordained of God."
Until their "seven times" shall end, the Kingdom of God
cannot come into universal dominion. However, like the
others, it must obtain power adequate to the overthrow of
these kingdoms before it shall break them in pieces.

So, in this "Day of Jehovah," the "Day of Trouble,"
our Lord takes his great power (hitherto dormant) and reigns,
and this it is that will cause the trouble, though the world
will not so recognize it for some time. That the saints
shall share in this work of breaking to pieces present kingdoms, there can be no doubt. It is written, "This honor
have all his saints—to execute the judgments written, to
bind their kings with chains, and their nobles with fetters
of iron "—of strength. (Psa. 149: 8, 9.) "He that over-
cometh, and keepeth my works unto the end, to him will I
give power over the nations, and he shall rule them with a
rod of iron; as the vessels of a potter shall they [the *empires*]
be broken to shivers."—Rev. 2: 26, 27; Psa. 2: 8, 9.

But our examination, in the preceding volume, of the great
difference in character between the Kingdom of God and
the beastly kingdoms of earth, prepares us to see also a
difference in modes of warfare. The methods of conquest
and breaking will be widely different from any which have
ever before overthrown nations. He who now takes his
great power to reign is shown in symbol (Rev. 19:15) as
the one whose sword went forth *out of his mouth*, "that with
it he should smite the nations; and he shall rule them with
a rod of iron." That sword is the TRUTH (Eph. 6: 17);

and the living saints, as well as many of the world, are now being used as the Lord's soldiers in overthrowing errors and evils. But let no one hastily infer a *peaceable conversion* of the nations to be here symbolized; for many scriptures, Such as Rev. 11:17, 18; Dan. 12:1; 2 Thes. 2:8; Psalms 149 and 47, teach the very opposite.

Be not surprised, then, when in subsequent chapters we present proofs that the setting up of the Kingdom of God is already begun, that it is pointed out in prophecy as due to begin the exercise of power in A. D. 1878, and that the "battle of the great day of God Almighty" (Rev. 16:14.), which will end in A.D. 1915, with the complete overthrow of earth's present rulership, is already commenced. The gathering of the armies is plainly visible from the standpoint of God's Word.

If our vision be unobstructed by prejudice, when we get the telescope of God's Word rightly adjusted we may see with clearness the character of many of the events due to take place in the "Day of the Lord"—that we are in the very midst of those events, and that "the Great Day of His Wrath is come."

The sword of truth, already sharpened, is to smite every evil system and custom—civil, social and ecclesiastical. Nay, more, we can see that the smiting is commenced: freedom of thought, and human rights, civil and religious, long lost sight of under kings and emperors, popes, synods, councils, traditions and creeds, are being appreciated and asserted as never before. The internal conflict is already fomenting: it will ere long break forth as a consuming fire, and human systems, and errors, which for centuries have fettered truth and oppressed the groaning creation, must melt before it. Yes, truth—and widespread and increasing knowledge of it—is the sword which is perplexing and wounding the heads over many countries. (Psa. 110:6.)

Yet in this trouble what a blessing is disguised: It will prepare mankind for a fuller appreciation of righteousness and truth, under the reign of the King of Righteousness.

As men shall eventually come to realize that justice is laid to the line and righteousness to the plummet (Isa. 28: 17), they will also learn that the strict rules of justice alone can secure the blessings which all desire. And, thoroughly disheartened with their own ways and the miserable fruitage of selfishness, they will welcome and gladly submit to the righteous authority which takes the control; and thus, as it is written, "The desire of all nations shall come"— the Kingdom of God, under the absolute and unlimited control of Jehovah's Anointed.

"We are living, we are dwelling,
　　In a grand and awful time.
In an age on ages telling,
　　To be living is sublime.
Hark! the rumbling in the nations,
　　Iron crumbling with the clay:
Hark! what soundeth? 'Tis creation
　　Groaning for a better day.

"Scoffers scorning, Heaven beholding,
　　Thou hast but an hour to fight.
See prophetic truth unfolding!
　　Watch! and keep thy garments white.
Oh, let all the soul within you
　　For the truth's sake go abroad!
Strike! let every nerve and sinew
　　Tell on ages—tell for God!"

STUDY V.

THE MANNER OF OUR LORD'S RETURN AND APPEARING.

THE VIEW just had, of the speedy close of Gentile Times, and the assurance that the consummation of the Church's hope must *precede* their close, only whets the appetite of those now waiting for the consolation of Israel. Such will be hungering for whatever information our Father may have supplied through the prophets, touching the "harvest," the end, or closing period of this age—the separating of wheat from tares among the living members of the nominal Church, and the time of the change of the overcomers, to be with and like their Lord and Head.

But in order to appreciate the reasonableness of the prophetic teaching on these deeply interesting subjects, it is absolutely necessary that we have clear views both of the *object* of our Lord's second coming, and of the *manner* in which he will be revealed. That the *object* of his coming is to reconcile "whosoever will," of the world, to God, by a process of ruling, and teaching, and disciplining, called judging and blessing, we trust all present readers have been convinced in the reading of Volume I. The *manner* of the

Lord's coming and appearing, therefore, is of paramount importance, before proceeding in our study of the time of the harvest, etc. The student must hold clearly in mind the object while studying the manner of our Lord's return; and both of these, when he comes to study the time. This is needful as an offset to the erroneous views, already pre-occupying many minds, based upon false ideas of both the object and the manner of our Lord's coming.

Grasp and hold in mind as firmly as possible the fact already demonstrated, that God's plan is one harmonious whole, which is being wrought out through Christ; and that the work of the second advent stands related to the work of the first as effect to cause: That is, that the great work of Restitution at the second advent follows the work of Redemption accomplished at the first advent as a logical sequence according to the divine plan. Therefore the Lord's return is *the dawn of hope for the world,* the time for the bestowment of the favors secured by the redemption —the Gospel Age being merely an intervening parenthesis, during which the bride of Christ is selected, to be associated with her Lord in the great work of restitution which he comes to accomplish.

And since the Church of Christ, which has been developing during the Gospel age, is to be associated with her Lord in the great restitution work of the Millennial age, the first work of Christ at the second advent must be the gathering of his elect Church, to which reference is made through the Prophet (Psa. 50 : 5), saying, "Gather my saints together unto me—those that have made a covenant with me by sacrifice." This gathering or harvesting time is in the lapping period of the two ages. As will be shown, it is a period of forty years, which both ends the Gospel age and introduces the Millennial age. (See Vol. I., pages 219–221; 234–237; and the Chart of the Ages.) This harvest period not only accomplishes the separation of wheat from tares in the nominal Gospel church, and the gathering and glorification of the wheat class, but it is also to accomplish the burning (destruction) of the tares (as tares, or imitation wheat—not as individuals: the fire of destruction is symbolic as well as the tares), and the gathering and destruction of the corrupt fruitage of "the Vine of the earth" (human ambition, greed and selfishness), which has been growing and ripening for centuries in the kingdoms of this world and in the various civil and social organizations among men.

Although, when treating of the object of our Lord's return, we showed that it would be a *personal* coming, let us again guard the student against confusion of thought in considering the two apparently conflicting expressions of our Lord—"Lo, I am with you alway, even unto the end of the world" (*aionos*, age), and, "*I go* to prepare a place for you, . . . and *will come again* and receive you." (Matt. 28: 20; John 14: 2, 3.) The following incident will serve as an illustration of the harmony of the two promises:—One friend said to another as they were about to part, Remember, I will be with you through all your journey. How? Certainly not in person; for there they took trains to go in opposite directions to distant points. The idea was that in love, and thought, and care one for another, they would not be separated. In a similar yet fuller sense, the Lord has always been with his Church, his divine power enabling him to oversee, direct and assist them, from first to last. But we are now considering, not our Lord's presence with us in this figurative sense, but the manner of his second personal presence and appearing, "when he shall come to be glorified in his saints and to be admired in all them that believe in that day."

The Scriptures teach that Christ comes again to reign; that he must reign until he has put down all enemies—all opponents, all things in the way of the great restitution which he comes to accomplish—the last to be overthrown being death (1 Cor. 15: 25, 26) ; and that he will reign for a thousand years. It is therefore only as should be expected, that we find a much larger space in prophecy devoted to the second advent and its thousand years of triumphant reign and overthrow of evil than to the thirty-four years of the first advent for redemption. And as we have found that prophecy touches the various important points of those thirty-four years, from Bethlehem and Nazareth to the gall and vinegar, the parted raiment, the cross, the tomb and the resurrection, so we find that prophecy likewise touches various points of the thousand years of the second presence, particularly their beginning and ending.

The second presence of our Lord will cover a much longer period of time than the first. The mission of his first advent was finished in less than thirty-four years, while it will require a thousand years to accomplish the appointed work of his second presence. And thus it may be seen at a glance that, while the work of the first advent was no less important than that of the second advent—yea, though it was *so important* that the work of the second advent *could never have been possible without it*—yet it was not so varied, and hence required less description than the work of the second advent.

In considering the second advent we must not, any more than at the first advent, expect all prophecies to mark one particularly eventful moment of our Lord's arrival and to call the attention of all men to the fact of his presence. Such is not God's usual method : such was not the case at the first advent. The first advent of Messiah was not marked by any sudden or surprising demonstration, out of the usual order of things, but it was manifested and proven by the gradual fulfilment of prophecy showing to thoughtful observers that the events which should be expected were being accomplished on time. And thus it will be at his second advent. It is of less importance that we discover the exact moment of his arrival than that we discern the fact of his presence when he has arrived, even as at the first advent it was important to be able to recognize his presence, and the sooner the better, but much less important to know the exact date of his birth. In considering the second advent, the act of coming and the moment of arrival are too frequently the thought, whereas it should be thought of as a *period of presence*, as was the first advent. The precise moment at which that presence would begin would then seem less important, and his object and work during the period of his presence would receive the greater consideration.

We must bear in mind, also, that our Lord is no longer a human being; that as a human being he gave himself a ransom for men, having become a man for that very purpose. (1 Tim. 2:6; Heb. 10:4, 5; 1 Cor. 15:21, 22.) He is now highly exalted, to the divine nature. Therefore Paul said, "Though we have known Christ after the flesh, yet now, henceforth, know we him [so] no more." (2 Cor. 5:16.) He was raised from the dead a life-giving *spirit* being (1 Cor. 15:45), and not a *man*, of the earth earthy. He is no longer human in any sense or degree; for we must not forget what we have learned (See Vol. I., Chap. 10)—that natures are separate and distinct. Since he is no longer in any sense or degree a human being, we must not expect him to come again as a human being, as at the first advent. His second coming is to be in a different manner, as well as for a different purpose.

Noting the fact that our Lord's *change* from human to divine nature at his resurrection was even a greater change than the one which occurred some thirty-four years previously, when he laid aside the glory of spiritual being and "was made flesh," we may with great profit consider very minutely his every action during the forty days after his resurrection before he went "to the Father;" because it is the resurrected Jesus of those forty days who is to come again, and not the *man* Christ Jesus who gave himself as our ransom, in death.   He who was put to death a flesh being was also in his resurrection quickened [made alive] a spirit being.—1 Pet. 3:18.*

At his second advent he does not come to be subject to the powers that be, to pay tribute to Cæsar and to suffer humiliation, injustice and violence; but he comes to reign, exercising all power in heaven and in earth.   He does not come in the body of his humiliation, a human body, which he took for the suffering of death, inferior to his former glorious body (Heb. 2:9); but in his glorious spiritual body, which is "the express image of the Father's person" (Heb. 1:3); for, because of his obedience even unto death, he is now highly exalted to the *divine nature* and likeness, and given a name above every name—the Father's name only excepted.   (Phil. 2:9; 1 Cor. 15:27.)   The Apostle shows that it "doth not yet appear" to our human under-standing what he is now like; hence we know not what we shall be like when made *like* him, but we (the Church) may

---

* In this passage, the words "in the" and "by the" are arbitrarily supplied by the translators, and are misleading. The Greek reads simply, —"Put to death flesh, quickened spirit." Our Lord was put to death a fleshly or human being, but was raised from the dead a spirit being. And since the Church is to be "*changed*" in order that she may be like Christ, it is evident that the change which occurred in the Head was of a kind similar to that described as in reservation for the overcomers, who shall be changed from human to spiritual nature, and made like him—"partakers of the divine nature." Hence, the following descrip-tion of the change of the saints is applicable also to their Lord; *viz*, —"It is sown in dishonor, it is raised in glory; it is sown in weakness, it is raised in power; it is sown a natural body, it is raised a spiritual body."

rejoice in the assurance that we shall one day be with him, and like him, and see him *as he is* (1 John 3 : 2)—not as he was at his first advent in humiliation, when he had laid aside his former glory and for our sakes had become poor, that we through his poverty might be made rich.

If we consider the wisdom and prudence of our Lord's methods of manifesting his presence to his disciples after his resurrection, as well as previously, it may help us to remember that the same wisdom will be displayed in his methods of revealing himself at his second advent, both to the Church and to the world—methods not necessarily similar, but in each case well suited to his object, which never is to alarm or excite men, but to *convince* their cool, calm judgments of the great truths to be impressed upon them. Our Lord's first advent was not a startling, exciting or alarming event. How quietly and unobtrusively he came ! So much so that only those who had *faith and humility* were enabled to recognize in the infant of humble birth, in the man of sorrows, in the friend of the humble and poor, and finally in the crucified one, the long-looked-for Messiah.

After his resurrection, the manifestation of his presence would in the nature of the case be a more astounding fact, particularly when his changed nature is taken into consideration. Yet the fact of his resurrection, together with the fact of his changed nature, had to be fully manifested, not to all the world at that time, but to chosen witnesses who would give credible testimony of the fact to succeeding generations. Had all the world been made acquainted with the fact then, the testimony coming down to our day would probably have been much less trustworthy, being colored and warped by men's ideas and mixed with their traditions, so that the truth might appear almost or quite incredible. But God entrusted it only to chosen, faithful and worthy witnesses ; and as we notice the account, let each mark how perfectly the *object* was accomplished, and how clear, positive and convincing was the proof of Christ's resurrection and change offered to them. Mark, too, the carefulness with which he guarded against alarming or unduly exciting them while making manifest and emphasizing these great truths. And be assured that the same wisdom, prudence and skill will be displayed in his methods of making known the fact of his glorious presence at his second advent. The cool, calm judgment will be convinced in every case, though the world in general will need to be brought by severe discipline to the proper attitude to receive the testimony, while those whose hearts are right will have the blessed intelligence sooner. All the proofs of his resurrection and change to spiritual nature were not given to his disciples at once, but as they were able to bear them and in the manner calculated to make the deepest impression.

During the three and a half years of our Lord's ministry, his disciples had sacrificed friends, reputation, business, etc., to devote time and energy to heralding Messiah's presence and the establishment of his kingdom. But they had necessarily crude ideas regarding the manner and time of their Master's exaltation, and of their promised exaltation with him. Nor was full knowledge then necessary : it was quite sufficient that they should faithfully take each step as it became due ; hence the Master taught them little by little as they were able to receive it. And near the close of his ministry he said, "I have yet many things to say unto you, but ye cannot bear them now. Howbeit, when he, the Spirit of truth, is come, he will guide you into all truth . . . and show you things to come, and bring all things to your remembrance, whatsoever I have said unto you."—John 16 : 12, 13 ; 14 : 26.

Who can tell their great disappointment, even though so far as possible they had been armed against it, when they

saw him suddenly taken from them and ignominiously crucified as a felon—him whose kingdom and glory they had been
expecting and declaring, and which only five days before
his crucifixion had seemed to them so near a realization.
(John. 12 : 1, 12–19.)   Though they knew him to be falsely
accused and wrongfully crucified, this did not alter the fact
that their long cherished national hopes of a Jewish king,
who would restore their nation to influence and power,
together with their own individual hopes, ambitions and
air-castles of important offices and high honors in the kingdom, were all suddenly demolished by this unfavorable
turn which matters had taken in the crucifixion of their king.

Well did the Master know how desolate and aimless and
perplexed they would feel; for thus it was written by the
Prophet, "I will smite the Shepherd, and the sheep shall
be scattered." (Zech. 13:7; Mark 14:27.) And during the
forty days between his resurrection and ascension, it was
therefore his chief concern to gather them again, and to
re-establish their faith in him as the long-looked-for Messiah, by proving to them the fact of his resurrection,
and that since his resurrection, though retaining the same
individuality, he was no longer human, but an exalted
spirit being, having "all power in heaven and in earth."—
Matt. 28 : 18.

He broke the news of his resurrection gradually to them—
first, through the women (Mary Magdalene, and Joanna,
Mary the mother of James and Salome, and others with
them—Mark 16 : 1; Luke 24 : 1, 10), who came early to
the sepulcher to anoint his dead body with sweet spices.
While they wondered whom they should get to roll away the
stone from the door of the sepulcher, behold, there was
an earthquake, and when they came they found the stone
rolled away, and an angel of the Lord sat upon it, who addressed them, saying, "Fear not, for I know that ye seek

Jesus which was crucified. He is not here; for he is risen, *as he said.* Come, see the place where the Lord lay. And go quickly and tell his disciples that he is risen from the dead; and behold, he goeth before you into Galilee; there shall ye see him."—Matt. 28: 5-7.

It seems that Mary Magdalene separated from the other women and ran to tell Peter and John (John 20: 1, 2), while the others went to tell the rest of the disciples, and that after she had left them Jesus appeared to the other women on the way, saying (Matt. 28: 9, 10), "All hail." And they came and held him by the feet and worshiped him. Then said Jesus unto them, "Be not afraid: go tell my brethren that they go into Galilee [their home], and there shall they see me." And with fear and joy they ran to tell the other disciples. In their mingled feelings of surprise, perplexity, joy and fear, and their general bewilderment, they scarcely knew how to report their strange and wonderful experience. When Mary met Peter and John she said sadly, "They have taken away the Lord out of the sepulcher, and we know not where they have laid him." (John 20: 2.) The other women told how at the sepulcher they had seen a vision of angels who said he was alive (Luke 24: 22, 23), and then how they afterward met the Lord in the way.—Matt. 28: 8, 10.

The majority of the disciples evidently regarded their story merely as superstitious excitement, but Peter and John said, We will go and see for ourselves; and Mary returned to the sepulcher with them. All that Peter and John saw was that the body was gone, that the grave clothes were carefully folded and laid by, and that the stone was rolled away from the door. So in perplexity they turned away, though Mary still remained there weeping. As she wept she stooped down and looked into the sepulcher and saw two angels, who said, "Woman, why weepest thou?" She answered, "Because they have taken away my Lord, and I know not where they have laid him." And as she turned about she saw Jesus standing, but did not know him. He inquired, "Woman, why weepest thou? whom seekest thou?" And she, supposing him to be the gardener, answered, "Sir, if thou hast borne him hence, tell me where thou hast laid him, and I will take him away." Then, in the old familiar tone which she quickly recognized, the Lord said, "Mary!"

That was enough to establish her faith in the statement of the angel, that he had risen, which until now had seemed like a dream or an idle tale; and in her joy she exclaimed, *"Master!"* Her first impulse was to embrace him, and to tarry in his presence. But Jesus gently informed her that there was a very important mission for her to perform now, in bearing witness to the fact of his resurrection, and that she should be in haste to carry the message and establish the faith of the other disciples, still in perplexity and uncertainty, saying, "Touch [Greek, *haptomai*, embrace] me not [do not tarry for further demonstration of your affection now]; for I am not yet ascended to my Father [I will be with you for a short time yet]: but go to my brethren and say unto them, I ascend unto my Father, and your Father, and to my God, and your God." (John 20 : 17.) Through the other women also he had sent them word that he would meet them in Galilee.

Next, he overtook two of the sad and perplexed disciples as they walked from Jerusalem to Emmaus, and inquired the cause of their sadness and despondency. (Luke 24 : 13–35.) And one of them answered: "Art thou only a stranger in Jerusalem, and hast not known the things which are come to pass there in these days? And he said unto them, What things? And they said unto him, Concerning Jesus of Nazareth, which was a prophet mighty in deed and word

8–B

before God and all the people: and how the chief priests and our rulers delivered him to be condemned to death, and have crucified him. But we trusted that it had been he which should have redeemed Israel: and besides all this, to-day is the third day since these things were done. [Here they were probably calling to mind John 2: 19, 21, 22.] Yea, and certain women also of our company made us astonished, which were early at the sepulcher. And when they found not his body, they came saying that they had also seen a vision of angels, which said he was alive. And certain of them which were with us went to the sepulcher, and found it even so as the women had said; but him they saw not."

No wonder they were perplexed; how strange it all seemed! how peculiar and thrilling had been the events of the past few days!

Then the stranger preached them a stirring sermon from the prophecies, showing them that the very things which had so disheartened them were the things which the prophets had foretold concerning the true Messiah: that before he could rule and bless and lift up Israel and all the world, he must first redeem them with his own life from the curse of death, which came upon all through Adam, and that afterward, raised to life and glory by Jehovah, their Master would fulfil all that was written by the prophets concerning his future glory and honor, as truly as he had fulfilled those prophecies which foretold his sufferings, humiliation and death. A wonderful preacher! and a wonderful sermon was that! It started new ideas and opened new expectations and hopes. As they drew near the village they constrained him to tarry with them, as it was toward evening and the day was far spent. He went in to tarry with them; and as he sat at meat with them, he took bread and brake and gave it to them. Then their eyes were opened; and he vanished out of their sight.

Not until that moment did they recognize him, though they had walked, and talked and sat at meat together. He was known to them not by face, but in the simple act of blessing and breaking bread in the old familiar way, thus assuring their faith in what they had already heard—that he had risen, and would see them again.

Then the two surprised and overjoyed disciples arose that same hour and returned to Jerusalem, saying to each other, "Did not our hearts burn within us while he talked with us by the way, and while he opened to us the Scriptures?" Arriving in Jerusalem they found the others rejoicing also, saying, "The Lord is risen indeed, and hath appeared to Simon." And they told what things were done in the way, and how he was known of them in breaking of bread. Probably they were nearly all there that evening, homes, business and everything else forgotten—Mary Magdalene with her tears of joy, saying, I knew him the moment he called my name—I could not credit the angel's assurance of his resurrection until then; and the other women telling their wonderful experience of the morning, and how they had met him in the way. Then Simon had his story to tell; and now here were two other witnesses from Emmaus. What an eventful day! No wonder they desired to meet together on the first day of every week after that, to talk the matter over and to call to mind all the circumstances connected with this wonderful event of the Lord's resurrection, and to have their hearts "burn" again and again.

While the excited and overjoyed little company were thus met and relating to each other their several experiences, the Lord Jesus himself suddenly stood in their midst (Luke 24: 36–49) and said, "Peace be unto you!" From where had he come? All such meetings were held secretly with closed doors, for fear of the Jews (John 20: 19, 26), but here was a sudden appearance without any visible approach;

and they were terrified, and supposed they had seen a spirit. Then he comforted them, told them to calm their fears, and showed them his hands and his feet, saying, "It is I, myself; handle me and see; for a spirit hath not flesh and bones, as ye see me have." And while they yet believed not for joy, and wondered, he said unto them, "Have ye here any meat?" and they gave him a piece of a broiled fish, and he took it and did eat before them. Then he opened their *understanding*, their mental eyes, and expounded the Scriptures to them, showing from the law and the prophets that these things had come to pass exactly as foretold. But Thomas was absent (John 20: 24); and when the other disciples told him that they had seen the Lord, he would not believe it, but said, "Except I shall see in his hands the print of the nails, and thrust my hand into his side, I will not believe."

Eight days passed without further manifestations, and they had time calmly to think and talk over the experiences of that wonderful day, when, the disciples being again assembled as before, Jesus stood in their midst, just as on the first evening, saying, "Peace be unto you." (John 20: 26.) This time Thomas was present, and the Lord addressed him, saying, "Thomas, reach hither thy finger, and behold my hands; and reach hither thy hand, and thrust it into my side; and be not faithless, but believing." He thus showed that he knew what Thomas had said without being told, and he gave that proof of his resurrection which Thomas had said would satisfy him; and with joy Thomas answered, "My Lord and my God!"

After this, there must have been quite a long interval before there was any further manifestation of the Lord's presence, and the disciples who were Galileans began to think of home and the future; and remembering the Lord's message by the women, that he would go before them into

Galilee, they went thither. Probably on their way, the Lord met them, as Matthew relates, in a mountain. They were perplexed; they no longer felt the same familiarity they once had toward him; he seemed so greatly changed since his crucifixion from what he used to be—he appeared and disappeared in such peculiar times and places; he no longer seemed like "the man Christ Jesus;" so Matthew says "they worshiped him—but some doubted." After a few words with them the Lord "vanished" from their sight, and left them to wonder what next would happen. For some time after their return to Galilee nothing unusual occurred, and there was no further indication of the Lord's presence. Doubtless they met together and talked over the situation, and wondered why he did not appear to them more frequently.

As they waited, the days and the weeks seemed long. They had long ago given up the ordinary pursuits of life, to follow the Lord from place to place, learning of him, and preaching to others, "The kingdom of heaven is at hand." (Matt. 10 : 5–7.) They did not now wish to go back to the old pursuits; and yet, how should they proceed with the Lord's work? They comprehended the situation clearly enough to know that they could no longer preach as formerly the kingdom at hand; for all the people knew that their Master and King had been crucified, and none but themselves knew of his resurrection. While all of the eleven were thus perplexed and anxious, waiting for something, they knew not what, Peter said, Well, it will not do to remain idle: I will go back to my old fishing business; and six of the others said, We will do the same: we will go with you. (John 21 : 3.) And probably the rest also turned again to their old employments.

Who can doubt that the Lord was invisibly present with them many times as they talked together, overruling and directing the course of circumstances, etc., for their highest good? If they should have great success and become swallowed up by interest in business, they would soon be unfit for the higher service; yet if they should have no success, it would seem like forcing them; so the Lord adopted a plan which taught them a lesson such as he often teaches his followers, viz.: that the success or failure of their efforts, in any direction, he can control if he please.

The old firm of fishermen reorganized: got together their boats, nets, etc., and went out for their first catch. But they toiled all night and caught no fish, and began to feel disheartened. In the morning a stranger on shore calls to them to know of their success. Poor success! We have caught nothing, they answer. Try again, said the stranger. Now cast your net on the other side of the boat. No use, stranger, we have tried both sides all night long, and if there were fish on one side, there would be on the other. However, we will try again and let you see. They did so, and got an immense haul. How strange! said some; but the quick and impressible John at once got the correct idea, and said, Brethren, the Lord only could do this. Don't you remember the feeding of the multitudes, etc.? That must be the Lord on shore, and this is another way that he has chosen to manifest himself to us. Don't you remember that it was just so when the Lord first called us? Then, too, we had toiled all night and caught nothing until he called to us, saying, "Let down your nets for a draught." (Luke 5 : 4–11.) Yes, surely that is the Lord, though, since his resurrection, we cannot recognize him by his appearance. He now appears in a variety of forms; but we know each time that it is he by some peculiar circumstance like this calling to mind some marked incident of our past acquaintance with him.

And when they got to shore they found that Jesus had

bread as well as fish, and they learned the lesson, that under his direction and care and in his service they would not be left to starve. (Luke 12 : 29, 30.) They did not ask him if he were the Lord; for on this as on other occasions, the *eyes of their understanding* being opened, they knew him, not by physical sight, but by the miracle. Then followed the instructions of that delightful hour, re-assuring Peter of his continued acceptance notwithstanding his denial of the Lord, for which he repented and wept. He now learned afresh of his Master's love, and of his continued privilege of feeding the sheep and the lambs. We seem to hear the Lord say, You need not go back to the fishing business, Peter: I called you once to be a fisher of men, and, knowing your heart to be still loyal and zealous, I renew your commission as a fisher of men.

"And, eating together with them, he commanded them that they should not depart from Jerusalem, but wait for the promise of the Father, which, saith he, ye have heard of me. For John truly baptized with water; but ye shall be baptized with the Holy Spirit not many days hence." (Acts 1 : 6—margin.) So they came to Jerusalem as instructed, and here it was, forty days after his resurrection, that he met with them for the last time and talked with them. They summoned courage this time to question him about the kingdom he had promised them, saying, "Lord, wilt thou at this time restore the kingdom to Israel?" This thought of the kingdom was the one uppermost in the mind of every Jew. Israel, they understood, was to be chief among the nations under Messiah, and they knew not of the long Times of the Gentiles, and they saw not yet that the chief blessing had been taken from fleshly Israel (Matt. 21 : 43; Rom. 11 : 7), and that they themselves were to be members of the new (spiritual) Israel, the royal priesthood and holy nation, through whom, as the body of Christ, the blessing of the world would come. They as yet understood none of these things. How could they? They had not yet received the holy Spirit of adoption as sons, but were still under condemnation; because, though the ransom-sacrifice had been made by the Redeemer, it had not yet been formally presented on our behalf in the Most Holy, even Heaven itself. (John 7 : 39.) Hence our Lord did not attempt any explanatory answer to their question, but merely said, "It is not for *you* [now] to know the times and seasons which the Father hath put in his own power. *But ye shall receive power* * after that the Holy Spirit is come upon you; and ye shall be witnesses unto me both in Jerusalem, and in all Judea, and in Samaria, and unto the uttermost part of the earth."—Acts 1 : 7, 8.

Then the Lord, who was walking with them, when they reached the Mount of Olives, lifted his hands and blessed them, and he was parted from them and went upward; and a cloud received him out of their sight. (Luke 24 : 48–52; Acts 1 : 6–15.) They began to see something more of God's plan now. The Lord who came down from heaven had returned to the Father, as he had told them before he died;—had gone to prepare a place for them and would come again and receive them;—had gone afar to receive the promised kingdom, and to return (Luke 19 : 12); and meantime they were to be his *witnesses* in all the earth to call and make ready a people to receive him when he would come to be glorified in his saints, and to reign King of kings and Lord of lords. They saw their new mission, of proclaiming to

---

* This promised power to know and to understand times and seasons, and all things pertaining to a proper *witnessing*, applies to the whole Church from first to last; and under the guidance and power of the holy Spirit, meat in due season concerning every feature of the plan is provided, in order that we may be his witnesses, even to the end of this age. —Compare John 16 : 12, 13.

every creature a coming king from heaven, " with all power in heaven and in earth," to be a much more important work than that of the preceding years, when they heralded "the man Christ Jesus," and followed him who was " despised and rejected of men." Their risen Lord was changed indeed, not only in his personal appearance—appearing sometimes in one way and place, and again in a different way and place, manifesting his "all power"—but he was changed in condition or nature also. No longer did he appeal to the Jews, nor show himself to them; for since his resurrection none saw him in any sense except his friends and followers. His words, " Yet a little while, and the world seeth me *no more*," were thus verified.

Thus was the faith of the apostles and of the early Church established in the fact of the Lord's resurrection. Their doubts were scattered, and their hearts rejoiced; and they returned to Jerusalem and continued in prayer and supplication and study of the Scriptures, waiting for the adoption promised by the Father, and their endowment with spiritual understanding, and with special miraculous gifts of power, to enable them to convince true Israelites, and to establish the Gospel Church, at the day of Pentecost.—Acts 1 : 14; 2 : 1.

Though our Lord at his second advent will not manifest his presence in the same way that he did during those forty days after his resurrection, yet we have his assurance that the "brethren shall not be in darkness." Nay, more : we shall have an aid which they could not and did not have to help them during those forty days, viz., "*power* from on high," to guide us into the understanding of every truth due to be understood, and, even as promised, to show us things *to come*. Hence in due season we shall have full understanding of the manner, time and attendant circumstances of his appearing, which, if carefully watched for and marked, will be no less convincing than were the evidences of our Lord's resurrection furnished to the early Church, although of a different kind.

That our Lord at his second advent *could* assume the human form, and thus appear to men, as he did to his disciples after his resurrection, there can be no question ; not only because he thus appeared in human form during those forty days, but because spirit beings have in the past manifested the power to appear as men in flesh and in various forms.   But such a manifestation would be out of harmony with the general tenor of God's plan, as well as out of harmony with the Scriptural indications given, relative to the manner of his manifestation, as we shall see.   Instead, it is the Lord's plan that his spiritual kingdom shall communicate, operate, and manifest its presence and power through human, earthly agencies.   Just as the prince of this world, Satan, though unseen by men, exercises a wide influence in the world through those subject to him, and possessed of and controlled by his spirit, so the new Prince of Peace, the Lord, will chiefly operate in, and manifest his presence and power through, human beings, subject to him and possessed of and controlled by his spirit.

Seeing with the natural eye and hearing with the natural ear are not all there is of seeing and hearing.   "No man hath seen God at any time" thus, yet all God's children have seen him, and known him, and held communion with him. (John 1 : 18 ; 5 : 37 ; 14 : 7.)   We *hear* God's call, our "high calling," we *hear* the voice of our Shepherd, and are constantly *looking* unto Jesus, and *see* the prize, the crown of life which he promises—not by natural sight and hearing, but by our understanding.   Far more precious is the sight we have of our glorified Lord as the spiritual, highly exalted King of glory, our Redeemer as well as our King, by the eyes of our understanding and faith, than the sight afforded to the natural eye before Pentecost.

There was a necessity for our Lord's appearing in the manner he did to his disciples, after his resurrection, which will not exist at his second advent. His object then will be better served in a different way. In fact, to appear so at his second advent would be detrimental to the purpose then to be accomplished. His object in appearing to his disciples after his resurrection was to convince them that he who was dead is alive forevermore, that they might go forth as witnesses to the fact of his resurrection (Luke 24: 48), and that their testimony might be a sure foundation for the faith of coming generations. Since no man can come to God acceptably, to receive the holy Spirit of adoption, without *faith* in Christ, it became necessary, not only for the sake of the disciples then, but for all since, that the *evidences* of his resurrection and change should be such as *natural men could grasp and appreciate.* After they had become partakers of the holy Spirit and understood spiritual things (See 1 Cor. 2 : 12–16), they could have believed the angels at the sepulcher, that he had risen from the dead condition, even if they had seen the fleshly body of the man Christ Jesus still lying in the tomb; but not so before —the body must be away to make faith in his resurrection possible to them. After the holy Spirit had enabled them to discern spiritual things, they could have believed the testimony of the prophets that he must needs die, and *would rise from the dead*, and that he would be highly exalted as King of glory, without its being needful for him to *appear as a man*, and assume various bodies of flesh as a garment, so that they could handle him and *see* him ascend. But all this was needful for them and for all natural men. By believing, we come to God by him and receive forgiveness of sins and the Spirit of adoption, to understand spiritual things.

Even while removing the *natural* obstacles to faith, by assuming human form, etc., our Lord *convinced* the disciples, and made them *witnesses* to others, not by their natural sight and touch, but by reasoning with them out of the Scriptures: "Then opened he their understanding, that they might understand the Scriptures, and said unto them, Thus it is written, and thus it behooved Christ to suffer and to rise from the dead the third day, and that repentance and remission of sins should be preached in his name among all nations, beginning at Jerusalem. *And ye are witnesses of these things.*" (Luke 24: 45–48.) Peter also states this object clearly, saying, "Him God raised up the third day, and *permitted him to become manifest*—NOT TO ALL THE PEOPLE, but to those witnesses previously chosen of God, to us, who did eat and drink with him after he arose from the dead. And he commanded us to proclaim to the people that this [the resurrected Jesus] is he who has been appointed by God the judge of the living and the dead."— Acts 10: 40–42. *Diaglott translation.*

With our Lord, after his resurrection, it was simply a question of expediency as to which way of appearing to his disciples would best accomplish his object, of making known his resurrection and change of nature. Had he appeared as *a flame of fire*, as the angel appeared to Moses in the burning bush (Exod. 3 : 2), he might indeed have conversed with them, but the evidence thus given would have been far from being as convincing as the method he did adopt, both to the apostles and to the world at large to whom they witnessed.

If he had appeared in the glory of the spirit form, as the angel did to Daniel (Dan. 10 : 5–8), the glory would have been greater than the witnesses could have borne. They would probably have been so alarmed as to be unable to receive instructions from him. To none except Paul did the Lord ever thus show himself; and Paul was so overcome by that glimpse of his glory that he fell to the ground

and was blinded by its brightness, which was above that of the sun at noonday.

In our examination of the method of manifestation adopted by our Lord during those forty days, we saw that he "*permitted*" himself to become manifest even to the chosen witnesses only a few times, and then but briefly. The entire time that he was manifest to them, had it all been crowded into one day instead of being at intervals during the forty days, would probably have been less than twelve hours, or one eightieth of that entire time. This being true, it is evident that he was present with them *unseen* about seventy-nine eightieths of that period of forty days. And even when they did have *manifestations*, they were not (except once to Thomas) in a form exactly like the one they had known so intimately for three years, and had seen but a few days before. It is not once intimated that they knew him by the familiar features of his face, nor even that he was recognized by the same appearance as in other manifestations.

Mary supposed him to be " the gardener." To the two on their way to Emmaus he was " a stranger." He was also a stranger to the fishermen on the sea of Galilee, and to the eleven in the upper room. On every occasion he was recognized by his actions, his words, or the familiar tones of his voice.

When Thomas declared that only the proof which addressed his natural sight and touch would be acceptable to him, the Lord, though he granted that demand, gently reproved him, saying, Because thou hast seen me, thou hast believed ; blessed are those who believe, *not having seen.* (John 20: 27–29.) The stronger evidence was that which was not addressed to natural sight, and more blessed are those who hold themselves in readiness to receive the truth through whatsoever proofs God is pleased to substantiate it.

He thus showed them, not only that he now had the power to appear in a variety of ways and forms, but also that no one of those bodies which they saw was his spiritual, glorious body, though the facts of his resurrection and presence were thus manifested to them. The different forms, and the long intervals of invisible presence with no outward manifestation, made evident the fact that though their Lord and teacher was alive and not yet ascended to the Father, he was now a spirit being, really invisible to human sight, but with ability to manifest his presence and power in a variety of ways at pleasure. *

The creating of the body and clothing in which he appeared to them, in the very room in which they were gathered, was proof unquestionable that Christ was no longer a human being, though he assured his disciples that the body which they saw, and which Thomas handled, was a veritable flesh and bone body, and not a mere vision or appearance. †

---

* The occurrence recorded by Luke (4 : 30) should not be regarded as a case parallel to his appearing and vanishing after his resurrection. That was not a disappearance in the sense of becoming invisible to the people. It was merely an adroit, prompt movement, by which he eluded the murderous design of his enemies. Before they had executed their plans for his death he turned about, and, passing through their midst, no man had courage or power to molest him, because his hour had not yet come.

† Let no one hastily suppose that we are here following Spiritism, Swedenborgianism or any other *ism*. We are simply following and logically connecting the apostolic account. The vast difference between the Bible teaching and that counterfeit of it promulgated by Satan, known as Spiritualism, we distinctly discern and shall examine in a succeeding volume. Suffice it here to point out that Spiritism affects to communicate between *dead men* and living men, while the Bible condemns this (Isa. 8 : 19), and teaches that such communications as were *true* have been made only by spirit beings, such as angels, and by our Lord; and not by our Lord while he was " the *man* Christ Jesus," nor while he was dead, but after his resurrection change, when he had become a life-giving or " quickening spirit" being.

As a human being he could not come into the room without opening the door, but as a spirit being he could, and there he instantly created and assumed such a body of flesh and such clothing as he saw fit for the purpose intended.

Nor can we for a moment admit the suggestion offered by some, that our Lord opened the doors without being observed; for the record is plain and clear that he came and stood in their midst *while the doors were shut*—probably very carefully barred and bolted too—"for fear of the Jews."—John 20: 19, 26.

The lesson of his changed nature was still further emphasized by his manner of leaving their sight: "He *vanished* out of their sight." The human body of flesh and bones, etc., and its clothing, which *appeared* suddenly while the doors were shut, did not go out of the door, but simply *disappeared* or dissolved into the same elements from which he had created them a few moments before. He *vanished* out of *their sight*, and was no longer *seen* of them when the flesh and bones and clothing in which he had manifested himself were dissolved, though doubtless he was still with them—invisibly present; and so also much of the time during those forty days.

On special occasions, for special instruction, God has granted similar power to other spirit beings, angels, enabling them to appear as men, in bodies of flesh and bones which ate and talked to those they instructed, just as our Lord did. See Gen. 18; Judges 6: 11–22; 13: 3–20; and the comments on these in Vol. I., pages 178 to 180.

The power manifested by our Lord, and the angels referred to, to create and dissolve the clothing in which they appeared, was just as superhuman as the creating and dissolving of their assumed human bodies; and the bodies were no more their glorious spiritual bodies than were the clothes they wore. It will be remembered that the seamless robe and other clothing which our Redeemer wore before his crucifixion had been divided among the Roman soldiers, and that the grave clothes were left folded away in the sepulcher (John 19: 23, 24; 20: 5-7), so that the clothing in which he appeared on the occasions mentioned must have been specially created, and probably was the most appropriate for each occasion. For instance, when he appeared as a gardener to Mary, it was probably in such apparel as a gardener would wear.

That the bodies in which our Lord appeared were real human bodies, and not mere delusions, he gave them clearly to understand when he ate before them, and invited them to handle him and see that the body was real flesh and bones, saying, "Why are ye troubled? . . . Behold my hands and my feet, that it is I myself: handle me and see; for *a spirit hath not flesh and bones,* as ye see me have."

Some Christians draw very absurd conclusions from this expression of our Lord as to the verity of his assumed flesh and bone body. They regard the assumed body as his spirit body, and declare that a spirit body is flesh and bones, and just like a human body, excepting that an indefinable something, which they call spirit, flows through its veins instead of blood. They seem to disregard the statement of our Lord, that this was not a spirit body—that a spirit being has not flesh and bones. Do they also forget John's statement, that "It doth not yet appear" what a spirit body is, and that we shall not know until we are changed and made like him and see him, not as he was, but as he is? (1 John 3:2.) Do they also forget the Apostle Paul's express statement that *"flesh and blood* cannot inherit the kingdom of God?"—and his further assurance that *therefore* all the heirs with Christ must also "be *changed?*"—1 Cor. 15:50, 51.

Many Christians have the idea that our Lord's glorious

spiritual body is the very same body that was crucified and laid away in Joseph's tomb: they expect, when they see the Lord in glory, to identify him by the scars he received on Calvary. This is a great mistake, which a very little consideration should make manifest—Firstly, It would prove that his resurrection body is not glorious or perfect, but scarred and disfigured: Secondly, It would prove that we do know what a spirit body is, notwithstanding the Apostle's statement to the contrary: Thirdly, It would prove that our redemption price was taken back; for Jesus said, "My flesh I will give for the life of the world." It was his flesh, his life *as a man*, his humanity, that was sacrificed for our redemption. And when he was raised to life again by the power of the Father, it was not to human existence; because that was sacrificed as our purchase price. And if that price had been taken back, we would still be under the condemnation of death, and without hope.

We have no more reason to suppose that our Lord's spirit body since his resurrection is a human body than we have for supposing that his spirit body prior to his first advent was human, or that other spirit beings have human bodies; for a spirit hath not flesh and bones; and, says the Apostle Peter, our Lord was "put to death in the flesh but made alive in spirit."

Our Lord's human body was, however, supernaturally removed from the tomb; because had it remained there it would have been an insurmountable obstacle to the faith of the disciples, who were not yet instructed in spiritual things —for "the spirit was not yet given." (John 7 : 39.) We know nothing about what became of it, except that it did not decay or corrupt. (Acts 2 : 27, 31.) Whether it was dissolved into gases or whether it is still preserved some- where as the grand memorial of God's love, of Christ's obedience, and of our redemption, no one knows;—nor is

9–B

such knowledge necessary. That God did miraculously hide the body of Moses, we are assured (Deut. 34 : 6 ; Jude 9) ; and that as a *memorial* God did miraculously preserve from corruption the manna in the golden bowl, which was placed in the Ark under the Mercy Seat in the Tabernacle, and that it was a symbol of our Lord's flesh, the bread from heaven, we also know (Exod. 14 : 20, 33 ; Heb. 9 : 4 ; John 6 : 51–58). Hence it will not surprise us if, in the Kingdom, God shall show to the world the body of flesh, crucified for all in giving the ransom on their behalf— not permitted to corrupt, but preserved as an everlasting testimony of infinite love and perfect obedience. It is at least possible that John 19 : 37 and Zech. 12 : 10 may have such a fulfilment. Those who cried, "Crucify him!" may yet, as witnesses, identify the very body pierced by the spear and torn by the nails and thorns.

To regard our Lord's glorious body as a body of flesh would not in the least account for his peculiar and sudden appearings during those forty days prior to his ascension. How could he so suddenly appear and then vanish? How was it that he kept himself almost constantly invisible during those forty days? And why was it that his appearance each time was so changed as not to be recognized as the same one seen on any former occasion, or as the one so well known and loved by all, before his crucifixion, only a few days previous?

It will not do merely to say that these were miracles, for then some use or necessity for the miracles should be named. If his body after his resurrection were flesh and bones, and the same body that was crucified, with all the features and scars, *why* did he perform miracles which not only did not establish that fact, but which were likely, we see, to teach the opposite?—that he himself was no longer human—flesh and bones—but a spirit being who could go and come as the wind, so that none could tell whence he came or whither he went, but who, for the purpose of instructing them, appeared *as* a man *in* various bodies of flesh and bones which he created and dissolved as occasion required.

Before our Lord's crucifixion, he had been on familiar terms with his disciples, but after his resurrection, though he loved them none the less, his manner toward them was more reserved. This was doubtless to impress them more forcibly with the dignity and honor of his high exaltation, and to inspire due reverence for his person and authority. Though as a man Jesus never lacked that dignity of deportment which commands respect, yet a greater reserve was necessary and expedient after his change to the divine nature. Such reserve has always been maintained by Jehovah toward his creatures, and is expedient under the circumstances. This reserve marked all our Lord's interviews with the disciples after his resurrection. They were very brief, even as he had said, "Hereafter I will not talk much with you."—John 14 : 30.

Those who believe that our Heavenly Father is a spirit and not a man should find no difficulty in realizing that our Lord Jesus, who is now exalted to the divine nature, and who is not only a moral likeness of God but in fact *"the express image of the Father's person,"* is no longer a man but a spirit being, whom no man hath seen nor can see without a miracle. It is just as impossible for men to see the unveiled glory of the Lord Jesus as it is for them to behold Jehovah. Think for a moment how even a reflection of the spiritual glory affected Moses and Israel at Sinai. (Heb. 12 : 21 ; Exod. 19 ; 20 : 19–21 ; 33 : 20–23 ; 34 : 29–35.) "So terrible was the sight," so overwhelming and fear-inspiring, "that Moses said, I exceedingly fear and quake." And though Moses was supernaturally strengthened to behold the glory of the Lord, so that for forty days and forty nights, alone with God, overshadowed by his glory and without either food or drink, he received and wrote the divine law (Exod. 34 : 28), yet when he desired to see the Lord face to face he was told, "Thou canst not see my face ; for there shall no man see me and live." (Exod. 33 : 20.) All that Moses ever saw, therefore, was an *appearance* representing God, and nothing more was possible. This accords, too, with the Apostle's statements: " No *man* hath seen God *at any time;*" he is the King immortal, invisible, *whom no man hath seen nor can* [*ever*] *see.* (1 Tim. 6 : 15, 16.) But that spirit beings can and do see God, who himself is a spirit being, is clearly stated.—Matt. 18 : 10.

If our Lord is still "the *man* Christ Jesus, who *gave himself* a ransom for all" (1 Tim. 2 : 5, 6)—if being put to death in the flesh he was raised again in the flesh, and not, as the Apostle declares, a life-giving spirit—then instead of being exalted higher than angels and every name that is named in heaven as well as in earth, he is still a man. And if he retains the form of a servant, which he took for the purpose of suffering death for every man, and is still a little lower than the angels, he never can see God. But how unreasonable such a view when fully examined in the light of apostolic testimony. Consider, too, that if our Lord's flesh, that was pierced and wounded with nail and spear and crown of thorns, and marked with sorrow, is his glorious spiritual body, and if the scars and marred human features are part and parcel of the exalted Lord, he would be far from beautiful, even if we should love the wounds endured for us. And if he thus bears an imperfect, scarred, marred body, and if we shall be *like him,* would it not imply that the apostles and saints who were crucified, beheaded, stoned to death, burned, cut to pieces and torn by beasts, as well as those who met with accidents, would each likewise bear his blemishes and scars? And in that view would not heaven present a most awful spectacle— to all eternity? But this is not the case, and no one could long hold so unreasonable and unscriptural a view. Spirit beings are perfect in every particular, and so the Apostle reminds the Church, who are heirs of heavenly or spiritual glory and honor, that, though sown [in death] in weakness [with marks and wounds, etc.] it [the being] is raised in power; though sown in dishonor [with lines of care and sorrow, etc.] it is raised in glory; though sown a natural body [literally, "an animal body"] it will be raised a spiritual body; and that as we have borne the image of the earthly father, we shall bear the image of the heavenly Lord. (1 Cor. 15: 42–51.) Our Lord Jesus for our sakes took and bore the image of the earthly also, for a while, that he might redeem us. But in his resurrection he became the heavenly Lord (Rom. 14: 9), and we, if faithful, shall soon bear the image of the heavenly Lord (spiritual bodies), as we now still bear the image of the earthly lord, Adam (human bodies).

Remember Paul's case—In order that he might be one of the apostles, he must be a *witness*—must see the Lord after his resurrection. He was not one of those who saw the manifestations of resurrection and presence during the forty days, hence he was given a special glimpse of the Lord. But he saw him, not as did the others—not veiled in flesh and garments of various forms. And the merest glance at the unveiled glorious person of our Lord caused him to fall to the ground blinded with a glory far "above the brightness of the sun at noon-day:" from which blindness, to restore him to even partial sight required a miracle. (Acts 9: 17, 18.) Did not Paul see the Lord as he *is*—a spiritual being? And did not our Lord during the forty days *appear* as he *was*, *i. e.*, as he had been previously, for the special purposes and reasons already pointed out? There is no room

to doubt this.   But the Lord had an object in appearing to
Paul thus, just as he had, and served another object by appearing differently to the others.   This object Paul shows,
saying : "Last of all he was *seen* of me also—*as* by one
BORN BEFORE THE DUE TIME."   (1 Cor. 15 : 8—literal rendering.)   As the resurrection of our Lord was his *birth*
from the dead, to the full perfection of spiritual being (Col.
1 : 18; Rom. 8: 29), so the resurrection of the Church, the
body of Christ, is here and elsewhere referred to as a birth.
In our birth or resurrection as spirit beings, we shall see the
Lord *as he is*, just as Paul saw him ; but we, being *changed*
or born then, as spirit beings, will not be stricken down
nor blinded with the sight of our Lord's glorious person.
Paul's statement means that he saw him *as* we shall see him
—"*as he is :*" he saw him *as* all the body of Christ shall
see him, but BEFORE THE DUE TIME, before he was born
from the dead, and therefore before able to endure it ;—yet
"*as*" each one so born shall in due time see him.

Moses, coming down from the mount to communicate to
Israel the Law Covenant, was a type of the greater Law-
giver and Mediator of the New Covenant, who at his second
advent shall come forth to rule and bless the world.   Moses
typified, therefore, the entire Church, of which our Lord is
the Head.   Moses' face was caused to shine, so that the
people could not look at him, and he must thereafter wear
a veil, as a type of the spiritual glory of Christ, an illustration of the point we are now examining.   Christ has the
real glory and brightness, the express image of the Father's
person, and we shall be like him, and no man can behold
that glory ; hence whatever manifestation of the Law-giver
there will be to the world when the glory of the Lord shall be
revealed, the glory of the spiritual persons cannot be seen.
They will speak through the veil—under the cover.   This, as
well as more, was meant by Moses' veil.—Exod. 34: 30–33.

As we give the matter careful study, we come more and more to recognize the divine wisdom displayed in the manner of revealing the resurrection of our Lord to the apostles, that they should be thoroughly satisfied and reliable witnesses, and that the meek of the world might be able to receive their testimony and believe that God raised our Lord from the dead—that they might recognize him as the one that was dead, but is now alive forevermore, and, believing, might come unto God by him. And as we consider him under the leadings of the holy Spirit of truth, our minds expand and we see him no longer the man Christ Jesus, but the Lord of glory and power, partaker of the divine nature. And thus we know him, for whose coming and kingdom the Church has so earnestly prayed and longed. And no one properly recognizing his great exaltation can expect at his second coming the man Christ Jesus in the body of flesh prepared for sacrifice and wounded and *given* in death as our ransom. Nor should we expect that at his second coming he would "appear," or *manifest* himself, in various flesh and bone forms to the world—that was needful for those early *witnesses*, but not so now. He will, as we shall see, manifest his second presence very differently.

From what we have seen regarding spirit beings and their manifestations in times past, it is evident that if our Lord were to manifest himself at his second advent either by opening men's eyes to behold his glory, as he did with Paul and Daniel, or by assuming a human body, it would be detrimental to the plan revealed in his Word. The effect of appearing in glory to the world, their eyes being miraculously wrought upon to enable them to see him, would be almost to paralyze them with the overwhelming sight, while to appear *as a man* would be to lower the standard of dignity and give a lower than the true estimate of the divine nature and form. As neither would seem to be necessary or advisable now, we cannot presume that either of these methods will be adopted.

On the contrary, we should expect that the Christ would be manifest in the flesh of mankind in the same manner that when the Lord was "*made flesh*" and dwelt among men, God was manifest in his flesh.   Human nature, when perfect and in harmony with God, is a *likeness of God* in the flesh ; hence the originally perfect Adam was a likeness of God, and the perfect man Christ Jesus was also ; so that he could say to the disciple Philip, who asked to *see* the Father, "He that hath seen me hath seen the Father"—he hath seen the likeness of God in the flesh, "God manifest in the flesh."

So, too, mankind in general, as its members come gradually back to the long-lost image of God, will be fleshly images and likenesses of the Father and of the Christ.   At the very beginning of the Millennium, as we have seen, there will be samples of perfect manhood before the world (Vol. I., pages 287–293): Abraham, Isaac and Jacob, and the holy prophets, already tried and approved, will be the "princes" among men, the exponents and representatives of the spiritual, invisible kingdom.   In these Christ will be manifested—in *their flesh*—even as the Father was manifested in his flesh.   And as "whosoever will" reaches perfection and comes into full harmony with the will of Christ, every such one will be an image of God and of Christ, and in each of these Christ will be manifested.

Because created in God's moral image, the perfect man, fully consecrated, will be able to appreciate perfectly the holy Spirit and Word of God ; and the glorified Church will direct him.   No doubt, too, visions and direct revelations, and general communication between the spiritual kingdom and its earthly representatives and exponents, will be much more free and general than similar communications ever were before—more after the order of the communions of Eden, before sin brought condemnation and separation from God's favor and communion.

Nothing, then, either in reason or in Scripture, demands that our Lord shall at his second advent appear in various bodies of flesh and bones. That such a procedure is not essential is evident from the success of Satan's kingdom, which operates through human beings as agents. Those who partake of the spirit of evil and error represent the great unseen prince, most fully. He is thus manifest in their flesh, though himself a spirit being, invisible to men.

The Christ "changed," made partakers of the divine nature, shall be spirit beings as truly as is Satan, and equally invisible to men. Their operations will be similar in manner, though directly opposite in character and results ; their honored agents, not bound and made slaves by ignorance and weakness, as are most of the servants of Satan, but made perfect, and "free indeed," will act intelligently and harmoniously, from choice and from love ; and their appointments will be rewards of righteousness.

Our Lord's presence will be manifested to the *world* by exhibitions of "power and great glory," not, however, merely to the natural sight, but to the eyes of their understanding, as they shall open to an appreciation of the great changes which the new Ruler shall effect. His presence and righteous authority will be recognized in both the punishments and the blessings that will flow to mankind from his reign.

It has long been generally believed that distress and trouble come as punishments for evil doing, upon the wicked. This seeming to be a natural and proper law, people in general have accepted it, thinking that it should be so, even if it is not ; yet the hard facts of experience agree with the Bible, that in the past it has been the godly who have oftenest suffered afflictions and persecutions. (2 Tim. 3 : 12.) But in the " Day of Trouble," the period of forty

years introducing Messiah's reign, this order will begin to be
reversed.   In that day, evil powers are to be overthrown,
and righteousness, established by a gradual process, shall
speedily work out a corresponding retribution to evil-doers,
and blessings to them that do good—"Tribulation and
anguish upon every soul of man that doeth evil, . . . but
glory, honor and peace to every man that worketh good"—
in that "day of wrath and revelation of the righteous judgment of God, who will render to every man according to
his deeds."   (Rom. 2 : 9, 10, 6, 5.)   And since there is so
much that is wrong now, the retribution will be very heavy
at first, making a "time of trouble such as was not since
there was a nation."   Thus, in vengeance, and trouble, and
wrath upon the nations, will the Lord reveal to the world
the fact of the change of dispensations, and the change of
rulers.   And thus, "When the judgments of the Lord are
in the earth, the inhabitants of the world will learn righteousness."   (Isa. 26 : 5–11.)   They will learn that under
the new order of things right-doers are to be exalted and
evil-doers restrained and punished.   For clear prophetic
testimony relative to this kingdom and its operation on
behalf of the humble, the upright, the poor, the needy and
the oppressed, and its overthrow of monopolies and every
system of injustice and oppression, and the general equal-
ization of human affairs, read carefully Psalm 72 : 1–19;
37 : 1–14.

Our King will thus reveal himself gradually : some will
discern the new Ruler sooner than others, but ultimately
"every eye shall see [*horao*—discern] him."   (Rev. 1 : 7.)
But "he cometh with clouds;" and while the clouds of
trouble are heavy and dark, when the mountains (kingdoms
of this world) are trembling and falling, and the earth (organized society) is being shaken, disintegrated, melted, some
will begin to realize what we now proclaim as already at

hand—that the great day of Jehovah has come; that the foretold day of trouble and wrath upon the nations is beginning; and that Jehovah's Anointed is taking to himself his great power and beginning his work, of laying justice to the line and righteousness to the plummet. (Isa. 28:17.) And "he must reign until" he shall have *put down* all authorities and laws on earth, contrary to those which control in heaven.

As the trouble increases, men will seek, but in vain, for protection in the "dens" and caves, the great rocks and fortresses of society (Free Masonry, Odd Fellowship, and Trades Unions, Guilds, Trusts, and all societies secular and ecclesiastical), and in the mountains (governments) of earth; saying, "Fall over* [cover, protect] and hide us from the face of him that sitteth on the throne, and from the wrath of the Lamb; for the great day of his wrath is come."— Rev. 6:15–17.

The idolatry of money in which the whole world has gone mad, and which is to have so prominent a place in the trouble, causing not only anxiety for its accumulation, but also for its preservation, is to be completely overthrown, as shown in Isa. 2:8–21; Ezek. 7:17–19.

The great day of trouble will be recognized, and from its storm all will seek protection, though few will recognize the judgments of the Lord then abroad in the world as the result of his *presence*, the setting up of his authority, and the enforcement of his laws. In the end, however, all shall

---

* The Greek word *epi*, here used, is generally translated *on*, but has also the significance of *over* and *about*, and is so translated many times in the common version. The thought is that of protection, not of destruction. The common view of this passage, that it teaches that wicked men will get faith enough to pray for literal mountains to fall, is absurd. The real fulfilment is already beginning: the great, the rich, and no less the poor, are seeking to the mountains and rocks and caves for shelter from the darkening storm of trouble which all see is gathering.

recognize ["*see*"] the King of glory; and all who then love righteousness will rejoice to obey him and conform themselves fully to his just requirements.

That will be a time of retribution upon all who by fraud or force, sometimes in the name of law and under its sanction, have unrighteously grasped the rights or property of others. The retribution, as we have seen, will come *from* the Lord, *through* the uprising of the masses of the people. In their distress, loth to part with a dollar or an acre, or an assumed right or dignity long enjoyed and long undisputed, yet seeing the approaching retribution, many will seek the covering of the hitherto powerful organizations—civil, social and ecclesiastical—to promote and shield their interests, feeling that alone they must fall. But these shall not be able to deliver them in the day of the Lord's anger. The approaching conflict and retribution will cause all the families of the earth to wail; for it will be a time of trouble such as was not since there was a nation— no, nor ever shall be again. It will be "*because of him*" that they will wail; because of his judgments producing in a natural way the great trouble; because the Lord ariseth to shake terribly the earth, and to destroy its corruptions. (Isa. 2 : 21.) So far-reaching will be the judgments and the trouble that none shall escape. Ultimately every eye shall discern the change, and recognize that the Lord reigneth. The trouble might be greatly lessened could men see and promptly act upon principles of equity, ignoring and relinquishing all unjust privileges of the past, even though legalized; but this, selfishness will not permit until the trouble shall break and overthrow the proud, humble the powerful and exalt the meek.

But not until the great day of trouble is about closing— not until the Gentile kingdoms are ground to powder and utterly removed, no place being found for them (A. D.

1915, as shown in the preceding chapter)—not until great Babylon is utterly overthrown and her influence over the world broken—will the great mass of mankind come to realize the true state of the case. Then they will see that the great trouble through which they will have passed was that symbolically termed "The battle of the great day of God Almighty" (Rev. 16 : 14); that in proportion as they have aided error and wrong, they have been battling against the law and forces of the new empire and the new Ruler of earth; and that in proportion as their tongues, and pens, and hands, and influence, and means, were used to support *the right* and the truth on any subject, they had been to that extent fighting on the Lord's side.

Some will learn the significance of the trouble more quickly than others, because more teachable. And during all the trouble there will be in the world those who will bear witness to its cause, declaring the Lord's presence and the setting up of his kingdom which is in opposition to the powers of darkness to be the real cause of the trouble and shaking and overturning of society, showing that all who oppose truth and righteousness are the enemies of the new kingdom, and that unless they quickly surrender they must soon suffer ignominious defeat. Yet the masses will be heedless of wise counsel, as they have always been, until completely humbled under the iron rule of the new kingdom, only at last realizing the folly of their course.

The true teacher and light bearer (Matt. 5 : 14), the true Church, the body of Christ, is not to be left in darkness to learn of her Lord's presence by the manifestations of his wrath and power, as the world will learn of it. For her enlightenment special provision has been made. By the sure word of prophecy, which shines as a light in a dark place, she is clearly and definitely informed just what to expect. (2 Pet. 1 : 19.) Through the prophetic word, she shall not only be shielded from discouragement, and enabled to overcome the besetments, snares and stumbling-stones so prevalent in "the evil day," and thus to stand approved of God, but she becomes the light-bearer and instructor of the world. The Church is thus enabled to point out to the world the cause of the trouble, to announce the presence of the new Ruler, to declare the policy, plan and object of the new dispensation, and to instruct the world as to the wisest course to pursue in view of these things. And though men will not give heed to the instruction until the lesson of submission has been forced upon them by the trouble, it will greatly aid them then in learning the lesson. It is to this mission of the "feet," or last members of the Church, who will declare upon the mountains (kingdoms) the *reign of Christ begun*, that Isa. 52 : 7 refers.

SEEMINGLY CONFLICTING SCRIPTURES.

There are some statements of Scripture with reference to the manner of the Lord's return and appearing which, until critically examined, appear to be contradictory of each other. And no doubt they have for centuries served the divine purpose of concealing the truth until the due time for it to be understood; and even then, from all except the special class of consecrated ones for whom it was intended.

For instance, our Lord said, "Behold, I come *as a thief;*" and, "As it was *in the days* of Noah, so shall it be also *in the days* of the Son of man [the days of his *presence*] : They did eat, they drank, they married wives, they were given in marriage," "and *knew not* until the flood came." "And when Jesus was questioned of the Pharisees when the Kingdom of God should come, he answered them and said, The Kingdom of God *cometh not with observation*" [*marginal reading,* "not with outward show"].—Rev. 16 : 15 ; Luke 17 : 26, 27, 20 ; Matt. 24 : 38, 39.

These scriptures plainly state and illustrate the manner of the Lord's coming. They show that he will be present unseen, doing a work of which the world for a time will be entirely unaware. His arrival must therefore be in a quiet manner, unobserved, and entirely unknown to the world, just "as a thief" would come, without noise or other demonstration to attract attention. As in the days of Noah the world went on with its affairs as usual, not in the least disconcerted, and without the slightest faith in the preaching of Noah with reference to the coming flood, so in the early part of the Day of the Lord, the world, having no faith in the announcement of his presence and of the impending trouble, will go on as usual, giving no heed whatever to any such preaching until, in the great flood of trouble, the old world—the old order of things—goes down, passes away, preparatory to the full establishment of the new order, the Kingdom of God under the whole heavens. —"As it was in the days of Noah, so shall it be also in the days [of the *presence*] of the Son of man."

On the other hand, we find scriptures which at first sight seem to be in direct conflict with these; as, for instance: "The Lord himself shall descend from heaven with a *shout*, with the *voice* of the Archangel, and with the *trump* of God."—"The Lord Jesus shall be revealed from heaven with his mighty messengers, in flaming fire, taking vengeance on them that know not God, and that obey not the gospel of our Lord Jesus Christ."—"They [the world] *shall see* the Son of man coming in the clouds of heaven with power and great glory."—"Behold, he cometh with clouds, and *every eye shall see him*."—1 Thes. 4:16; 2 Thes. 1:7, 8; Matt. 24:30; Rev. 1:7.

As seekers after truth, it will not do for us to say, in view of these passages, that the *majority* of them seem to favor whatever view we incline to prefer, and then to ignore the others.   Until we have a view of the matter in which every Bible statement finds a reasonable representation, we should not feel sure that we have the truth on the subject. One statement of God is as true, and as firm a foundation for faith, as a hundred.   And it would be wiser to seek for a harmonious understanding than to arrive at a conclusion or adopt a theory based on a one-sided interpretation, and thus to deceive ourselves and others.

Christians generally make no effort to harmonize these statements, and therefore their ideas are one-sided and incorrect.   The last group of statements is just as positive as the first, and apparently teaches the very reverse of a quiet, unobserved, thief-like manner in the Lord's coming and presence.   In addition to these statements, we are referred to two other illustrations of the manner of his coming, viz.: "This same Jesus, which is taken up from you into heaven, shall *so come*, IN LIKE MANNER as ye have seen him go into heaven," and, "As the lightning cometh out of the east, and shineth even unto the west, so shall also the coming of the Son of man be." (Acts 1:11 ; Matt. 24:27.) To reach a correct conclusion, these also must be given due weight.

In our examination of the subject we should note that while our Lord stated, as a positive fact, that his kingdom would be established without outward show, and that his coming, his presence, would be *as* a thief, requiring close, attentive watching to apprehend and discern it, all of the above texts generally cited as proof of an outward, visible manifestation are in *highly figurative language*, except the one which says that he will come in like manner as he went away.   The symbolic must always bend in interpretation to the plainer, more literal statements, as soon as their symbolic character is recognized.   Whenever a literal interpretation would do violence to reason, and also place the passage in direct antagonism to *plain statements* of Scriptιre, such passage should be considered figurative, and its interpretation as a symbol should be sought in harmony with obviously plain and literal passages, and with the general character and object of the revealed plan. By recognizing and thus interpreting the symbols in this case, the beautiful harmony of all the statements is manifest. Let us now examine them and see how perfectly they agree with the statements which are not symbolic.

(*a*) "The Lord himself shall descend from heaven with a *shout*, with the *voice of the Archangel*, and with the *trump of God*." (1 Thes. 4: 16.) The voice and the trumpet here mentioned correspond in every way with the same figures used in Rev. 11 : 15–19—"The seventh angel *sounded;* and there were great *voices* in heaven, saying, The kingdom of this world is become the kingdom of our Lord, and of his Christ, and he shall reign forever and ever. . . . And the nations were angry, and thy wrath is come, and the time of the dead, that they should be judged," etc. The same events are referred to in Daniel's prophecy :—"And at that time shall Michael [Christ] stand up [assume control], the great Prince, . . . and there shall be a time of trouble such as never was since there was a nation, . . . and many of them that sleep in the dust of the earth shall awake." And Paul adds to his mention of the voices and the trumpet the statement, "And the dead in Christ shall rise first." In 2 Tim. 4: 1 he further states that Christ shall judge the quick (the living) and the dead, at this time of his appearing and kingdom ; and the beginning of this judgment of the living nations is everywhere described as the greatest time of trouble the world has ever known.—Dan. 12: 1.

Thus Paul, John and Daniel evidently refer to the same time, the time of our Lord's appearing, and the establishment of his kingdom in the midst of a great time of trouble, and to the events preceding and introducing it. The same result is shown by each writer to follow the standing up of Michael, the voices and the trumpet: namely, trouble and wrath upon the nations and the resurrection of the dead. Next, mark the figure used:—

"WITH A SHOUT."—The Greek word here translated "shout" is *keleusma*, which signifies *a shout of encouragement.* A shout implies a public message designed for the ears, not of a few, but of a mixed multitude. It is generally designed either to alarm and terrify or to assist and encourage. Or it may have the one effect upon one class, and the reverse effect upon another, according to circumstances and conditions.

The aspect of affairs in the world for the past fifteen years very strikingly corresponds with this symbol, in the outbursts of world-wide encouragement for all men to wake up to a sense of their rights and privileges as men, and to consider their mutual relationships, the principles upon which they are based and the ends which they should accomplish. Where on the face of the earth is the civilized nation that has not heard the shout, and is not influenced by it! The entire civilized world has, in the past few years, been studying political economy, civil rights and social liberties as never before in the annals of history; and men are encouraging each other, and being encouraged, as never before, to probe these subjects to the very foundation. The shout of encouragement started by the increase of knowledge among men has already encircled the earth, and under its influence men are banding themselves together, encouraged and assisted by men of brain and genius, to contend and strive for both real and fancied rights and liberties; and as their organizations increase and multiply, the shout grows louder and longer, and will by and by result as foretold, in the great time of trouble and tumult of angry nations. This result is graphically described by the Prophet —"The noise of a multitude in the mountains [kingdoms] like as of a great people; a tumultuous noise of the king-doms of nations gathered together: the Lord of hosts mustereth the host of battle.''—Isa. 13:4.

"THE VOICE OF THE ARCHANGEL"—is another striking symbol of similar import. The name "archangel" signi-fies *chief messenger;* and our anointed Lord himself is Jeho-vah's Chief Messenger—the "Messenger of the Covenant." (Mal. 3:1.) Daniel refers to the same personage, calling him Michael, which name signifies *who as God*—an ap-propriate name for him who is "the express image of the Father's person," and the representative of his authority and power. The voice of the Archangel represents Christ's authority and command. This symbol, then, represents Christ as taking control, or beginning his reign and issuing his commands, his official orders, announcing the change of dispensation by the enforcement of the laws of his kingdom.

The same thought is differently expressed by Daniel, when he says, Then shall Michael, the great Prince, *"stand up."* To stand up signifies to assume authority, to give commands. See *"ariseth,"* Isa. 2:19, 21. Another illustration of this symbol is from David, who says of Christ prophetically, "He uttered his voice; the earth melted." The great time of trouble will be precipitated, and the earth (organized so-ciety) will melt, or disintegrate, under the change of ad-ministration going into effect when the new King utters his voice of command. At his command, systems of error, civil, social and religious, must go down, however old or firmly entrenched and fortified they may be. The sword out of his mouth shall cause the havoc: The truth on every subject, and in all its varied aspects, shall judge men, and, under his power and overruling, shall cause the overturn-ing of evil and error in all their thousand forms.

" THE TRUMP OF GOD."—Many seem thoughtlessly to entertain the idea that this trumpet will be a literal sound on the air. But this will be seen to be an unreasonable expectation, when it is noticed that Paul here refers to what the Revelator designates "The Seventh Trumpet," the "Last Trump" in *a series* of symbolic trumpets. (Rev. 11:15; 1 Cor. 15:52.) The proof that these references are to the same trumpet is found in the record of the events connected with each. Paul mentions the resurrection, and the establishment of the Lord's Kingdom, as connected with "the trump of God," and the Revelator mentions the same with even greater minuteness. The propriety of calling the "seventh," or "last trump," the "trump of God," is evident, too, when we remember that the events mentioned under the preceding six trumpets of Revelation refer to humanity's doings, while the seventh refers specially to the Lord's work, and covers the "Day of the Lord." Since the six preceding trumpets were symbols—and this is generally admitted by commentators and students who make any claim as expositors of Revelation—it would be a violation of reason and common sense to expect the seventh, the last of the series, to be a literal, audible sound on the air. And not only so, but it would be out of harmony with the Lord's general methods, as well as with those statements of Scripture indicating the *secrecy* of his coming; for a thief never sounds a trumpet to announce his arrival.

The seven trumpets of Revelation are all symbolic, and represent seven great periods of time and their events. The examination of these we leave for a subsequent volume. Suffice it here to say that we find ourselves to-day in the midst of the very events which mark the sounding of the seventh trumpet. The great voices, the increase of knowledge, the angry nations, etc., taken in connection with time-prophecies, establish this as a fact. Many events are yet to transpire before this seventh or last trumpet ceases to sound; as, for instance, the rewarding of the saints and prophets, the resurrection of all the dead, etc. In fact, it covers the entire period of the Millennial reign of Christ, as indicated by the events which are to transpire under it. —Rev. 10:7; 11:15, 18.

Thus we find the "*shout,*" the "*voice of the Archangel*" and "*the trump of God*" all symbols, and now in process of fulfilment. Note carefully, too, the fact that each of the three prophecies just referred to (Dan. 12:1; Rev. 11:15; I Thes. 4:16) declares the Lord's *presence* at the time when the events mentioned transpire. They were foretold for the very purpose of indicating the manner in which his *invisible presence* would be manifested to those who have faith in the word of prophecy. Paul says, "The Lord *shall descend* with [literally *in*, or *during*] a shout," voice, trumpet, etc.; John says that the kingdoms of this world become his, during the time of these events; and Daniel says, "At that time shall Michael, the great Prince [Christ], stand up" (be *present*) and take to himself his great power. If, therefore, we can recognize the shout, the voices and the sounding of the great trumpet, we should accept them as indications, not that the Lord will come soon, but rather that he has come and is now present, and that the harvest work of gathering the wheat and burning the tares is already under way. This we shall soon see is abundantly proved by time-prophecies. Yet it is not to the natural vision, but only to the eye of faith, through the sure word of prophecy, that his presence and work can be discerned.

Just here another fact should not be overlooked, namely, that the "Shout," the "Voice of the Archangel," and the "Trump of God," as above explained, are all instrumentalities for the accomplishment of the harvest work of the Gospel age. If, therefore, we see not only the meaning of these symbols, but the foretold *results* actually taking place, we have additional proof both that we have rightly interpreted the symbols, and that we are now in this period called the "harvest," in which the Gospel age and the Millennial age lap—the one closing and the other opening. Many will need no aid in tracing a *separating work* now going on between the truly consecrated and the merely nominal Christians.   Many can see the symbolic fire already under way, and can discern the "shout" of the people, the command of the new King Immanuel and the events called the "seventh trumpet," and the "clouds" of trouble, in which the Lord comes, and from and in which his power is to be manifested—subduing all things unto himself.

We have already (Vol. I., p. 237) called attention to the fact, that the recognition of the harvest work in actual process is proof of the Lord's presence, since he declared that he would be the chief reaper and director of the entire work, and that this would be his first work.—"Behold, a white cloud, and upon the cloud one sat like unto the Son of man, having on his head a golden crown, and in his hand a sharp sickle. . . . And he that sat on the cloud thrust in his sickle on the earth; and the earth was reaped."—"In *the time* of the harvest *I* will say to the reapers, gather" etc. (Rev. 15:14, 16; Matt. 13:30.)   The harvest work will occupy forty years for its full accomplishment, ending with A. D. 1914.   Its various features will be accomplished gradually, but all of its days are "days of the Son of Man"— days of our Lord's presence and power—recognized in the end by all, but at first only by the class specified by the Apostle—"Ye, brethren—not in darkness."

"IN FLAMING FIRE."—The next of these symbolic statements can be readily understood, if the meaning of the symbols, fire, etc., already explained (Vol. I., p. 317), be borne in mind.   It reads, "The Lord Jesus shall be revealed from heaven with his mighty angels, in flaming fire, taking vengeance on them that know not God, and that obey not the gospel of our Lord Jesus Christ."—2 Thessalonians 1:8.

Expressed literally, we understand this to signify that in his day (the Millennial age) our Lord's presence will be revealed or manifested to the world from his position of spiritual control ("heaven"), in the wrath and punishment then visited upon evil and evil-doers. It will be consuming wrath, as indicated by the symbol, *fire*, and will leave neither root nor branch of evil systems, error, oppression, or wilful sinners; and all the proud, and all evil doers, shall be burned up as stubble in that Millennial day. In its beginning—in this "harvest" period—this fire will burn very fiercely, consuming pride and evil, now of such rank growth. Happy those who will surrender their pride and evil to be destroyed, that they themselves be not destroyed also (in the "second death"), as some resisters will evidently be, during the Millennial age. It is of this time that we read, "Behold, the day cometh that shall burn as an oven; and all the proud, yea, and all that do wickedly, shall be stubble: and the day that cometh shall burn them up, saith the Lord of hosts, that it shall leave them neither root nor branch."—Mal. 4:1.

The "mighty angels," messengers, or agents of his power, are various, and may properly be understood as applying to and including all the various agencies, animate and inanimate, which shall be used by our Lord in the overthrow of the evil systems of the present, and in the chastisement of evil-doers.

While the wrath or vengeance of the Lord is thus to be expressed in flaming fire, in consuming trouble, such as never before was known—so general and wide-spread, and so destructive of evil—righteousness and the righteous will begin to be favored. And as these dealings become more and more apparent, men will begin to draw the inference that a new power has taken control of human affairs;

and thus the *presence* of our Lord as King of kings shall be revealed to the world.   " He shall be revealed in flaming fire, taking vengeance [both] on them that know not God [who are not really acquainted with God, but who nevertheless fail to obey the light of conscience, which all to some extent possess], and [also on those who, while knowing God, yet] obey not the Gospel of our Lord Jesus Christ."

Under the chastisements and increasing light and favorable opportunities of the Millennial day, all will be brought to such a clear knowledge of the truth and the way of righteousness as to be without the excuse of ignorance, or of inability to obey the truth; and those who persistently *continue* enemies of God and righteousness shall be punished with *lasting destruction* [a destruction from which there shall be no resurrection] from the presence of the Lord and from the glory of his power.

"IN POWER AND GREAT GLORY."—The next statement is to the effect that the world will see the Son of man *coming,* before his kingdom is fully set up or his joint-heirs are all gathered and exalted with him.   And, seeing his coming, all the tribes of the earth will mourn—"They shall see the Son of man coming with power and great glory."

Already the world sees the clouds of trouble gathering and darkening; they realize that a power is now at work in the affairs of men, with which they cannot cope; the near future, from the present outlook, is dark and ominous to all who have sufficient intelligence to mark the trend of events. Thinking men observe the persistency with which questions of right and wrong, justice and injustice, are *forced* upon their consideration, *demanding* an expression of their individual principles.   Many recognize the *glory and power* of earth's new Ruler, yet because clouds and darkness are round about him they do not recognize the King himself.   Men see *the clouds*, and therefore see him coming in the clouds with power and great glory [the glory of power and justice], but they do not recognize *him*. Not until the clouds have let fall hail stones and coals of fire (Psa. 18 : 12, 13) to batter down men's pride, and selfishness, and prejudices, and consume these, will the clouds disappear, and reveal the full majesty and glory of Christ's presence. If men would consider, and hearken to the voice of the Lord, which now directs the course of justice, and warns of impending retribution, the great disasters of the near future would be averted ; but "God speaketh once, yea, twice, yet man perceiveth it not. . . . Then he openeth the ears of men [in the thunder tones of "the day of trouble"] and sealeth their instruction, that he may withdraw man from his [own] purpose, and hide pride from man."

"Behold, he cometh with clouds," and in due time "every eye shall see [discern] him," shall recognize his presence, power and authority; and all must submit to it, whether willing or unwilling, until the loosing of Satan for a little season, in the close of the Millennium, when after full experience their willingness or unwillingness will be fully tested, and the unwilling will be destroyed—the second death, symbolically called the lake of fire.—Rev. 21:8.

Thus seen, all of these symbolic explanations of the manner of our Lord's coming accord perfectly with the plain statements which declare that his presence will be a secret for a time, known only to those watching.

IN LIKE MANNER.

What, now, is taught by the statement of the angel at the time of our Lord's departure—Acts 1 : 11—"This same Jesus which is taken up from you into heaven shall so come, in like manner, as ye have seen him go into heaven"?

A careful examination of this text will manifest its harmony with the foregoing. Many seem to think the passage reads, As you *see* the Lord ascend into heaven, so, in like manner, you shall *see* him come again.   Such should read it again and again, until they note the fact that it does not say that those who saw him go will *see* him come, nor that any one else will *see* him come.   What it does say is, that the *manner* of his coming will be *like* the *manner* of his going.   What, then, was the manner of his going? Was it with great splendor, and with great demonstration?   Was it with trumpet sound and voices and a great shout rending the air, and the Lord's person shining in supernatural glory and brightness?   If so, we should expect his coming again to be "*in like manner.*"   On the other hand, was it not as quietly and secretly as was possible, consistent with his purpose of having thoroughly convinced witnesses of the fact? None saw him, or knew of the fact, except his faithful followers.   His statement (John 14:19), "Yet a little while and the world seeth me no more," has never yet been disproved ; for none but the brethren saw even his manifestations after his resurrection, and no others witnessed his ascension.   And in *like manner* as he went away (quietly, secretly, so far as the world was concerned, and unknown except to his followers), *so*, in this manner, he comes again. And as when he went away he lifted up his hands and blessed them, so, when he comes again, it is that their joy may be full, as he said : "I will come again, and receive you unto myself;" "I will see you again, and your heart shall rejoice, and your joy no man taketh from you."— Luke 24 : 50, 51 ; John 14 : 3 ; 16 : 22.

The angel seemed also to give special emphasis to the fact that the coming again would be the coming of this very "*same Jesus*"—the same one who left the glory which he had with the Father before the world was, and became man—became poor that we might be made rich ; the same Jesus that died on Calvary ; the same Jesus that arose a quickening spirit the third day; the same Jesus that had manifested his *change* during the forty days—THIS same Jesus now ascended up on high. Yes, it is the *same* Jesus who has experienced two changes of nature—first from spirit to human, and then from human to divine. These changes of nature have not destroyed his individuality. His identity was preserved, as the angel thus assures us, whether the philosophy of that fact be understood or not; and though we shall know him no more after the flesh (as a man), but should remember his exaltation, that he is now of the divine, spiritual nature, and should anticipate his coming in harmony with this change and exaltation, yet we may remember that he is *the same loving Jesus*, and not changed in this respect. It is "this same Jesus," who, though present forty days after his resurrection, was seen of the disciples only, and by them but briefly, who in his second presence will be as invisible to the world as during the forty days preceding his ascension. We must remember that he does not come to give himself as a sacrifice, and hence that he has no further use for a human body prepared for sacrifice. (Heb. 10: 5.) That is all over now: he dies no more, but now comes to rule and bless and uplift the redeemed race.

Our Lord furnished us a most beautiful illustration of the manner in which his presence will be revealed, when he said, "As the bright-shining emerges from the east, and illuminates even unto the west, so will be the *presence* of the Son of man." (Matt. 24: 27.) That most translations of this verse are faulty in using the word lightning, where sunlight is meant, is evident; for lightning flashes do not come out of the east and shine unto the west. They just as frequently come from other quarters, and rarely, if ever, flash clear across the heavens. The Lord's illustration, and the only one which will comport with his words, is the sun's brightness, which does invariably emerge from the east and

shine even unto the west.   The Greek word *astrape*, here
used, is thus shown to be improperly translated in this
text, and also in the account of the same words by Luke
(17 : 24).   Another instance of the use of this word *astrape*
by our Lord is found in Luke 11 : 36, where it applies
to the brightness of a candle, and in the common version is rendered "bright-shining."   Incorrect ideas of the
manner of our Lord's coming and revealing, firmly fixed
in the minds of translators, led them into this error of
translating *astrape* by the word "lightning."   They supposed
that he would be revealed suddenly, like a flash of lightning, and not gradually, like the dawning sunlight.   But
how beautiful is the figure of sunrise, as illustrating the
gradual dawning of truth and blessing in the day of his
presence.   The Lord associates the overcomers with himself
in this figure, saying, "Then shall the righteous shine forth as
the Sun in the Kingdom of their Father."   And the Prophet, using the same figure, says, "The Sun of righteousness
shall arise with healing in his beams."   The dawning is
gradual, but finally the full, clear brightness shall thoroughly
banish the darkness of evil, ignorance, superstition and sin.

An imperfect translation of the word *parousia* has further
tended to obscure the sense of this passage.   In the Emphatic Diaglott and in Prof. Young's translation it is rendered
presence; in Rotherham's it is *arrival;* while in the common version it is rendered *coming*.   And though the text
of the Revised Version retains this last erroneous rendering—*coming*—yet in the marginal reading it acknowledges
"*presence*" to be the true definition of the Greek.   The
Greek word *parousia* invariably signifies personal presence,
as having come, having arrived ; and it should never be
understood as signifying to be on the way, as the English
word *coming* is generally used.   The text under consideration therefore teaches that as the *sunlight* gradually dawns,

so shall the *presence* of the Son of man be gradually manifested or revealed.

Together with this illustration, our Lord coupled words
of caution to guard us against certain errors which would
be advanced about the time of his second advent, calculated
to lead his Church astray. "Behold, I have told you before.
Wherefore, if they shall say unto you, Behold, he is in the
desert; go not forth: behold, he is in the secret chambers;
believe it not. For as the bright shining [sun] cometh out
of the east and [gradually] shineth even unto the west, so
shall be the *presence* of the son of man." Thus does our
Lord put us on guard against two errors rapidly growing in
our day. One is the claim that our Lord will come in the
flesh, in the wilderness or desert of Palestine; and, so believing, many have gone thither, and are waiting to see
Jesus in the *flesh*, with the scars, as when crucified. Expecting him as he *was*, and not "as he is," they seriously
err, and blind themselves to the truth, as did the Jews at
the first advent. These false expectations lead this class to
interpret literally the statement of the prophet (Zech. 14:4),
"His feet shall stand in that day upon the Mount of Olives,"
etc. * Blinded by false expectations, they do not see that
the "feet" in this passage are figurative, as truly as in
Psa. 91:12; Isa. 52:7; Psa. 7:6; 110:1; Eph. 6:15;
Deut. 33:3; and in many other passages. If they knew
what to expect, they would know not to go to Jerusalem
to look for the *man* Christ Jesus; for the highly exalted
king comes as the sunlight, making his presence and influence felt the world over. Wherefore, "Go not forth."

"If they shall say, Behold, he is in the secret chambers;
believe it not." Spiritism, ever ready to deceive by counterfeits, and ever ready to use advanced truths as a garment of light (2 Cor. 11:13, 14), has not hesitated to

* We leave the examination of this prophecy for another occasion.

claim that we are in a period of dispensational change, the dawning of a glorious age. Among other such things some of them even teach that Christ is *present*, and, we doubt not, ere long they will give *seances* at which they will claim to show him in the *secret chambers*. Should the error present itself in this form, or any other, let us remember our Lord's words and repudiate all such claims as false, knowing that not thus will he *reveal* his presence, but "as the sunlight," emerging gradually—"the Sun of righteousness shall arise with healing in his beams."

OUR LORD'S PAROUSIA IN THE HARVEST.

The Greek is a very exact language: a fact which greatly enhances its value in giving exact expression to truth. Thus, for instance, in our common English Bibles, the word *come* is used to translate thirty-two Greek words, each of which has a fine shade of difference. Instances:—*ephistemi* signifies *to overtake*, as in Luke 21:34—"*come* upon [overtake] you unawares;" *sunerchomai* signifies *to gather*, or *come together*, as in 1 Cor. 11:18—"*come* together in the church;" *proserchomai* signifies *to approach*, or *come toward*, as in Heb. 4:16—"Let us therefore *come* boldly;" *heko* signifies *to arrive*, or *have come*, or *came*, as when the action of coming is completed, as in John 2:4—"Mine hour is not yet come;" *enistemi* signifies *to be present*, and is so translated, except in two instances where it should be so rendered: 2 Tim. 3:1—"Perilous times *shall come*"—be present; and 2 Thes. 2:2—"That the day of Christ *is at hand*"—present. *Parousia*, too, signifies *presence*, and should never be translated *coming*, as in the common English Bible, where it is twice rendered properly, *presence*. (2 Cor. 10:10; Phil. 2:12.) The "*Emphatic Diaglott*," a very valuable translation of the New Testament, renders *parousia* properly, PRESENCE, in almost every occurrence of the word.

The two Greek words, *heko* and *parousia*, and their use in the New Testament, are what we desire to notice at present, and particularly the latter of these; because a correct appreciation of their significance sheds light upon the manner of our Lord's return, through passages in which they occur, while the common but erroneous translation beclouds the very point it should illuminate.*

With the correct thought as to the meaning of *parousia* in mind—not that of *coming*, as being on the way, but *presence*, as after arrival—let us examine some passages in which the word is used. And from these we will learn that *presence* does not necessarily imply sight, but that it is applicable also to things present but unseen. Thus, for instance, angels, spirit beings, can be present with us, yet unseen, as our Lord was *present* in the world and often with the disciples during the forty days after his resurrection, without being seen of the world, or by his disciples except on the few brief occasions already referred to. Those days were days of his *parousia* (presence), as much as the preceding thirty-three and a half years had been.

In the conversation previous to the question of Matt. 24:3, our Lord had foretold the destruction of the temple, and the rejection of Israel after the flesh until a time when they would gladly recognize him as their Messiah and say, "Blessed is he." He had told his disciples that he would go away, and come again and receive them unto himself. He called their day the "harvest," or end of that age, and he had told them of a future "harvest" at the time of his

---

* The word *parousia* occurs twenty-four times in the Greek Testament, and is only twice in the English com. ver. (2 Cor. 10:10; Phil. 2:12) correctly translated *presence*. The other occurrences, in which it is mistranslated *coming*, are as follows:—Matt. 24: 3, 27, 37, 39; 1 Cor. 15:23; 16: 17; 2 Cor. 7:6, 7; Phil. 1: 26; 1 Thes. 2: 19; 3:13; 4:15; 5:23; 2 Thes. 2: 1, 8, 9; James 5: 7, 8; 2 Pet. 1:16; 3:4, 12; 1 John 2:28.

second coming. (Matt. 9:37, 38; 13:39, 40.) Doubtless remembering that few recognized him as the Christ at his first advent, they wanted to know *how* he might be surely recognized at his second advent—expecting probably that his second advent would occur in their day. Hence their inquiry, "What shall be the sign [indication] of thy *parousia* [presence] and of the end of the age?"

Because of their disposition to mix the closing events of the Jewish age, or harvest, in which they already were, with the then future "harvest," or end of the Gospel dispensation, our Lord gave quite a detailed account of events which must intervene, indicating a lapse of a considerable *period* between, yet giving no clear idea of its length; for even he did not then know how long it would be.—Mark 13:32.

Our Lord's reply in verses 1 to 14 covers the entire Gospel age; and his words in verses 15 to 22 have a double application—literally to the close of the Jewish age, and figuratively to the end of this Gospel age, of which the Jewish age was a shadow. Verses 23–26 contain words of warning against false Christs, and in verse 27 he reaches their question regarding his *parousia*, and declares [properly translated], "As the bright shining [the sunlight] cometh out of the east and shineth even unto the west, so shall the *parousia* [the PRESENCE] of the Son of man be." The sunlight becomes present instantly, yet noiselessly; and it is first discerned by those who are first awake.

Leaving other intermediate features of our Lord's discourse for examination in their appropriate place, we note his second reference to their question regarding his *parousia* in verses 37 and 39. He says, "As the days of Noah, so shall also the *parousia* [PRESENCE] of the Son of man be." Notice, that the comparison is not between the *coming* of Noah and the *coming* of our Lord, nor between the *coming* of the flood and the *coming* of our Lord. The *coming* of Noah is not referred to at all ; neither is the *coming* of our Lord referred to; for, as already stated, *parousia* does not mean *coming*, but *presence*. The contrast, then, is between the time of the presence of Noah among the people "*before* the flood," and the time of the presence of Christ in the world, at his second advent, *before* the fire—the extreme trouble of the Day of the Lord with which this age ends.

And though the people were wicked in Noah's day, *before* the flood, and will be wicked in the time of our Lord's presence, *before* the hot fire of trouble comes upon them, yet *this is not* the point of comparison or likeness to which our Lord refers; for wickedness has abounded in every age. The point of comparison is stated clearly, and is readily seen if we read critically: The people, except the members of Noah's family, were *ignorant* of the coming storm, and *unbelieving* as to the testimony of Noah and his family, and hence they "*knew not;*" and this is the point of comparison. *So* shall also the PRESENCE of the Son of man be. None but those of the family of God will believe here: others will " know not," until society, as at present organized, begins to melt with the fervent heat of the time of trouble now impending. This is illustrated by the words, "As in the days that were *before* the flood, they were eating, drinking and marrying [Luke (17 : 28) adds "planting and building "], until the day Noah entered into the ark, and knew not, . . . so shall also the *parousia* [the presence] of the Son of man be." In the time of the *presence* of the Son of man, therefore, the world will go on with its eating, drinking, planting, building and marrying—not mentioned as sinful doings, but as indicative of their *ignorance of his presence*, and of the trouble that will prevail in the world. This, then, is our Lord's answer to the question of the disciples—What shall be the sign [indication] of thy

11–B

[*parousia*] presence and of the end or harvest of the age?
In substance, he says: There will be no sign for the worldly
masses; they will not know of my presence and the new
dispensational changes. Only the few will know, and they
will be taught of God (in a way not here explained) before
there is any *sign* (indication) which the worldly could
discern.

Luke's account of this same discourse (Luke 17:26-29),
though not in the same words, is in perfect accord. Luke
does not use the word *parousia*, but he expresses this exact
thought, saying: "As it was *in the days of Noe*, so shall it
be also *in the days of the Son of man*"—in the days of his
presence. Not *before* his days, nor *after* his days, but *in*
(*during*) his days, the world will be eating, drinking, marrying, buying, selling, planting and building. These Scriptures, then, clearly teach that our Lord will be *present* in the
end of this age, entirely unknown to the world, and unseen
by them.

Though there shall never be another *flood* to destroy the
earth (Gen. 9:11), it is written that the whole earth shall
be devoured with the *fire* of God's jealousy (Zeph. 3: 8);
—not the literal, physical earth in either case, but the existing *order of things* in both cases: in the first instance accomplished by drowning all the people except Noah's family; in the last, by burning all except the family of God
in the symbolic fire—the great trouble of the Day of the
Lord. The faithful children of God shall be counted worthy
to escape all those things coming on the earth (Luke 21:36);
not necessarily by being taken away from the earth, but possibly by being rendered fire-proof, as in the typical illustration of the three Hebrews who walked in the midst of the
fiery furnace heated seven times, on whose garments, even,
was not the smell of fire; because one like unto the Son of
God was present with them.—Dan. 3:19-25.

Next we will notice scriptures which teach that many in the Church will, for a time, be ignorant of the Lord's presence, and of the "harvest" and ending of this age, while he is actually present, and the harvest work in progress.

The closing verses of Matt. 24, from verse 42 on, are very significant. In verse 37 our Lord had shown that the world would not know of the *parousia* of the Son of man; and now he cautions his professed disciples that, unless on their guard, they will be similarly in darkness relative to his *parousia*. He says, "Watch, therefore; for ye know not what hour your Lord doth come [*erchomai*—arrive]." If people were expecting a thief at a definite time, they would stay awake so as not to be taken unawares: so you should be ever awake, always ready, and always watching for the first evidence of my *parousia*. In reply to your question, "*When* shall these things be?" I merely tell you to watch and be ready, and when I arrive, when I am *present*, I will communicate the fact to all who are watching and faithful, and they only will have any right to know. All others should and must be in outer darkness, and must learn with and as the world—through trouble.

Who, *then* [in the "harvest"], is a faithful and wise servant whom his Master shall make * ruler over his household, to give them meat in due season? Blessed that servant whom his Master on coming [*erchomai*—when he arrives*] shall find so doing. Verily, I say unto you, he shall make him ruler over all his goods" —all the vast storehouse of precious truth shall be opened to such faithful servants, to arm and supply and feed the entire household of faith.

But if the servant's heart is not right, he will say, My Master tarries [has *not arrived*], and may smite [oppose and contradict] his fellow servants [those who differ with him; those, therefore, who are declaring the opposite—My

---

* Sinaitic and Vatican MSS. read "*shall make.*"

Lord does not tarry, but *has come*, is *present.*] Such may eat and drink with the intemperate [become intoxicated with the spirit of the world], but the Master of that servant will come [Greek, *heko*—will have arrived] in a day not expected, and in an hour in which that servant *is not aware,* and will cut him off [from being one of the servants privileged to hand meat in due season to the household], and will appoint him his portion with the hypocrites. [Though not a hypocrite but a genuine servant, he must, because unfaithful and overcharged, have his portion with the hypocrites in the perplexity and trouble coming upon Babylon.] "There shall be weeping and gnashing of teeth."

The foregoing, carefully examined, clearly teaches us that in the end of this age there will be one class denying that the Lord *is present* (not denying that he will come sometime, but that he has come), and smiting or harshly opposing those fellow servants who must therefore be teaching the opposite—that the Lord has come. Which is the faithful, truthful servant, and which the one in error, is clearly stated by our Lord. The faithful one whom he finds giving seasonable "meat" will be exalted and given fuller stewardship over the storehouse of truth, with increased ability to bring it forth to the household, while the unfaithful one will be gradually separated and drawn into closer and closer sympathy with the mere professors or hypocrites. And note the fact that the unfaithful is thus cut off, or separated, at a time of which *he is not aware*—in the harvest time—while his Lord is really *present* unknown to him, searching for and gathering his jewels.— Matt. 13 : 30 ; Psa. 50 : 5 ; Mal. 3 : 17 ; Matt. 24 : 31.

We particularize here, merely to show that, in answer to the question of the disciples about signs and evidences of his second *presence*, our Lord taught that neither the world nor the unfaithful servants would be aware of it, until the intense fire of trouble is at least commenced. And the faithful evidently will *see him present* merely by the eye of faith—through the Scriptures written aforetime for their learning, to be apprehended as they become due. Present truths on every subject are parts of "his goods" and treasures new and old which our Lord had laid up for us and now freely gives us.—Matt. 24:45–47.

While thus, by foretold indications, the Lord made ample preparation to enable the Church to recognize his presence when due, though they should not see him with the natural eye, he also carefully warned us against deceptions which should arise—deceptions which should appear so plausible as to deceive the very elect, if it were possible. But it is not possible, because all the elect give earnest heed to the warning, and studiously acquaint themselves with the foretold indications of his presence, and are watching for their fulfilment. Those otherwise minded are not of the elect class. Only the overcomers are to reign with the Lord. These deceptions, as will be shown in a succeeding chapter, are already in existence, and are deceiving many. But, thank God, the elect are forewarned and forearmed, and shall neither be deceived nor disheartened. Though clouds and darkness are round about him, they recognize his presence, and rejoice that their deliverance draweth nigh. If any man should say unto you, Lo, here is Christ, or there [in any particular *place*], believe it not. And if they shall say unto you, Behold, he is in the desert, go not forth : behold he is in the secret chambers, believe it not; for as [like] the bright shining sunlight, which gradually dawns upon and fills the earth, *so shall his presence be.* (Matt. 25 : 23, 26, 27.) It will be manifested as foretold, by the dawning light of truth—truth on every subject, as we now see it so rapidly and gloriously unfolding. A few years more, and the Sun of righteousness will have fully risen with healing in its beams to bless and raise up the death-stricken world.

In view of the evidences presented in this and the preceding and following chapters, we have no hesitation in announcing the heart-cheering intelligence, that the harvest of the Gospel age is upon us, and that the Master is again present as the Chief Reaper—not in the flesh, as in the Jewish harvest, but in power and great glory, as the "highly exalted," divine Christ whose glorious body is now "the express image of the Father's person," though his glorious person is graciously vailed from human sight. He is inaugurating his reign of righteousness; his sickle of truth is separating; he is gathering together into oneness of heart and mind the ripe first-fruits of spiritual Israel; and soon that elect "body" complete shall rule and bless the world.

This announcement is here made, in order that as we proceed the reader may have the clearer idea of what the time-prophecies most particularly indicate, when it shall be shown that the harvest, and all its attendant events, are *now* chronologically due, and coming to pass as foretold.

Thus seen, these time-prophecies and all this particularity of instruction with reference to the manner and the attending circumstances of the Lord's appearing were not given to alarm the world, nor to satisfy idle curiosity, nor to awaken a sleeping nominal church; but they were given in order that those who are not asleep, and not of the world, but who are awake, consecrated and faithful, and earnest students of their Father's plan, may be informed of the significance of transpiring events, and not be in darkness on a subject and with regard to *events in no other way discernible with certainty*—the harvest, the presence of the great Reaper, the threshing and sifting of the true wheat, the bundling and burning of the tares in the time of trouble, etc.

SCOFFING FORETOLD.

The Apostle Peter describes how some of the unfaithful servants and hypocrites will scoff during the *presence* of the Lord, even as they scoffed in the days of Noah. (2 Pet. 3:3, 4, 10, 12.) Notice that the Apostle wrote to the Church, and that the scoffers he describes are *in* the nominal church and professedly interested in the Lord's work and plan, and believers, therefore, that he *will come some time.* The scoffing described is on the very subject here noticed, and such as we hear and shall hear from professed Christians, whenever the subject of the Lord's presence and harvest work, etc., is presented. Christians generally, until they investigate the subject, have such ideas of literal manifestations of fire, trumpets, voices, etc., and of seeing the Lord descending through the air, a shining body of flesh, that when they hear of his invisible *presence*, without taking time to investigate a subject upon which they feel so sure, busied with worldly plans, and intoxicated with the spirit of the world, they will dismiss the matter quickly as unworthy of investigation.

It is to this class of professed Christians that the Apostle refers, saying, " In the last days [in the closing years of the Gospel age—in the "harvest"] shall come scoffers, walking after their own desires [plans, theories, etc.], asking, *Where is the promise of his presence* [*parousia*]? for ever since the fathers fell asleep, all things continue as at present from the beginning of creation." When referred to our Lord's statement (Matt. 24:37–39; Luke 17:26) that in *his days*, in the days of his *presence*, things would indeed continue as before; and that, as in Noah's day, men would be eating, drinking, marrying, planting and building; and that, as then, the world would *know not* of his presence, and read not the signs of the speedy and great changes just at hand, they are too busy to consider the testimony carefully, and only continue to scoff.

Ah! says Peter, they forget the great change which occurred in the days of Noah; and then, under the symbol of fire, he describes the overwhelming flood of trouble which shall shortly overtake the whole world, utterly over-throwing all civil and ecclesiastical rule [the heavens] and melting the entire social fabric [the earth]—producing anarchy and social chaos until the new heavens [ruling powers—the Kingdom of God] shall be fully established, as well as a new earth [society organized on a new and better basis, of love, equality and righteousness]. The Apostle then reminds us (verse 8) that this Day of the Lord's *presence,* for which the Church has long hoped and looked, is a thousand-year day—the Millennium of Christ's reign.

In verse 10 he assures us that "the Day of the Lord will *arrive* [Greek, *heko*] *as a thief*" * [unobservedly, quiet-ly: it will be present, while some are scoffing and smiting those fellow-servants who declare the truth]. The Apostle then exhorts the saints to separateness from the world; that they be not swallowed up by politics, money-getting, etc., but that they set their affections on higher things. He says, Seeing that in God's plan present earthly conditions are only temporary and will soon give place to the better order, what manner of persons ought we to be, in respect to holy conduct and piety?—"*looking for the* PRESENCE [*parousia*] of the Day of God"—watching for the evidences (signs) to prove that it has come.

And, thanks be to God, his provision is so abundant that all those of piety, who are *looking* for that day, will know of it before the full bursting forth of the fire of wrath. Through Paul he assures us that none of the children of the light will be left in darkness, that that day should come

---

* Old Manuscripts omit here the words, "*in the night.*"

upon them unawares. (1 Thes. 5 : 4.) Hence, though we are already *in* the day of the Lord's *presence*, and in the beginning of the great fire of trouble, we see that it is even as shown us in symbol (Rev. 7 : 1, 2)—the storm is held in check until the faithful servants of God are "sealed in their foreheads:" *i. e.*, until such are given an intellectual appreciation of the *time*, *presence*, etc., which will not only comfort them, and shield them, but also be a *mark*, seal or evidence of their sonship, as indicated by our Lord when he promised that the holy Spirit should show to the faithful "things to *come*."—John 16 : 13.

Some take Peter's statement literally, that "the heavens being on fire shall be dissolved and pass away with a great noise;" and also the Revelator's description of the same events, by a very similar symbol, "The heaven departed as a scroll when it is rolled together." It would seem, however, that one glance upward at the myriad gems of night shining through millions of miles of space, with nothing between to roll away, or to take fire, should be argument enough in one moment to convince such that they had erred in supposing these statements to be literal—should convince them that their expectation of a literal fulfilment is absurd in the extreme.

So, then, God veiled from mankind under figures of trumpets, voices, fire, etc, information (which was not for the worldly to know, but only for the "little flock" of consecrated saints) regarding the harvest, the Lord's presence, his spiritual kingdom, etc.; and yet he arranged them so that, in due time, they would speak clearly and emphatically to the class for whom he intended the information. As at the first advent, so to a similar consecrated class it may now be said, in the time of the second advent—"Unto you it is given to know the mysteries of the kingdom of God ; but unto them that are without, all these things are done in parables "—in figures and dark sayings—in order that, even though having the Bible before them, others than the consecrated may not really see and understand.—Mark 4:11, 12.

The world is not ignorant of the unprecedented events and circumstances of the present time, and their increasing noteworthiness with every passing year ; but not perceiving the grand outcome, these only fill their minds with dark forebodings of evil.   As foretold, they are in fear, looking forward to those things that are coming on the earth ; for already the powers of the heaven (the present ruling powers) are being shaken.

CONNECTING THE PROPHETIC CHAIN.

In the preceding chapter we presented evidence showing that the "Times of the Gentiles," or their lease of dominion, will run fully out with the year A. D. 1914, and that at that time they will all be overturned and Christ's Kingdom fully established.   That the Lord must be present, and set up his Kingdom, and exercise his great power so as to dash the nations to pieces as a potter's vessel, is then clearly fixed; for it is "in the days of these kings"—before their overthrow—*i. e.*, before A. D. 1914—that the God of heaven shall set up his Kingdom.   And IT *shall break in pieces and consume all these.* (Dan. 2 : 44.)   And in harmony with this, we see all about us evidence of the beginning of the smiting, shaking and overturning of the present powers, preparatory to the establishment of the kingdom "which cannot be moved"—the strong government.

The next chapter will present Bible evidence that 1874 A. D. was the exact date of the beginning of the "Times of Restitution," and hence of our Lord's return.   Since that date he has been verifying his promise to those in the proper attitude of watchfulness— "Blessed are those servants whom the Lord when he cometh shall find watching : Verily, I say unto you, that he shall gird himself, and make them to sit down to meat, and will come forth and serve them." (Luke 12:37.) Even so, he has opened unto us the Scriptures, showing us truth concerning his present glorious nature, the object, manner and time of his coming, and the character of his manifestations to the household of faith and to the world. He has drawn our attention to the prophecies which definitely locate us on the stream of time, and has shown us the order of his plan of operations in this harvest time. He has shown us, first of all, that it is a harvest of the saints, a time for their full ripening, and for their separation from the tares ; and secondly, that it is a time for the world to reap its whirlwind harvest—for the reaping of the vine of the earth, and the treading of its fruitage in the winepress of the wrath of Almighty God. He has shown us that both of these ripenings (Rev. 14:1–4, 18–20) will be completed in a period of forty years, ending with the year A. D. 1915.

But while the reader is thus informed of what will be proved in succeeding chapters, he must not expect to have passages of Scripture pointed out in which these matters and these dates are plainly written. On the contrary, he must bear in mind that all these things have been *hidden* by the Lord, in such manner that they could not be understood or appreciated until the due time had come, and then only by his earnest, faithful children, who esteem truth as more precious than rubies, and who are willing to seek it as men search for silver. Truth, like silver, must be not only mined, but also refined, separated from dross, before its value can be appreciated. The things here stated in few words will be proved point by point ; and while many may prefer to take a statement without the trouble of verifying it from the Scriptures, this will not be the case with the real truth-seeker. He must, so far as possible, make every point, argument and proof his own, direct from God's Word, by tracing all the connections, and thus convincing himself of the truthfulness of the account presented.

Though the Lord provides it, and the servants bring forth the " meat in due season for the household," yet each, to be strengthened thereby, must eat for himself.

———

"Mine eyes can see the glory of the coming of the Lord;
  He is trampling out the winepress where His grapes of wrath are stored;
  I see the flaming tempest of His swift-descending sword.
            Our King is marching on.

"I can see His coming judgments, as they circle all the earth,
  The signs and groanings promised, to precede a second birth;
  I read His righteous sentence in the crumbling thrones of earth.
            Our King is marching on.

"The 'Gentile Times' are closing; for their kings have had their day;
  And with them sin and sorrow will forever pass away;
  For the tribe of Judah's *'Lion'* now comes to hold the sway.
            Our King is marching on.

"The seventh trump is sounding, and our King knows no defeat:
  He will sift out the hearts of men before His Judgment Seat.
  Oh, be swift, my soul, to welcome Him, be jubilant, my feet.
            Our King is marching on."

STUDY VI.

EARTH'S GREAT JUBILEE.

"THE TIMES OF RESTITUTION OF ALL THINGS" FORETOLD BY MOSES.—THE DATE OF THEIR BEGINNING INDICATED.—THEY CANNOT BEGIN UNTIL THE GREAT RESTORER HAS COME.—EVIDENCE FROM THE LAW.—CORROBORATIVE TESTIMONY FROM THE PROPHETS.—LOGICAL CONCLUSIONS DRAWN FROM THESE AS SEPARATELY AND UNITEDLY CONSIDERED.—HARMONY OF PRESENT INDICATIONS.

VERILY I say unto you, Till heaven and earth pass, one jot or one tittle shall in no wise pass from the Law, till all be *fulfilled*."—Matt. 5 : 18.

It is only when we recognize the typical character of God's dealings with Israel that we can rightly appreciate the wonderful history of that people, or understand why their history, in preference to that of all other nations, is so particularly recorded by the Prophets and the New Testament writers. In them, as the New Testament writers show, God has given striking illustrations of his plans, both for the Church and for the world. Their Tabernacle service, so minutely prescribed in the divinely given Law, with its bleeding beasts and all its peculiar appointments, their festivals and holy days, their Sabbaths, and all their ceremonies, as types pointed forward to antitypes, larger, higher and grander far than those shadows. And the Apostle Paul assures us that those antitypes will be laden with blessings for mankind, when he says that the Law foreshadowed "GOOD THINGS *to come*" (Heb. 10:1; 8:5; Col. 2:17); while our Lord, in the above expression, assures us that all the good things foreshadowed are sure of fulfilment.

However, in considering types, we should carefully avoid the error of many well-meaning people, who, when they

173

begin to see that there are significant types in the Scriptures, run to the extreme of treating every Bible character
and incident as typical, and are thus led into error by mere
curiosity and ingenuity. On no such unsafe ground do we
build when examining the ceremonies of the Jewish Law,
given specially as types and declared by the apostles to be
such. Nor can we afford to let these types pass without
due consideration and careful study of the lessons they
teach, any more than we can afford to spend time in spec-
ulating, and in building faith upon mere conjecture.

When our Lord said that not one jot or tittle of the Law
should pass away until fulfilled, he referred not only to the
fulfilling of its covenant obligations for all under that Law
Covenant, finishing its hold upon them, by meeting its
demands against them in full with his own life, but he
meant more than this : He meant, further, that all the
blessings expressed in it typically would also be sure of fulfilment upon an antitypical scale. In all the Jewish ceremonies, God caused no type to be made which will prove
meaningless, or pass unfulfilled ; and the observance of all
types was kept up until their fulfilment *at least began.* All
types must be continually repeated until their antitypes appear ; for the keeping of a type is not the fulfilling of it.
The fulfilling is reached where the type ceases, being dis-
placed by the reality, the antitype.

Thus, for instance, the slaying of the paschal lamb was
fulfilled in the death of Christ, the "Lamb of God," and
there began the special blessing upon the antitypical first-
born, the believers of the Gospel age. The blessing, foreshadowed in that type, is not yet completely fulfilled, though
the fulfilment began with the death of Christ, our Passover
Lamb. In like manner, every ceremony prescribed in the
Law proves to be full of typical significance. And the particularity with which the observance of every detail of the

types was enforced throughout the Jewish age gives emphasis to our Lord's words quoted above—that every minute particular, every jot and tittle, must be as particularly fulfilled as it was carefully enforced in the ceremonies of the Law.

In this chapter we propose to examine that typical feature of the Mosaic Law known as the Jubilee, and to show that it was intended to foreshadow the great Restitution, the recovery of mankind from the fall, to be accomplished in the Millennial age; that in its character it was an illustration of the coming Restitution ; and that in the manner of its reckoning it furnishes time regulations which, when understood and applied, indicate clearly *the time for the beginning of the antitype*, the "Restitution of all things."— Acts 3:19–21.

Since the Jubilee was a part of the Law, and since repeating does not fulfil it, and since our Lord declared that the type could not pass away without fulfilment ; and moreover, since we know that no such restitution of all things as that foretold "by all the holy prophets since the world began," and prefigured in this type, has ever yet occurred, we know that it must be *fulfilled* in the future.

ISRAEL'S JUBILEE YEAR.

The year of Jubilee was a Sabbath of rest and refreshing, both to the people and to the land which God gave them. It was the chief of a series of Sabbaths or rests. *   They had a Sabbath *day* every seventh day ; and once every year these typical Sabbath days reached a climax—*i. e.*, a cycle of seven of these Sabbaths, thus marking a period of forty-nine days (7 x 7 = 49), was followed by a *Jubilee day*, the fiftieth day (Lev. 23:15, 16), known among the Jews as Pentecost.   It was a day of rejoicing and thanksgiving.

---

* The word "Sabbath" signifies *rest*.

The Sabbath *year* occurred every seventh year.   In it the land was allowed to rest and no crops were to be planted. A climax of these Sabbath [rest] years was reached in the same manner as the Pentecost or fiftieth day-Sabbath. Seven of the Sabbath years, embracing a period of seven times seven years, or forty-nine years ($7 \times 7 = 49$), constituted a cycle of Sabbath years; and the year following, the FIFTIETH YEAR, WAS THE YEAR OF JUBILEE.

Let us examine the account of it and mark its fitness as an illustration of the great millennium of restitution.

When Israel came into Canaan, the land was divided among them by lot, according to their tribes and families. Success thereafter might increase, or adversity decrease, their individual possessions, as the case might be.   If a man became involved in debt, he might be obliged to sell a part or even all of his property, and with his family go into servitude.   But God made a bountiful provision for the unfortunate : He arranged that such adverse circumstances might not continue forever, but that all their accounts— credits and debts—must be reckoned only to the Jubilee Year, when all must be freed from old encumbrances, etc., to make a fresh start for the next term of fifty years. *

Thus every fiftieth year, counting from the time of their entrance into Canaan, was to Israel a year of Jubilee, a time of rejoicing and restitution, in which broken families were re-united and lost homesteads were restored.   No wonder that it was called a Jubilee.   If property had been sold for debt, it was to be considered merely as a grant of

---

* A somewhat similar arrangement under a *Bankrupt Law* has been found expedient in our day and land, thus endorsing the principle then enunciated.   Nor does it follow, that a cancellation of debt every *fifty years*, and the Jewish *form*, would serve us better than the methods of to-day; for in their case, the time, circumstances, etc., were not *specially* for themselves, their convenience, and their circumstances, but *specially* as prophetic figures and lessons relating to God's plan in its future development.

such property until the Jubilee year; and the price it would bring if sold depended on whether the coming Jubilee was near or far distant.

The account of this observance is found in Leviticus 25. Verses 10 to 15 read thus: "Ye shall hallow the fiftieth year, and proclaim liberty throughout all the land, unto all the inhabitants thereof. It is a Jubilee unto you, and ye shall return every man unto his possession and ye shall return every man unto his family. . . . And if thou sell aught to thy neighbor, or buyest aught of thy neighbor's hand, ye shall not oppress one another. According to the number of years after the Jubilee thou shalt buy of thy neighbor, and according unto the number of years of the fruits he shall sell unto thee. According to the multitude of the years thou shalt increase the price thereof, and according to the fewness of the years thou shalt diminish the price of it."

This arrangement provided by God through their leader and typical mediator, Moses, though itself a blessed boon, foreshadowed a still greater blessing which God had in view—the release of all mankind from the debt of sin and its bondage and servitude, through Christ our Lord, the greater Mediator and Deliverer, whom Moses typified. (Deut. 18:15.) It was thus, in types, that Moses wrote of Christ and the blessings to come through him (John 5:46; 1:45)—the Great Restitution and Jubilee to come to all the race, now groaning under the bondage of corruption and slavery to Sin.

If the shadow brought happiness and joy to the typical people, the substance, the real restitution, will cause boundless joy and will indeed be a grand Jubilee to all people —all the world, including Israel, being typified by that people, even as their priesthood represented the Church, the "royal priesthood." Even if we were not definitely in-

12–B

formed, what would be more reasonable than to surmise that the same infinite love which provided for the temporary welfare of Israel, a "stiff-necked generation," would much more make provision for the lasting welfare of the whole world, which God so loved as to redeem while yet sinners? And here it may be well to note what will be more fully shown hereafter, that while in one aspect the Israelites were typical of the believers of the Gospel age, in another they represented all who, in any age, shall believe God and accept his leading. And in this character we are now viewing them. Their covenant, sealed with the blood of bulls and goats, was typical of the New Covenant, sealed with the precious blood of Christ, under which the reconciling of the world shall be effected in the next age. Their day of atonement and its sin-offerings, though in type to that people, and for their sins only, typified the "better sacrifices" and the actual atonement *"for the sins of the whole world."* But note that the Jubilee applied not to Israel's priesthood (typical of the Gospel Church), but to the *others only;* for the priesthood was given no possessions, and hence could neither lose any nor have any restored. The Jubilee was for all the people except the priestly tribe, and hence typifies, not those blessings which are to come to the Church, the "Royal Priesthood," but the restitution blessings—earthly blessings—in due time to come to all those who become believers in and followers of God.

The teaching of this type is in perfect accord with what we have learned in our examination of the divine Plan of the Ages. It points unmistakably to "The Times of Restitution of all things, spoken by the mouth of all the holy prophets since the world began." Moses was one of the prophets ; and here particularly *he* speaks to us of the coming restitution of man's first estate and liberty, long lost, sold under sin. By the failure of our first parents all was lost: all rights were forfeited, and all became slaves to the tyrant Sin and were unable to free themselves. The family circle has been sadly broken by the bondage of corruption—death. Thank God for the promised time of release! The Jubilee is at hand, and soon the captives of Death and slaves of Sin shall have back their first estate, perfect manhood, and their first inheritance, the earth— the gift of God through Jesus Christ, the mediator and ratifier of the New Covenant.

While in the typical Jubilee Year many restored liberties and blessings were at once entered upon, yet probably most of the year was required to straighten out affairs and get each one fully installed again in all his former liberties, rights and possessions. So, too, with the antitype, the Millennial age of Restitution. It will open with sweeping reforms, with the recognition of rights, liberties and possessions long lost sight of; but the work of completely restoring (to the obedient) *all that was originally lost* will require all of that age of restitution—a thousand years.

It is certain that no antitype of the Jubilee answering to the features of this type has yet occurred; and, on the strength of our Lord's assertion, we are equally sure that the type could not pass away unfulfilled: "It is easier for heaven and earth to pass, than for one tittle of the Law to fail." (Luke 16:17.) But, *apparently*, this feature of the Law has failed. As a matter of fact, the type, which was observed regularly every fiftieth year as long as the Israelites were in their own land, has not been observed since their captivity in Babylon. *Apparently*, therefore, this feature of the Law did "pass away" without even *beginning* a fulfilment. What shall we answer in the face of this apparent contradiction of the Lord's statement? But is it really so? or can any antitype of the Jubilee be found, beginning where the last observance of the typical Jubilee ended? Yes, we answer; a clearly defined antitype had its beginning at that exact point, and on a larger and grander scale, as antitypes always are. We see, by actual fulfilment, that the *cycles*, as well as the Jubilee Years in which they culminated, were included in the type; and that the same *method* by which the typical Jubilee was pointed out (by multiplying) was to be observed in calculating the time for the antitype—Earth's Great Jubilee. When the last typical Jubilee had been observed and had passed away, *the great cycle began to count*, the close of which will usher in the antitypical Jubilee or Restitution age.

We have already referred to the method of counting the Sabbaths—that the multiplying of the Sabbath or seventh day by seven ($7 \times 7 = 49$) pointed out Pentecost, the Jubilee Day which followed; and the multiplying of the seventh year by seven ($7 \times 7 = 49$) made the cycle which pointed out and led to the fiftieth or Jubilee Year. And the same system carried out would indicate that to reach the great antitype which we seek we should in like manner square the Jubilee—*i. e.*, multiply the fiftieth year by fifty. That is to say, the antitypical cycle, by the method of multiplying here taught us, should be reckoned by multiplying the typical Jubilee or fiftieth Sabbath year by fifty, just as in reaching it we multiplied the seventh year Sabbath by seven.—Lev. 25: 2–13.

Following this divinely indicated method of reckoning, wonderful results open before us, which assure us that we have the correct key and are using it as was intended by him who formed this treasure-casket. Fifty times fifty years gives the long period of twenty-five hundred years ($50 \times 50 = 2500$), as the length of that great *cycle*, which began to count when Israel's last typical Jubilee ended, and which **must culminate** in the great antitypical Jubilee. We know that such a cycle must have *begun to count* where the type ceased ; because, if not one jot or tittle of the Law could pass away without a fulfilment at least commencing, then the Jubilee type, which was far more than a jot or tittle, indeed a large and important feature of the Law, would not have been permitted to pass away until the right time for its antitype to begin. That the antitype of the Jubilee did not in any sense begin when the Israelites ceased to observe it, is evident ; hence that a grand *cycle* began to *count* then, we may be certain. The new, long cycle began there, though Israel and all the world are ignorant both of the fact that a great cycle has been counting and also of the great antitypical Jubilee by which it will be terminated. We are not to look for the great Jubilee of Jubilees to begin *after* this cycle, but as the antitype to take the place of the fiftieth or last Jubilee of the cycle. An antitype never *follows* its type but takes its place upon the same date. Hence the 2500th year, which would be the great 50th Jubilee, must be the antitype, the real Jubilee or Restitution. But instead of being a year, as in the type, it will be larger ; it will be the beginning of the great thous-and-year Jubilee—the Millennium. Just so it has been in the fulfilment of every type in which *time* was a feature. Thus the Pentecostal outpouring of the holy Spirit came upon the typical day of Pentecost—or fiftieth day. Christ, our Passover-sacrifice, died in the same night in which the typical lamb was appointed to be killed—a day before or a day after would not answer. So here, not the year after nor the year before the 2500th, or closing of the typical cycle, would do ; but that very year, beginning October, 1874, must have begun the antitype or Restitution times.

The observance of the type could not cease until the great cycle (50 x 50) began to count. The important point to be ascertained, then, is the *exact date* when the last typical

Jubilee was observed by Israel.   With that date definitely established, it becomes a very simple matter to count the great cycle of fifty times fifty or twenty-five hundred years, and thus locate definitely the date of the beginning of the great Jubilee of Earth—the "Times of Restitution of all things."

But we must look for beginnings only of this stupendous work of restoring all things.   The first few days in the typical Jubilee Year would see comparatively little accomplished ; and so we must expect in the first few years in the dawning of the great Millennial Jubilee to see but little accomplished.   The first work in the typical Jubilee Year would naturally be a searching out of former rights and possessions and the ascertaining of present lacks.   Tracing the parallel of this, we should expect in the antitype just what we now see going on all about us ; for, as will shortly be shown, we have already entered upon the great antitypical Jubilee period, and have been in it since October, A. D. 1874.   What do we see about us ?   We see investigation on the part of the people of their original, God-given inheritance, and their present lacks, rights, etc., many in ignorance and selfishness claiming what others have ; and the attempt to hold on to as much as possible on the part of those who have possession—causing disputes, controversies, strikes and lock-outs, with more or less justice and injustice on both sides, which must finally be left to Christ's adjudication, as disputes under the Law were settled by Moses, and after his death by those who sat in Moses' seat. (Matt. 23 : 2.)   With these fixed conclusions and expectations, let us seek the date which God evidently hid for us in this type, "that we might know the things freely given unto us of God," now due to be understood.

We have no *direct* Bible record of Israel's observance of their typical Jubilees which would show which was the last one observed.   We fix upon the date for the Jubilee immediately preceding the Babylonian captivity and seventy years desolation of their land, as the last one, for two reasons: First, It could not have been this side of that desolation, because there, surely, the *type* ceased, "passed away;" for the land being desolate seventy years and the people in captivity in a foreign land, a Jubilee must have been due somewhere in the midst of those seventy years and *must have gone unobserved.* A glance is sufficient to show that the commands and provisions relative to the Jubilee Year could not be complied with while they as a nation were in captivity and the land was desolate. Hence we say the type either passed away then, or before that interruption: it could not be this side of it. And whenever the observance of the type ceased, the *cycle* of the great antitype must have begun to count. One such failure to observe the type would indicate that the *type had ceased* and that the cycle leading to the antitype had begun. Besides, never since the Babylonian captivity has Israel had full control of the land: they and their land have ever since been subject to Gentile dominion.

Secondly, In every captivity previous to that one, God evidently delivered them from their enemies in time to get back into their own land to celebrate the Jubilee Year, and thus to perpetuate it as a type until the right time for the great (50 x 50) cycle to begin counting; for their previous captivities, though frequent, it seems never lasted longer than forty years, thus permitting them, according to the Jubilee arrangement, to go free and to receive back every man his inheritance every Jubilee Year. Besides, when we shall shortly show that, reckoned from the beginning of the seventy years desolation under Babylon, the great cycle ends with the year A. D. 1875, it will be manifest to all that it could not have commenced at an earlier date, prior to that Babylonian captivity; for if we place it even one Jubilee earlier, it would locate the termination of the cycle fifty years earlier than A. D. 1875, namely A. D. 1825 ; and surely no Jubilee age of restitution began with that year.

Satisfied thus that the last typical Jubilee, from which the great (50 x 50) cycle counts, was not earlier, and *could not be since* the captivity in Babylon, and hence that the one immediately preceding that captivity was the last typical Jubilee Year, and that at its close the great, silent cycle began to count, we proceed to locate the exact time of that last typical Jubilee, thus:—

The system of year Sabbaths being identified with their *land*, Canaan, and their inheritance in it, the first cycle of forty-nine years, leading to the first Jubilee, should begin to count from the time they entered Canaan. This reasonable inference is made positive by the Lord's words— "When ye *come into the land* which I give you, then shall the land keep a Sabbath [observe the Sabbath system] unto the Lord: Six years shalt thou sow thy field, and six years shalt thou prune thy vineyard and gather in the fruit thereof; but in the seventh year [from entering the land] shall be a Sabbath of rest unto the land." So, then, the cycle of seven times seven, or forty-nine years (7 x 7 = 49), began to count *at once*, and the fiftieth year after entering Canaan was the first typical Jubilee. *

---

* Some have suggested that as there were six years consumed in war before the division of the land was finished, therefore the counting of the Jubilee cycles did not begin until then. But no, the land was entered upon when they crossed over Jordan, and the command reads, "When ye come into the land," and not, When ye have divided the land. It was divided parcel by parcel during the six years, but they did not get *possession* of all of it during those years, nor for an indefinite time afterward —until the enemies were driven out, which in some cases was never done. (See Joshua 18:2, 3; 17:12, 13; 23:4, 7, 13, 15.) Hence, had they waited for full possession before beginning to count the cycles, they would never have begun.

It will be seen, by reference to the table of Chronology, that 969 years elapsed between the entering of Canaan and the seventy years desolation.

To the division of the land, . . .	6 years.
Period of the Judges, ...	450 "
Period of the Kings, ...	513 "
Total	969 "

We may know how many Jubilees they had observed up to that time by dividing 969 years by 50. There are 19 fifties in 969, showing that number of Jubilees, and the remaining 19 years show that their nineteenth, which was the last of the typical Jubilees, occurred just nineteen years before the beginning of the seventy years of desolation of the land while they were in captivity in Babylon, and nine hundred and fifty years after entering Canaan.

There, then, just nineteen years before the "seventy years desolation" of their land, at the close of their last Jubilee—the nineteenth—the great cycle of 2500 years (50 x 50 = 2500) *began to count;* and it becomes a very simple matter to reckon where those 2500 years terminated, and consequently where the twenty-five hundreth year, the beginning of the great antitypical Jubilee, began. Thus:—

From the last or nineteenth Jubilee to the beginning of the desolation of the land, .	19 years.
Period of the desolation, ...	70 "
From the restoration of Israel by Cyrus, to the date known as A. D. (Anno Domini— the year of our Lord), ...	536 "
Hence, from their last Jubilee to A. D. 1, .	625 "
The number of years since A. D. 1, necessary to complete the cycle of 2500 years, .	1875 "
From the last observed Jubilee—Total, .	2500 "

THE JUBILEE AS A TYPE IN THE LAW.

SEE PAGE 184.

CHRONOLOGICAL TABLE.

Jubilee type dates from entering Canaan:—

To the division of the land,	6	yrs.
Period of Judges,	450	"
" " Kings,	513	"
To the desolation,	969	"
19 Jubilees, =	950	"
Remainder:	19	yrs.

From last Jubilee to the desolation,	19	yrs.
Period of desolation, and captivity of *all* in Babylon,	70	"
From Restoration to their land by Cyrus, to A. D. 1,	536	"
From year A. D. 1 to A. D. 1875 (Jewish time, beginning Oct. 1874),	1874	"
	2499	yrs.

Thus, the year which began October 1874 was the 2500th year, but since the antitype is larger than the type—1000 years instead of one year—1875 (beginning Oct. 1874), instead of being a Jubilee year was the first of the 1000 years of Jubilee.

TYPICAL CYCLES AND JUBILEES, NINETEEN, CONTINUED UNTIL THE GREAT CYCLE WAS DUE TO BEGIN TO COUNT.

WHERE THE TYPICAL CEASED, THE GRAND CYCLE BEGAN ITS FIFTY TIMES FIFTY YEARS TO THE GREAT ANTITYPE, THE JUBILEE OF EARTH—THE TIMES OF RESTITUTION OF ALL THINGS SILENTLY TO COUNT

19 x 50 = 950 years.

50 x 50 = 2500 years.

THE GREAT ANTITYPE—EARTH'S JUBILEE.

ONE GRAND CYCLE CULMINATING IN

= JUBILEE.

Thus we find that the *twenty-five hundredth year* began with the beginning of the year A. D. 1875, which in Jewish civil time, by which this is reckoned (Lev. 25:9), began about October, 1874. So, then, if the great Jubilee were to be only *a year*, like its type, it would have commenced October, A. D. 1874, at the end of 2499 years, and would have ended October, A. D. 1875. But this is not the type, but the reality: it was not a *Jubilee Year*, but the antitypical *Thousand years of Restitution of all things,* which commenced October, A. D. 1874.

Thus we see that not only did Israel's Jubilee clearly and forcibly prefigure the great "TIMES OF RESTITUTION OF ALL THINGS which God hath spoken by the mouth of all the holy prophets since the world began," but that also the manner of its reckoning just as clearly indicates the date of the beginning of Earth's Great Jubilee. If we fail to accept these conclusions, we see no other alternative than that this type passed away without fulfilment, notwithstanding the most positive assertions of our Lord that it could not—that it would be easier for heaven and earth to pass than for one jot or tittle of the Law to pass away without reaching a fulfilment. (Matt. 5:18.) We accept the facts thus divinely indicated, however astounding the conclusions which we must reasonably draw therefrom.

But what are the reasonable conclusions from these Bible teachings? Let us consider what must follow, from the standpoint of reason, and then see if any other scriptures will either warrant or contradict those conclusions. First, we infer that when the "Times of Restitution" are due to begin, the presence of the GREAT RESTORER is also due. This would be a very reasonable inference, but it amounts to much more than inference when it is indorsed by the Apostle's positive inspired statement, that "*When the* [*appointed*] *times of refreshing* shall come from the presence* of the Lord [Jehovah], . . . he shall send Jesus Christ, which before was preached unto you, whom the heaven must retain *until* THE TIMES OF RESTITUTION OF ALL THINGS, which God hath spoken by the mouth of all his holy prophets since the world began.''—Acts 3:19–21.

On the strength of this inspired statement alone, we have clear evidence of the fact that our Lord's second advent *was due* when the Times of Restitution *were due* to begin, viz., in October, A. D. 1874, as marked by the Jubilee arrangement.   It seems evident, indeed, that the Jubilee, like all other things of that dispensation, was arranged ''for *our* admonition [*our* instruction] upon whom the ends of the ages are come.'' (1 Cor. 10:11.)   One thing seems clear—if they do not profit us, they have been thus far almost profitless; for the Scriptures inform us that the Jews never *fully* and properly observed the type, even during the first nineteen Jubilees. (Lev. 26:35.) They no doubt found it almost impossible to restrain their love of wealth.   It, like all prophecies and types, was no doubt arranged to cast light when and where needed on the path of the just —to guide the '' feet '' of the body of Christ.

---

* The word here rendered *presence* is not *parousia*, but *prosopon ;* and *apo prosopon*, rendered *from the presence*, does not signify *as a result of presence*, but rather *out from the face of*.   The thought is common to us, and was much more common in eastern countries long ago: To show the face was a mark of favor, while to turn the back was a mark of disfavor. Thus of our Lord at his first advent it was written, ''We hid as it were our faces from him,'' *i. e.*, we were ashamed of and would not acknowledge him.   Thus, too, Jehovah ''would not look upon sin,'' and hid his face from sinners.   Now, however, since the *ransom* has been given, Jehovah waits to be gracious, until the appointed time.   Then he will no longer disregard men and treat them as sinners, turning his back upon them, but will send them refreshment from his face, his favor, and will send Jesus, his agent in the restitution of all things.   We have the same thought in our hymns: ''Show thy reconciled face;'' and ''Show thy face and all is bright.''

Now call to mind what was shown in the preceding chapter concerning the manner of our Lord's return and appearing, lest you stumble here because of erroneous ideas on that point. Remember, that "As the days of Noah were, so shall also the *presence* [Greek, *parousia*] of the Son of man be; for as in the days that were before the flood they . . . *knew not,* . . . so shall also the presence of the Son of man be." (Matt. 24:37-39.) Remember, also, what we have already gathered from the inspired teaching—that only those faithfully watching unto the sure word of prophecy, and loving and looking for his appearing, will be *able* to discern his presence, until he makes it manifest to the world "in flaming fire, taking vengeance"—in the great time of trouble. The fact, then, that *his presence* is not known and generally recognized by the world, or even among Christians, is no argument against this truth. The world has no faith in prophecy, and of course cannot see anything in its light. And lukewarm Christians (and such are the large majority) are paying no attention to the "sure word of prophecy;" and many who profess to be watching are reading the prophecies through the colored glasses of old and long cherished errors, and with their eyes miserably crossed by prejudice. All such should go to the Great Physician for some of the "eye salve" of meekness (Rev. 3:18), and forever discard the colored glasses of the traditions of men, and all theories of their own and of others which will not harmonize with every testimony of God's Word.

But neither the world's ignorance and unbelief nor the lukewarm indifference and prejudice of the great majority of professed Christians shall prove stumbling blocks to God's elect—to those who in simple, child-like faith accept the testimony of his blessed Word. Such cannot stumble; nor is it possible that *they* should be deceived. By their faith and God's leading such will overcome all. Fear not, precious Jewels of the Lord's own choosing: lift up your heads and rejoice, knowing that your deliverance, your exaltation and glory, draweth nigh.—Luke 21 : 28; 12: 32.

Another reasonable expectation, if the Times of Restitution actually began with October, A. D. 1874, and if our Lord's second presence was then due, would be, that those watching should see some distinguishable indications of what the Scriptures explain to be the first work of his presence, viz., the harvesting of the fruit of the Gospel age, the gathering together of his elect (in mental association and spiritual communion), and at least some preparatory steps toward the establishment of Christ's Kingdom. Some of these evidences we have already briefly hinted at; but there is so much to be observed on this point that we must leave its consideration for a subsequent chapter. The harvest of the Church is indeed upon us; the wheat is being separated from the tares; and affairs in the world are rapidly shaping themselves, making ready for the permanent establishment of the Redeemer's Kingdom. The foretold signs, in the exact manner and order of their prediction, are made clearly manifest to those watching; but this we leave for the present—because we wish first to bring other prophetic testimonies to view. *Suffice it to say here that the sickle in the "harvest" of this age, as in the Jewish "harvest," is the truth; and that the "messengers" who use the sickle now are disciples or followers of the Lord, though many of them now, as then, realize but slightly the magnitude of the work in which *they* are engaged.

PROPHETIC EVIDENCES

CORROBORATIVE.

While the foregoing evidence is strong and clear just as it stands, we now present *prophetic testimony* which proves that we began counting the Great Cycle (50 x 50) at the right point.   Our Heavenly Father knew the fear and trembling with which our faith would grasp these exceeding great and precious promises, and hence he has doubled the already strong cord of evidence, furnished in the Law, by additional testimony through the prophet.   And our dear Redeemer and Lord, who hands us this cord, and whose *presence* this testimony points out to us, as he comes to us in the early dawn of the Millennial Day, seems to say, as he once said to Peter (Matt. 14: 25–32), "O thou of little faith, wherefore didst thou doubt?"   Learn that I am a spirit being, no longer visible to human sight.   I thus reveal myself by the lamp of the Word to the eyes of thine understanding, that as in coming days I shall walk upon the stormy sea of the world's unparalleled trouble, *thou* needst not fear, but "Be of good cheer."   Remembering that it is I, be not afraid.

This truly marvelous prophetic corroboration, which we now proceed to consider, lay hidden in its own simplicity until the appreciation and application of the Jubilee type, as above, gave it significance.

The seventy years, usually referred to as the *seventy years captivity* in Babylon, is Scripturally styled the *"seventy years desolation of the land."*   This desolation God had predicted by Jeremiah the Prophet, thus:—"And this whole land shall be a desolation, and . . . shall serve the king of Babylon seventy years." (Jer. 25:11.)   "Thus saith the Lord, that after seventy years be accomplished at Babylon, I will visit you, and perform my good word toward you, in causing you to return to this place." (Jer. 29:10.)   In 2 Chron. 36:17–21 the fulfilment of this prophecy is recorded; and the reason *why* it was just seventy years, and why it was made completely *desolate*, is stated thus: "He brought upon them the king of the Chaldees [Nebu-

chadnezzar, king of Babylon], . . . and them that had
escaped from the sword carried he away to Babylon, where
they were servants to him and his sons until the reign of the
kingdom of Persia: to fulfil the word of the Lord by the
mouth of Jeremiah, *until the land had enjoyed her Sabbaths;
for* AS LONG AS SHE LAY DESOLATE SHE KEPT SABBATH, *to
fulfil threescore and ten* [70] *years.*"

From this we see that Israel had failed to observe properly the Sabbatic years, of which the Jubilees were the
chief. It certainly was a severe test of obedience toward
the Heavenly King, to a people so notably avaricious, to
be commanded to let the land rest, to restore to former
owners lands acquired and possessed for years, and to restore to servants their liberty—especially when obedience
was only commanded, and not summarily enforced by com-
pulsion. God had forewarned them, through Moses, that if
they were disobedient to the laws to which as a nation they
had pledged themselves, he would punish them for it. In the
same chapter in which he tells them of the punishment of *seven
times* under Gentile rule, he tells them, also, that if they
would neglect the year Sabbaths he would punish them for
it by *desolating their land.* (And, as a matter of fact, the
seventy years desolation was also the beginning of the *seven
Gentile Times*, as already shown.) The Lord's threatening
reads thus: "Your land shall be desolate and your cities
waste. Then shall the land enjoy her Sabbaths, as long as
it lieth desolate and ye be in your enemies' land, . . *because
it did not rest in your Sabbaths when ye dwelt upon it.*"
—Lev. 26:34, 35, 43.

God permitted for a while their half-hearted and half-
way obedience, but finally removed them entirely from the
land, made it desolate, without an inhabitant, and gave it
the *full number* of its Jubilee Years—not only for those they
had imperfectly observed, but also for the entire future

number which would elapse, according to his arrangement, before the antitypical Jubilee, the Restitution or Millennial age, would be due.

And since the *entire number* of typical Jubilees, designed to precede the antitype, is thus proved to be seventy, we are thus furnished another means of calculating when the antitype is due to begin. The calculating of this prophetic statement of the entire number of Jubilees is simple and easy; and, as we should expect, its results *agree exactly* with those already obtained by the method of counting furnished by the Law.

The entire number being seventy, and nineteen of these having been observed in a half-hearted way by Israel before the desolation, it follows that the remaining fifty-one ($70 - 19 = 51$) mark the period from the last Jubilee which Israel imperfectly observed, down to the great antitype. But here note a difference in the manner of counting. Under the Law reckoning, we counted the future as well as the past cycles of forty-nine years with the fiftieth or Jubilee Year *added;* for the Law shows things as they would have been, had Israel carried them out properly. But prophecy records things just as they will actually occur. We are now examining the *prophetic* statement, remember, and hence should now reckon these cycles as they *have occurred* —cycles of forty-nine years, without Jubilees; for Israel did not observe a Jubilee since their nineteenth one. The first nineteen cycles had Jubilee Years, but the fifty-one since have had none; hence we must reckon fifty-one cycles of forty-nine years each, or 2499 years ($49 \times 51 = 2499$), from the last typical Jubilee observed by Israel to the antitype. This calculation, though entirely distinct from the other, ends exactly as shown by the Law method of reckoning previously examined—October, A. D. 1874.

Let us state this last proof in another form, for the benefit of some, thus:—The full number of Jubilee cycles which God had ordained was seventy, as shown by the plain statements relative to the reason for the *seventy years desolation* of their land. This was to include those that Israel had observed in an unsatisfactory manner, which we have seen were nineteen, as well as all the cycles to follow, up to the antitype. We will now reckon all these from their commencement on entering Canaan, and see where they end.

19 Cycles with Jubilees added (50 years each) = 950 years.
51 Cycles without Jubilees (49 years each) = 2499 "

70 Cycles, therefore, cover a period of   3449 "

This period of 3449 years, reckoned from the entering of Canaan, ends as the foregoing, October, A. D. 1874, thus:—

From entering Canaan to division of the land,	6 years.
Period of the Judges to Saul the king,	450 "
Period of the kings,	513 "
Period of the desolation,	70 "
From the restoration to A. D.,	536 "

Total number of years before the date known as A. D.,   1575 "

Years since A. D., to complete above period of 3449 years, are 1874 full years, which would end (Jewish time) October,   1874 "

The period of the 70 cycles, as shown above, from the beginning of the Jubilee system, on entering Canaan, until the antitype, the Great Jubilee, or Times of Restitution, began, Oct., A. D. 1874,   3449 years.

The logical conclusion, if these matters are accepted as of divine arrangement, is easily drawn. And if not divinely arranged, whence came they? We do not *put* them into the inspired Word: we merely find them *there* in all their simplicity and beauty, and, like all the other precious and

THE JUBILEE VIEWED PROPHETICALLY.

JER. 25:9-12 AND 2 CHRON. 36:21.

TOTAL NUMBER OF JUBILEE CYCLES—SEVENTY.

CHRONOLOGICAL TABLE.

—SEE PAGE 194.—

From entering Canaan:—

To the division of
the land, . . 6 years.

Period of Judges, 450 "

" " Kings, 513 "

To the Desolation, 969 "
19 Jubilees, = 950 years.

19 years.

Thus their last Jubilee was observed 19 years before the Desolation.

PERIOD SINCE LAST JUBILEE.

Before the "Desola-
tion" as above, 19 yrs.

Years of Desolation, 70 "

From the Restora-
tion by Cyrus to
A. D. 1, . . . 536 "

Years from A. D. 1
to A. D. 1874,
Oct. 10th (the
end of year—
Jewish time), . 1874 "

2499 yrs.

51 cycles (without Jubi-
lees) as they actually occurred and were mentioned in proph-
ecy, 49 years each = 2499 years.—Or, total years from entering Canaan to October 1874 = 3449 years.

The Period of 19 cycles and Jubilees (950 years) and 51 cycles alone (2499 years) = 3449 years.

CYCLES WITH JUBILEES OBSERVED, BUT UNSATISFACTORILY, NINETEEN.

19 x 50 = 950 years.

CYCLES OF 7 x 7 = 49 YEARS EACH, AFTER THE DESOLATION OF THE LAND, WHEN NO JUBILEES WERE ATTEMPTED, FIFTY-ONE.

51 x 49 = 2499 years.

To 950 YEARS OF JUBILEE OBSERVANCE ADD 2499 YEARS SINCE = 3449 YEARS;

THE FULL PERIOD FROM THE COMMENCEMENT OF THIS TYPICAL JUBILEE SYSTEM TO THE ANTITYPE—EARTH'S GREAT JUBILEE, THE TIMES OF RESTITUTION OF ALL THINGS—OCTOBER, A. D. 1874.

OCT., A. D. 1874, DATE OF BEGINNING OF EARTH'S GREAT JUBILEE.

rich food from the storehouse, which our Lord is now serving us according to his promise (Luke 12:37), this is nourishing "strong meat"—not especially intended for "babes in Christ," but for those more developed, "who have their senses exercised" (Heb. 5:14) to discern and appreciate this meat now in "due season." If not of divine arrangement and intended for our instruction, how and why come the double proofs, matching and corroborating each other so perfectly? To convince yourself of their divine arrangement, notice that in no other place and way can these seventy years of Sabbaths in desolation be made to harmonize with the (50 x 50) cycle of the Great Jubilee. Try it. Prove it. Suppose either a mistake, or a change of *one* of the nineteen Jubilees kept by Israel: Suppose that eighteen (one *less*) or twenty (one *more*) had elapsed before the *seventy years desolation* began. Calculate, and you will see that these *two lines* of evidence, which so perfectly unite in the testimony that 1875 (beginning October, A. D. 1874) is the date of the beginning of the Times of Restitution, and the date, therefore, from which we may know that the heavens no longer retain our Lord, the great Restorer, cannot be united elsewhere, without doing violence to themselves, to the chronology, and to other prophecies yet to be examined.

If these time-prophecies teach anything, it is that the Great Jubilee, the Times of Restitution of all things, has begun, and that we are already in the dawn of the Millennial age, as well as in the "harvest" of the Gospel age—which ages lap one upon the other for forty years—the "day of wrath." We are already fourteen years into this forty-year-day of wrath; and preparations for the struggle are progressing rapidly. The coming twenty-six years, at the present momentum, will be quite sufficient for the accomplishment of "all things written."

Let no reader hastily conclude that there are no evidences of Restitution about us, nor that the Sun of Righteousness is not already gilding the watch towers of Zion and enlightening the world. Let him, on the contrary, reflect that we are already in the day when the hidden things are being made manifest; and let him remember that the first work of Restitution is properly a breaking down of the old and decaying structure which stands in the place which the new is to occupy. Remember that the first work of the tenderest physician is often to open the wounds, and to cleanse and amputate according to the necessities of the patient, in order to make thorough work of the healing. That such service causes pain and is seldom appreciated by the patient at the time, none need be told; and so it is with the work of the great Physician, the Restorer, the Life-giver: He wounds to heal, and the trouble and sifting in the Church and the world are but the lancing and cleansing needful, and a most important part of the Restitution work.

In the type, the Trumpet of Jubilee was to be sounded when the Jubilee Year began, to proclaim liberty throughout all the land, unto *all* the inhabitants thereof. (Lev. 25 : 10.) The antitype is ushered in with the sounding of the (symbolic) " Seventh Trumpet," the " Trump of God," the " Last Trump." It is indeed the great trumpet: it announces liberty to every captive; and while at first it means the surrender of many expired claims and privileges, and a general time of disturbance and unsettling of usages, habits, etc., its full import, when rightly appreciated, is *"good tidings of great joy which shall be unto all people."*

In the early commotion, each one who hears the Jubilee Trumpet of the new dispensation is forcibly struck by some one of its many features and heeds no other. One sees the propriety of, and calls for, governmental reforms, the aboli-

tion of standing armies and their burdensome tax.   Another calls for the abolition of titled aristocracy and the
recognition of every man by his manly qualities.   Others call
for the abolition of landlordism, and demand that landhold-
ing shall be as at first, according to necessity, and ability
and willingness to use.   Others call for temperance reform,
and by prohibitory and other laws, by Law and Order Societies, seek to chain this great evil, and begin to restrain
men who for the love of money would ensnare, enslave
and destroy fellow men, and who, fastening their fangs into their weaknesses, would fatten and luxuriate upon their
blood.   Others form Humane and Anti-Cruelty Societies,
to prevent those who have the ability from injuring the
weak and dependent.   Others form societies for the sup-
pression of vice and of demoralizing literature.   Others form
Anti-Adulteration Societies to examine into adulterations
of food, and to expose and prosecute and punish those
who for love of greater gain adulterate food and make it
even injurious to health.   Laws are enacted for the protection of the lives and the health of the people.   Miners must
have pure air, no matter what the cost ; they must have two
ways of escape in case of fire.   Working people, powerless
to help themselves or to choose their places of work, are
cared for by the public laws.   They can no longer be paid
when the employer may please, and in store-orders, but the
law now demands that pay-day shall be at least every two
weeks and in cash.   They can no longer be crowded into
buildings where in case of fire they would be liable either
to burn to death or to maim themselves for life by jumping ;
for "fire-escapes" are compulsory, and for any death or
injury traceable to carelessness on the part of the employer,
he is held responsible, and is punishable, either by fines,
damages or imprisonment.   Wealthy corporations, such as
own railroad and steam-ship lines, are compelled to care for

the lives and interests of *the people*, the poor as well as the rich. These reforms are the results of the awakening of the people by the Jubilee Trump of knowledge and liberty, and are not traceable to pure benevolence on the part of the more favored class. For though all in the favored or wealthy class who are benevolent, and such as love righteousness, can and do rejoice in these beginnings of reform, others, and the majority, regretfully yield from necessity. True, such laws and arrangements are not yet perfected, nor are they universal; but the beginnings noticed rejoice our hearts, and give evidence of what may be expected in the exalting of the humble and lowly, and the abasing of the proud, when the Jubilee regulations are fully in operation. All these things are parts of the reform commotion ushering in Earth's Great Jubilee; and though much has been demanded, and much has been gradually conceded, yet kings, and emperors, and queens—political, social, ecclesiastical and financial—will not submit to the great leveling process of this Jubilee or Restitution age without a great and severe struggle, such as the Scriptures point out as just before us, and which, though severe, is unavoidable, and will work out ultimate good.

The spirit of "*liberty* throughout all the land" is indeed sometimes carried to an unreasonable extent by the ignorant and the hot-headed; and yet it is all part of the great unavoidable Jubilee excitement, occasioned by the ignorance and oppression of the past. None but the Lord's "little flock" is fully and correctly informed as to the grand scope of the Restitution. These see the minor changes, the straightening out of the lesser affairs of men, but they see also what can be seen from no other standpoint than God's Word—that the great enslaver, Sin, is to be shorn of his power, that the great prison-house of Death is to be opened and a release presented to each prisoner, signed in the precious blood of the Lamb of God which taketh away the sin of the world, the great Redeemer and Restorer. Glad tidings indeed it *shall be* to *all* people, not only to the living, but also to all that are in their graves. Before the end of this great Jubilee every human being may go entirely free—may get back to man's first estate, "very good," receiving back through Christ all that was lost in Adam.

THE SEVENTH TRUMPET.

"Blow ye the Trumpet, blow
 The gladly solemn sound;
Let all the nations know,
 To earth's remotest bound,
The Jubilee of Earth is come,
Returning ransomed sinners home.

"Jesus, our great High-Priest,
 Hath full atonement made.
Ye weary spirits, rest;
 Ye mournful souls, be glad.
The Jubilee of Earth is come,
Returning ransomed sinners home.

"Ye who were sold for naught,
 Whose heritage was lost,
May have all back unbought,
 A gift at Jesus' cost.
The Jubilee of Earth is come,
Returning ransomed sinners home.

"The Seventh Trumpet hear,
 The news of heavenly grace;
Salvation now is near;
 Seek ye the Savior's face.
The Jubilee of Earth is come,
Returning ransomed sinners home."

STUDY VII.

THE PARALLEL DISPENSATIONS.

THE JEWISH AGE A TYPE OF THE GOSPEL AGE.—REMARKABLE PARALLELISM OR CORRESPONDENCY BETWEEN THE TWO DISPENSATIONS.—YET THEY ARE DISTINCT.—SUPERIORITY OF THE CHRISTIAN EPOCH, THE ANTITYPE.—FLESHLY AND SPIRITUAL ISRAEL CONTRASTED.—PROMINENT PARALLELS EXAMINED.—TIME PARALLELS SPECIALLY NOTICED.—PERIOD OF FLESHLY ISRAEL'S FAVOR.—TIME OF THEIR CUTTING OFF FROM FAVOR.—THE PERIOD OF DISFAVOR SHOWN FROM PROPHECY TO BE EQUAL TO THE PERIOD OF FAVOR.—APOSTOLIC TESTIMONY THAT THEIR PERIOD OF DISFAVOR IS THE PERIOD FOR THE HIGH CALLING OF SPIRITUAL ISRAEL.—THE LENGTH OF THE GOSPEL AGE THUS SHOWN INDIRECTLY BUT CLEARLY.—HARMONY OF THE BIBLE CHRONOLOGY, JUBILEE TESTIMONY, GENTILE TIMES, AND OTHER PROPHECIES WITH THE LESSONS OF THESE PARALLELS UNANSWERABLE, CONCLUSIVE AND SATISFYING.

IN previous chapters the fact has been referred to, that God's dealings with the nation of Israel were of a typical character; yet few have any adequate conception of how fully this was the case. It has doubtless been observed by many that the apostles, particularly Paul, in instructing the Christian Church, frequently refer to some striking features of type and antitype in the Jewish and Christian dispensations. But a closer attention to the Apostle's teachings will show that he does not only make use of a few illustrations drawn from the Jewish economy, but that in his close reasonings he calls up the whole Jewish system as divinely instituted (ignoring entirely the "traditions of the elders," which were no part of that system), and shows that in all its features it was typical of the then dawning Christian dispensation, mapping out most clearly the course of the Christian Church in the Gospel age, as well as pointing out its glorious work in the Millennial age.

Many presume that the Jewish and Christian ages are really one, and that God has been selecting the Christian Church from the very beginning of human existence. This is a serious mistake, which beclouds and hinders the correct and clear apprehension of many truths. Jesus was the head and forerunner of the Christian Church, which is his body (Eph. 5 : 23 ; Col. 1 : 24); consequently none preceded him as members of the Church. Had any preceded him, he could not properly be styled the *forerunner*. The "high calling" to become joint-sacrificers, and finally joint-heirs with him, was not made known in other ages. (Eph. 3 : 2, 5, 6.) Good men who lived and died prior to the *actual payment* of our ransom by the precious blood knew nothing of this "high calling." And since the gifts and callings of God are unmerited favors, no injustice is done to those of other ages, in not offering them the same favor. The call and favor to those of past ages, as they will also be to those of the coming age, were to earthly honors, and earthly glory, and everlasting life as earthly (human) beings; while the call and favor of the Gospel age are to heavenly honors and glory, to a *change of nature* from human to divine, and to power, honor and dominion in heaven and in earth, as joint-heirs and co-workers with Christ. And since the Church thus called out, separated from the world, and developed during this age, is in the age to come to be the agent of Jehovah in the full execution of his great plan of the ages—a plan which compasses the interests not only of humanity, but of all creatures in heaven and in earth— wonderful have been the preparations made in the ages past for their training and instruction. And no less wonderful has been the care with which these, called to be *heirs* of divine glory, have during this age been trained, disciplined, guided and protected through the long, difficult, narrow way, first opened up by their Lord and Forerunner, in whose footprints they are directed to tread—as he set the example.—1 Pet. 2 : 21.

Our Lord spent the three and a half years of his ministry in gathering out from Israel, and in training and instructing, the few disciples who should form the nucleus of the Christian Church. When about to leave them alone in the world he gave them the promise of the holy Spirit, which, during the entire age, should guide the Church into all truth, and show them things to come, and bring freshly to remembrance what he had taught—which promise began to be verified at Pentecost. It is also written that the angels are all ministering spirits sent forth to minister to these heirs of this great salvation (Heb. 1 : 14), and that our Lord's special care is over them, even to the end of the age. (Matt. 28 : 20.) All the writings of the apostles are addressed to the Church, and not to the world, as many seem to think; and they are full of *special* instructions, encouragements and exhortations, needful only to the saints who during this age are walking in the narrow way. And our Lord's revelation, which God gave him after he had passed into glory, he sent and signified [*signified*—told in signs, symbols, etc.] to his Church, through his servant John. (Rev. 1 : 1.) We are also told that the prophecies given aforetime by holy men of old were given, not for themselves, nor for others of their day and age, but exclusively for the instruction of the Christian Church.— 1 Pet. 1 : 12.

In this chapter we purpose to show that the whole Jewish nation, during that entire age, was unwittingly engaged, under God's direction, in furnishing for our instruction a typical view of the entire plan of salvation in all its workings, even as we have just seen its Jubilees pointing out the final consummation of the plan in the blessing of all the families of the earth. It is by our drawing upon this storehouse of truth, so abundantly and specially provided for the Church, that the Spirit of God feeds us and leads us gradually into a more and more nearly complete understanding of his plan, as rapidly as that knowledge becomes needful to us. And from this great storehouse God is now supplying much of the special light and food needful to us in this "harvest" time at the consummation of the age. Since such has been God's care and abundant provision for the Christian Church above all other people of past and future ages, how important in his estimation must that knowledge be to us, and how eagerly should we avail ourselves of it.

While we will not in this chapter or volume enter into a *detailed* examination of the typical features of God's dealings with Israel, as set forth in the Tabernacle, and Temple, and ordinances and sacrifices, etc., we do now invite close attention to some of the marked and prominent outlines of *correspondency* between the Jewish and Christian dispensations as type and antitype; for all that the Christian Church actually experiences and accomplishes, the Jewish Church prefigured. And many of these features of correspondency are parallel not only in character, but also in their relative *time* of occurrence. Even in their national history, and in the history of many particular individuals of that nation, we find correspondencies marked by the Scriptures. Some of these, Christian thinkers have long noticed, and others have been entirely overlooked. Here a beautiful and fruitful field of thought and study opens before us.

Paul designates the Jewish Church "Israel after the flesh," and the Christian Church "*The* Israel of God." (1 Cor. 10 : 18 ; Gal. 6 : 16.) We may thefore properly designate them Fleshly Israel and Spiritual Israel. The higher plane of the spiritual house is also pointed out by the Apostle when he describes Fleshly Israel as a house [family] of *servants*, and Spiritual Israel as a house of *sons*. (Heb. 3 : 5, 6 ; Rom. 8 : 14.) The fleshly house was the honored servants of the spiritual house in various ways, but chiefly in that they unconsciously, under God's arrangement, furnished pantomime illustrations of spiritual things, which, if studied and heeded, greatly bless and enlighten the house of sons.

In both cases there have been a Nominal Israel and a Real Israel, in God's estimation, though to men they have appeared as one ; the nominal and the real not being clearly distinguishable until the end or harvest time of their respective ages, when the truth then due and brought to light accomplishes the separation, and makes manifest which are of the real and which of the merely nominal Israel. Of the fleshly house Paul said, "They are not all Israel which are [nominally] of Israel" (Rom. 9 : 6) ; and our Lord recognized the same fact when of Nathaniel he said, "Behold an Israelite *indeed*, in whom is no guile," and also when in the time of harvest he separated the real from the nominal, and called the former valuable wheat, and the latter mere chaff—though, comparatively, the wheat was only a handful, and the chaff included nearly all of that nation. In a similar proportion, and under a similar figure, the nominal and the real members of Spiritual Israel of the Gospel age are pointed out ; and their separation, too, is in the time of harvest—in the end of the Gospel age. Then only the wheat—a comparatively small number, a "little flock"—will be separated from the masses of nominal Spiritual Israel, while the great majority, being tares and not real wheat, will be rejected as unworthy of the chief favor to which they were called, and will not be counted among the Lord's jewels.—Rom. 9 : 27 ; 11 : 5 ; Luke 12 : 32 ; Matt. 3 : 12 ; 13 : 24–40.

The head of the fleshly house was Jacob, surnamed Israel (a prince) ; and through his *twelve* sons he founded the house which bore his name, the House of Jacob, the House of *Israel.* So with the Spiritual House: its founder, Christ, established it through the *twelve* apostles; and this house also bears the name of its founder—The Church of Christ. In point of time, God called Fleshly Israel first; but in point of favor, and in time of realization, Spiritual Israel comes first. Thus the first becomes last, and the last first. (Luke 13: 30.) The Scriptures clearly mark these two houses of Israel as being the fleshly seed of Abraham and the spiritual seed of Jehovah—the Heavenly Father whom Abraham typified.

Some are blinded to important truths by the supposition that the expression, "both the houses of Israel," refers to the two divisions of Fleshly Israel, after the split in the days of Solomon's son, Rehoboam. Such need only be reminded that after the captivity in Babylon, upon their restoration to Palestine, all Israelites of all the tribes then captives in all the universal domain of Medo-Persia, includ- ing the land of Syria or Babylonia, were given liberty to return to their own land if they chose. (Ezra 1: 1–4.) Many of the faithful Israelites of *all* the tribes, who had respect to the promises of God associated with the holy land and the holy city, returned to the various cities of Pales- tine. The tribe of Judah, the principal tribe, in which was vested the kingly office, and in whose territory Jerusa- lem, the chief city, was located, naturally took a leading part in its rebuilding; but after that return from Babylon, Israel was no more a divided nation, but dwelt together as at first, as one people, and were known by the one original name, Israel.—See Neh. 11: 1, 20 ; Ezra 2 : 70.

This is further emphasized in the New Testament. The Lord and the apostles speak of Fleshly Israel as *one.* Paul says that *Israel* sought, but that only a "remnant" was found worthy. (Rom. 10:1–3; 9:27; 11:5–12, 20–25; Acts 26:7.)

Our Lord said that he was "sent to [all] the lost sheep of the [one] house of Israel ;" yet when he would not permit his disciples to go outside of Palestine to seek them (Matt. 10:5, 6; 15:24), it is evident that those living in Palestine represented *all* Israel. Peter, too, speaks of fleshly Israel as one house ; and addressing the people at Jerusalem he said, "Let all the house of Israel know," etc. James also speaks of the twelve tribes as one people. (Acts 2:36; Jas. 1:1.) Many of all the tribes dwelt in Palestine, and many of all the tribes dwelt in surrounding nations. Thus Paul met and preached to Israelites in nearly every city which he visited in Asia Minor and Italy, but they were always recognized as one nation, spiritual Israel being the only other Israel.

God has made special covenants or promises to both these houses of Israel. The promises to the fleshly house were all *earthly*, while those to the spiritual house are all *heavenly*. Though the promises to the fleshly house were (and still are) grand and precious, the promises to the spiritual house are characterized as "better promises," and "*exceeding great and precious promises.*" (Heb. 8:6; 2 Pet. 1:4.) To the fleshly house it was said, "If ye will obey my voice indeed, and keep my covenant, then ye shall be a peculiar treasure unto me above all people ; for all the earth is mine. And ye shall be unto me a kingdom of priests, and a holy nation." And though all Israel answered and said, "All that the Lord hath spoken we will do" (Exod. 19:5-8), and then failed to keep their covenant, yet the faithful among them, who earnestly endeavored in their weakness to keep it, will in the Millennial age be "princes in all the *earth*," members of the earthly phase of the Kingdom of God.—See Vol. I., chapter xiv.

To the spiritual house, on the contrary, it is said, "Ye are built up a *spiritual house*, a holy priesthood, to offer up sacrifices * acceptable to God by Jesus Christ. . . . Ye are a chosen generation, a royal priesthood, a holy nation, a peculiar people, that ye should show forth the praises of him who hath called you out of darkness into his marvelous light; which in time past were not a people, but are *now* THE PEOPLE OF GOD.''—1 Pet. 2 : 5, 9, 10.

Fleshly Israel had by God's appointment a Tabernacle made with hands, which was typical both in itself and in all its services. (Heb. 9 : 1, 2, 9, 10.)   But Spiritual Israel has "the *true* [the antitypical] Tabernacle, which the Lord pitched and not man.'' (Heb. 8 : 2.)   For the services of the typical Tabernacle a typical priesthood was ordained, of which Aaron was the head, which offered typical sacrifices for the sins of the typical people, and accomplished a typical cleansing or justification each year.   The antitypical Tabernacle has its priesthood, which offers up better sacrifices (Heb. 9 : 23), which actually and forever cancel the sins of the whole world.   And of this priesthood our Lord Jesus is the head priest—the High Priest of our profession [or order]—the Church which is his body being the under-priests.   The entire nominal church is not this priesthood—but the true Church, the faithful in Christ Jesus, who follow the footsteps of our great High Priest in sacrifice.

Another marked feature of this correspondency as type and antitype, noted in the Scriptures, is that both the houses of Israel (fleshly and spiritual) were carried away captives into Babylon.   This will be more clearly seen when in a succeeding chapter we come to view "Babylon the Great, the Mother of Harlots.'' (Rev. 17 : 5, 6.)   We merely notice here the correspondence.   Fleshly Israel was taken

---

* The word *spiritual* before sacrifices in this text (verse 5) is omitted in the oldest Greek manuscript—the Sinaitic.   The correctness of this omission is evident when we reflect that not spiritual things are sacrificed, but earthly or human privileges, rights, etc.

captive into literal Babylon, which was built upon the literal river Euphrates, while in the Gospel age mystic or figurative Babylon, which carried away captive Spiritual Israel, is portrayed as sitting upon the mystic Euphrates. In the type, the golden vessels of the Temple were carried away and profaned by literal Babylon: in the antitype, the precious, divine (golden) truths, pertaining to the service of the true Temple, the Church (1 Cor. 3:16, 17; Rev. 3:12), were far removed from their proper places, perverted and misapplied by mystic Babylon. Literal Babylon being built upon the river Euphrates, which materially contributed to its wealth and resources, its overthrow was accomplished by the turning aside of those waters. So mystic Babylon sits upon, is supported by, many waters (peoples, nations), and its fall is predicted, through the turning aside of its supporters and sustainers, the people.—Rev. 16: 12.

TIME PARALLELS
MEASURING
SHADOW AND SUBSTANCE—TYPE AND ANTITYPE.

We now come to the consideration of that most wonderful feature of this typical correspondency, viz., the time element, which in every instance sustains and corroborates the dates indicated by the Jubilees, the Chronology, and the foretold close of Gentile Times. And it is for this purpose particularly that this subject is here introduced—that the force of this wonderful parallelism may increase and confirm the faith of God's children in the time element of his plan, as it was evidently intended to do.—Heb. 9:9, 23; 10:1.

Of all the prophecies and time-proofs there is none more striking and convincing than this one. The lesson it teaches is startling because of its very simplicity, and carries conviction to the hearts of the humble. Not only were Fleshly Israel and its ceremonies typical, but the Jew-

14-B

ish *age* was typical of the Gospel *age*. They are of exactly the same length, and correspond to each other ; so that, seeing and appreciating the Jewish age, its length, and the peculiarities of its harvest or close, we may know the exact length of the Gospel age, its antitype, and may understand what to look for, and when, in the harvest of the Gospel age. But let us now proceed to show this ; for though we might take it for granted on general principles, and say that as the various features of the Jewish system correspond to those of the Gospel age, so too the *time* should correspond, yet God has not left us thus to *infer this*, but has clearly though indirectly told us so.

Paul tells us that God has cast off the fleshly house from favor, during the time of the selection of the spiritual house ; and that when the spiritual house has been selected, then God's favor will return to the fleshly house. He says: "I would not, brethren [brethren of the Church, or spiritual Israel], that ye should be ignorant of this mystery, lest ye should be wise in your own conceits, that blindness in part is happened to Israel [natural, or fleshly] *until* the fulness of the Gentiles * be come in. As it is written : There shall come out of Zion the [promised] Deliverer [the Christ— our Lord, the head, and the remnants or faithful few, of both the nominal houses of Israel, which shall compose his body, the Church] and shall turn away ungodliness from

---

* None should confound this "Fulness of [or, from out of] the Gentiles" with the "Times of the Gentiles," mentioned heretofore. The "Times of the Gentiles," as has been shown, is the period of time during which the Gentiles are permitted to rule the world; while the "Fulness of the Gentiles" refers to the *full number* to be selected out from among the Gentiles, to complete the Gospel Church—who, with the "remnant" selected from among the Israelites (which would include the apostles), shall constitute the Church of Christ, the Holy Nation, the Royal Priesthood, the Kingdom of God, to whom the kingdom and dominion of earth shall be committed.

Jacob. And so all Israel shall be saved (for this is my covenant unto them) *when I shall take away their sins.* As concerning the gospel [the high calling of this age], they are enemies [cast off] for your sakes [that you may have the preference and inherit the choicest, the spiritual parts of the promises] ; but as touching the election [by which they were chosen to receive special earthly favors from God, promised to their father Abraham and his natural seed], they are beloved for the fathers' sakes; for the gifts and calling of God are not things to be repented of." What God has promised is sure of fulfilment. Knowing the end from the beginning, Jehovah never made a covenant which he would need or wish to break.

In this prophecy the Apostle gives an intimation of the length of the Gospel age, by showing that it began with the casting off of Fleshly Israel, and that it will end with their restoration to favor. Placing the statements of Paul and Peter (Rom. 11 : 27 and Acts 3 : 19, 20) together, we learn that the time for the return of favor to Israel will be in the beginning of the Times of Restitution, at the second advent of our Lord. Paul says the return of favor to that people will be when God shall *take away their sins,* which Peter says he will do in the times of refreshing or restitution which shall come when our Lord comes the second time, when the heavens no longer retain him.

The date of our Lord's second advent, and the dawn of the Times of Restitution, we have already shown to be A. D. 1874. We should expect, therefore, to see some marks of God's returning favor to Fleshly Israel shortly after A. D. 1874, as one of the first features of restitution work. And, surely enough, we do see favor beginning to return to them. And every fresh evidence of the removal of Israel's blindness, and of divine favor toward them, is, when measured by the Apostle's words, a fresh proof that the Gospel age is closing and that the "little flock" is about complete. But we have further proof which furnishes us with the *exact date* when favor should begin to return to Israel. Thus far we have merely seen that the measure of Fleshly Israel's *cast off* condition is the measure of the time of *special* favor to others, for the calling of other people (Gentiles) to be joint-heirs with Christ, which call ends *in* the beginning of the Times of Restitution; but not (other prophecies show) *at* the very beginning of it.

But pause a moment—let there be no misunderstanding on this point: When the *call* to the high privilege of becoming members of the Church, the bride and joint-heir of Christ, ceases, it by no means signifies that all of those already called are sure to be counted worthy, and therefore to be chosen; for "Many are *called*, but few are *chosen*," because only a few of the called ones comply with the conditions of the call. Nor does it imply that those not thereafter called to that "high calling" will be offered no other favors. The fact is, that when this "high calling" ceases, it is because the great Designer of the plan of the ages has almost completed *that part* of his plan intended to be accomplished in the Gospel age—viz.: the selection of the Gospel Church, the bride of Christ. All men were not called to that high honor. We are specially informed that God's design was to select for this purpose only a limited number, a "little flock," as compared with the mass of mankind. After enough have been called and the time for calling ends and it is no longer proper to extend *this* call to others, it will still be possible for those already called, who have accepted the call, to make their calling and election sure, by faithfulness to their covenant of entire consecration to God, even unto death; and it will still be possible for these to fail of so doing. This call, which must end when enough have been invited from which to complete the favored "little flock," the body of Christ, is far from being the limit of God's love and favor and calling. Its end will merely close the heavenly or "high calling." For where this call ends, where this door of opportunity and favor closes, another door begins to swing open—the door of opportunity to enter the highway of holiness, and to go up thereon —not to the divine nature, to which the Gospel Church was called, but to everlasting life and perfection as human beings.—See Vol. I., chapters x. and xi.

But now for the *exact date* of the return of favor to Israel, which marks the exact end of the heavenly *call*—from which date Israel will begin gradually to see, and to have increasing evidences of returning divine favor, and from which date also God's call to heavenly honors will cease, and only these already called will be privileged to win that prize by faithfulness to the close of life:—

Fleshly Israel, like Spiritual Israel, was called of God to be his peculiar people, a peculiar treasure unto him above all other people (the one an earthly treasure, and a type of the other, which is a heavenly treasure). Separated from the world, they were the recipients of special favor from God for eighteen hundred and forty-five (1845) years. This period began with the beginning of their *national life,* at the death of Jacob, the last of the patriarchs, when they were first recognized as a nation, and called "The Twelve Tribes of Israel," a national name. See Gen. 49:28; 46:3; Deut. 26:5. These eighteen hundred and forty-five years of national life and favor ended with their rejection of Messiah—A. D. 33—when, five days before his crucifixion, he presented himself to them as their king, and, not being received, declared, "*Your house is left unto you desolate.*" (Matt. 23:38.) This, the end of their favor, was the point of their fall, which continued for **thirty-seven (37)** years, and ended A. D. 70 in the total destruction of their national polity, as well as of their city, temple, etc. It should be noted, however, that God continued his favor to individuals of that nation, after the nation, as a nation, had been cut off; for the gospel call was *confined* to individuals of that nation for three and a half years after Pentecost, after the death of Christ—not reaching Cornelius, the first Gentile so favored (Acts 10), until that time. This was the full end of the seventy weeks of favor promised through Daniel, as it had been written, " He shall confirm the covenant with many for one week." That seventieth week of years began at our Lord's baptism ; his cross, as predicted, marked its middle ; and favor was confined to Fleshly Israel until its close.

During their long period (1845 years) of national favor, during which other nations were ignored, Israel had chastisements and blessings combined. But even their chastisements for sins were evidences and elements of God's favor and fatherly care over them. He sent trouble upon them, and frequently allowed them to be carried away into captivity, when they forgot and disobeyed him ; yet when they repented and cried unto the Lord he always heard and delivered them. The entire history of that people, as recorded in Exodus, Joshua, Judges, Chronicles and Samuel, attests the fact that God did not long hide his face from them, and that his ear was ever open unto their repentant cry—down to the day their house was left desolate. Even on that day, God was forgiving them more than ever, and had sent them the long-promised Messiah, the Deliverer, in the person of our Lord, his Son. The unfitness of that nation longer to be his special treasure, or in any measure to represent God's Kingdom on earth, was manifested in their rejection of the holy, harmless, undefiled one, and their desire of a murderer in his stead.

Thus, because of their unfitness, the day of their greatest

favor became the day of their rejection and fall from favor. And the great favor of becoming joint-inheritors with Messiah, which Israel, except the faithful *"remnant"* (Isa. 1:9; 10:22, 23; Rom. 9:28, 29; 11:5), thus missed by their blindness and hardness of heart, was offered to believing Gentiles: not to Gentile nations, but to justified believers of every nation—though the favor was at first, for three and a half years, confined exclusively to believers of the nation of Israel. Blinded as a people by national prejudices, the great prize which they were offered first, but of which they were unworthy, goes to a holy nation, a peculiar people, composed of a worthy "remnant" of their nation, with others called out from Gentile nations, whom in their arrogant pride they once despised as "dogs." And God's promised favor will not return to them as a people, to remove their blindness, and to lead them as a first-fruits of the nations into earthly blessings, *until* the full number of the "peculiar people" have been called from the Gentiles—*until* the fulness of the Gentiles be come into this higher favor.

Thus, as Paul declared (Rom. 11:7), Fleshly Israel did not obtain that for which they sought, viz., the chief favor. Supposing the chief favor to be the earthly blessings, and in their pride of heart claiming that chief blessing as their natural birth-right, and as further merited by their works, they blindly stumbled over and rejected it as a *favor* through Christ. As David had foretold, their table—so bountifully spread with the rich promises and blessings offered them *through Christ*—became "a snare, and a trap, and a stumbling block, and a recompense unto them," because of their hardness of heart. (Rom. 11:9, 10; Psa. 69:22–28.) Christ, who came to redeem and who would have exalted them to a position of glory beyond their ability to desire or imagine, was to their pride "a stone of stumbling and a rock of offence."—Rom. 9:32, 33; Isa. 8:14.

Yet the blindness of Israel was only a "blindness in part," and not a total loss of sight; for the testimony of the Law, the prophets and the apostles was open to all, whether Jew or Gentile; and during the Gospel age any Jew who would resolutely brush away the films of prejudice and pride, and humbly and thankfully accept the favor of God with his Gentile brother, might do so. Yet few have ever been able to do so; and no *favor* will be granted, and no *special* effort to convince them as a nation of the truth, or to overcome their prejudices, will be exerted, until the fulness of the Gentiles has come in; or, in other words, until Spiritual Israel is complete.

Since their rejection of Messiah—since their house was left desolate—Israel has had no marks of God's favor. Even Jews themselves must admit that their tears and groans and prayers have gone unanswered; and, as foretold by their prophets, they have been "a by-word and a hissing" unto all nations. Though formerly God heard their prayers, and marked their tears, and returned them to their own land, and continually favored them, since then he heeds them not and shows them *no favor*. Since they said, "His blood be upon us and upon our children," theirs has been one continuous chastisement: they have been scattered and persecuted among all nations, as foretold. These are the facts as all may read them on the pages of history. Now let us turn to the prophets and see how particularly these facts were foretold, and what the same prophets have to say concerning their future.

Through the prophet Jeremiah (chapter xvi.), after telling Israel how they had forsaken him, the Lord says: "Therefore will I cast you out of this land into a land that ye know not, neither ye nor your fathers; and there shall ye serve other Gods [rulers] day and night, where I *will not show you favor.*" (Verses 9-13.) These days came when they rejected Messiah. How literally this threat has been fulfilled all may judge, and they themselves must admit. This prophecy cannot refer to any of their previous captivities to surrounding nations—Syria, Babylon, etc. Such an inference is guarded against in the expression, "Into a land which ye know not, *neither ye nor your fathers.*" Abraham came from Ur of the Chaldees—Babylonia—and Jacob from Syria. (Deut. 26 : 5.) Israel's dispersion among all nations since the close of their 1845 years of favor, and no other of their captivities, fits this pointed expression—a land which *ye* and your fathers have not known. So then this, together with the *no favor*, positively marks this prophecy as relating to Israel's present dispersion among all nations.

But though he cast them off from all favor for a while, God will not leave them cast off forever, but says—Jer. 16 : 13–15 : "Behold, the days come, saith the Lord, that it shall no more be said, The Lord liveth, that brought up the children of Israel out of the land of Egypt ; but, The Lord liveth, that brought up the children of Israel from the land of the north [Russia, where nearly one half of the Hebrew race resides], and from all the lands whither he had driven them : and I will bring them again into their land that I gave unto their fathers."

We might multiply quotations from the prophets and apostles concerning the final return of God's favor to Jacob, or Israel after the flesh, after the selection of the full number for "the body of Christ" from the Gentiles, but the student can do so by the use of a Concordance or a Reference Bible. Among the very pointed references to this favor to be restored to Israel, in the New Testament, is that by James, Acts 15 : 14–16, and by Paul, Rom. 11 : 26. But first, they must drink the very last dregs of their chastisement ; and thus it is expressed in this remarkable proph-

ecy (verse 18); "And first [before the favor will come] I
will recompense their iniquity and their sin *double*." The
Hebrew word here rendered "double" is *mishneh*, and
signifies a second portion, a repetition. Thus understood,
the Prophet's declaration is, that from the time of their being cast off from all favor until the time of their return to
favor would be a repetition, or *duplication in time*, of their
previous history, during which time they had enjoyed
divine favor.

As shown in the accompanying diagram, the period of
their favor, from the commencement of their national existence at the death of Jacob, down to the end of that
favor at the death of Christ, A. D. 33, was eighteen hundred and forty-five (1845) years; and there their "double"
(*mishneh*)—the repetition or duplication of the same length
of time, eighteen hundred and forty-five (1845) years, *without favor*—began. Eighteen hundred and forty-five years
since A. D. 33 shows A. D. 1878 to be the end of their period
of disfavor. A. D. 33 plus 1845 = A. D. 1878.

All these prophetic points in the past are clearly marked,
and we should expect some evidence of God's returning
favor to Fleshly Israel ("Jacob") in or about A. D. 1878.
This we do find, in the fact that the Jew is now permitted
privileges in Palestine denied him for centuries past. And
it was in that very year—1878 A. D., when their "*double*"
was full, and God's favor was due to return to that people—
that the "Berlin Congress of Nations" was held, in which
Lord Beaconsfield (a Jew), then Prime Minister of England, was the central figure and took the leading part.
There England assumed a general protectorate over the
Asiatic provinces of Turkey, among which is Palestine;
and the Turkish government amended its laws relating to
aliens, which greatly ameliorated the condition of the Jews
then residing in Palestine, as well as partially opened the

"BOTH THE HOUSES OF ISRAEL.

—TIME PARALLELS.—

B.C. 1813.	A.D. 33.

PERIOD OF THE NATIONAL EXISTENCE OF THE CHILDREN OF JACOB, SURNAMED ISRAEL, DATING FROM THE DEATH OF THE PATRIARCH JACOB.

PERIOD OF CHRISTIAN FAVOR AND HIGH CALLING TO BELIEVERS, DATING FROM MESSIAH'S DEATH TO THE REJECTION AND FALL OF BABYLON.

JEWISH FAVOR, WAITING FOR THE KINGDOM

1845 + 3½ YEARS.

CHRISTIAN FAVOR, WAITING FOR THE KINGDOM

DURING JEWISH "DOUBLE"—1845 + 3½ YEARS.

A.D. 29.	A.D. 1874.

7 OTH WEEK

THE KING CAME IN.

THE KING CAME IN.

A.D. 33.	A.D. 1878.

A.D. 36.	A.D. 1881.

ISRAEL FALLS.

DAYS OF VENGEANCE.

LUKE 21 : 22.

A TIME OF TROUBLE AND FINAL OVERTHROW.

BABYLON FALLS.

DAYS OF VENGEANCE.

DAN. 12 : 1.

"A TIME OF TROUBLE SUCH AS WAS NOT SINCE THERE WAS A NATION."

JEWISH HARVEST

3½ + 3½ + 33 = 40 YEARS.

CHRISTIAN HARVEST

3½ + 3½ + 33 = 40 YEARS.

A.D. 70.	A.D. 1915.

door for others to locate there, with the privilege of holding real estate. Previously, the Jew was but "a dog," to be cuffed, kicked and abused by his Mohammedan ruler, and was denied the most ordinary privileges of existence, in the land sacred to him with memories of the past, and with promises touching the future.

At the same time that the door to Palestine thus opened before them, a fierce persecution arose in Roumania and Germany, and specially in Russia, where it still continues —increasingly. By one regulation after another they have been despoiled of rights and privileges by these governments, as well as mobbed by their neighbors, until they are being compelled to leave in large numbers. But this persecution is doubtless a favor also, as it will tend, and has already tended, to cause them to look toward Jerusalem and the covenants, and to remind them that they are heirs of certain rich earthly promises.

But we must remember that the year A. D. 1878 was but the turning point of returning favor to Fleshly Israel. We have already learned, from our study of "The Times of the Gentiles," that Jerusalem and its people will continue to be trodden down—controlled and oppressed by the Gentiles—"*until* the Times of the Gentiles be fulfilled," and hence, though favor was due and began in A. D. 1878, the Jew will not be received back into *full favor* until A. D. 1914. Thus their rise again to favor will be gradual, as was their fall from it. It is remarkable, too, that these two periods of their falling and rising are of exactly the same length—the falling was gradual, with increasing momentum, for *thirty-seven* years, from A. D. 33, where their national favor ceased, to A. D. 70, where their national existence ended, the land was desolated and Jerusalem totally destroyed. History thus marks the beginning and ending of their fall, while prophecy marks both ends of their rising—1878 and 1914—showing an exact parallel of thirty-seven years. This is a further part of their *mishneh* ("double") mentioned by the prophet.

Though the turning points of the Jewish and Gospel ages are thus clearly marked at A. D. 33 and A. D. 1878 respectively, by Israel's rejection and returning favor, yet the work of each of these ages laps over upon the age succeeding it. Thus the turning point of the Jewish age being reached, their age thereafter was *lapped* upon by the opening Gospel age, just as their returning favor, which is one of the opening features of the Millennial age, laps over upon the close or harvest of the Gospel age. For thirty-seven years (from A. D. 33, the end of their national favor, to A. D. 70, their complete overthrow) Israel, except the faithful remnant, was falling, and the believing Gentiles were rising—the Jewish age was ending and the Gospel age was beginning; and for thirty-seven years (from A. D. 1878 to A. D. 1914) the Gospel age is ending, and woes are preparing and coming upon so-called Christendom, except the faithful remnant, while the restitution work for Israel and all people is preparing. That is to say, the dates A. D. 33 and A. D. 1878 mark when the work of the respective new ages began, though the work of harvesting the preceding age, and destroying the refuse, was allowed to continue thirty-seven years into the new, in both cases. Thus the lap of the dispensations, as well as the end-marks of each, is clearly defined.

A double work belongs to each of these lapping periods: the pulling down of the old and the establishment of the new arrangement or dispensation. And as the Jewish age and people were but the types or shadows, we must expect the results here to be much more extensive than there; and so we shall find them. This twofold work is shown in the statement of the prophet Isaiah—"For (1) the day of vengeance is in my heart, and (2) the year of my redeemed is come."—Isa. 63 : 4.

Nor is it a cunningly devised correspondency, arranged to suit the facts; for many of these parallels, and other truths, were seen from prophecy, and were preached as here presented, several years prior to A. D. 1878—that year being announced as the time of returning favor to Israel, before it came, and before any event marked it so. The author of this volume published these conclusions drawn from Scripture, in pamphlet form, in the spring of A. D. 1877.

The testimony could scarcely be stronger, and yet be kept secret until the present *due time* for knowledge to be increased, and for the wise [in truly heavenly teaching] to understand. The exact year of Israel's rejection—yes, even the very day—we know; that they were to have a *mishneh* or double, the Prophet explicitly declares; that this parallel period is eighteen hundred and forty-five years long, and that it ended A. D. 1878, we have shown clearly, we think; and that it was marked by favor is an indisputable fact. And bear in mind, too, that it is since the end of their "double" that Prof. Delitzsch has published his Hebrew translation of the New Testament, which is already in the hands of thousands of Hebrews and awakening much interest. And further, remember that the greatest Christian movement among the Hebrews since the days of the apostles, headed by Rabinowitsch and others, is now in progress in Russia. And it had its start about as long a time after A. D. 1878, where Israel's *"double"* ended, as the time of the awakening among the Gentiles was after Israel's rejection in A. D. 33.

Now call to mind the Apostle's words which show clearly that they were cast off from divine favor, and from EARTHLY COVENANTS, STILL THEIRS, *until* the fulness or complete number from the Gentiles has come in—until the *end of the Gospel call*—and then you will see that 1878 is a marked date, of deep interest to Spiritual Israel—no less important than to Fleshly Israel.

However, as none but our Lord Jesus knew the import of the end of the Law age and the beginning of the Gospel age (even the apostles knew only in part and saw dimly until after Pentecost), so we can now expect only the body of Christ, anointed with the same spirit, to see clearly the ending of the Gospel age and its weighty import. The poor Jews and many professed Christians do not even yet know of the great dispensational change which occurred at the first advent—the ending of the Jewish age and the opening of the Gospel age. And likewise now, few know, or will come to know, until outward evidences prove it to their natural sight, that we are now in the end or "harvest" of the Gospel age, and that A. D. 1878 marked so important a point as it did. Nor was it intended that others than the faithful few should see and know, and not be in darkness with the world—"To *you* it is given to know," said our Lord.

But some perhaps may say, Though Jeremiah was truly a prophet of the Lord, whose testimony as to the *"mishneh"* or duplication of Israel's experiences should be respected, we should consider the evidence still stronger if another prophet had mentioned the same thing. To such we reply that the statement of one reliable prophet is good and sufficient ground for faith, and that many of the notable proofs at the first advent were foretold by only a single prophet ; nevertheless, God, who is rich in mercy and very pitiful, considered our weakness of faith, and has answered the prayer of our hearts in advance, providing more than the one testimony.

Turn now to Zechariah's prophecy (9 : 9-12). In prophetic vision he walks beside Jesus as he rides into Jerusalem—A. D. 33—five days before his crucifixion (John 12 : 1-12), and to the people the Prophet cries, "Rejoice greatly, O daughter of Zion ! Shout, O daughter of Jerusalem ! Behold, thy king cometh unto thee ! He is just, and

having salvation : lowly, and riding upon an ass." Mark
the clear fulfilment of these words—Matt. 21 : 4–9, 43;
John 12 : 12–15 ; Luke 19 : 40–42. Every item was fulfilled, even to the shouting. When the people shouted
Hosanna ! the Pharisees asked Jesus to rebuke them, but
he refused, saying, "If these should hold their peace, the
stones would immediately cry out." Why ? Because it had
been prophesied that there would be a shout, and every item
of prophecy must be fulfilled. Let this particularity of detail
in prophetic fulfilment give us confidence in the further
statements of this and other prophets.

After briefly noting the evil consequences to follow a
rejection of their king (Zech. 9 : 10), the Prophet, speaking
for Jehovah, addresses them thus (verse 12) : "Turn you to
the strong hold [Christ], ye prisoners of hope : *even to-day*
do I declare that I will render DOUBLE unto thee." The
word double, here, is the same word used by Jeremiah—
"*mishneh*"—a repetition, or another equal portion. Israel
had for years been under the Roman yoke, but they were
"prisoners of hope," hoping for a coming king who would
deliver them and exalt them to the promised dominion of
earth. Now their king, their strong tower, had come, but
so meek and lowly that they in their pride of heart could
not recognize him as such a deliverer. And much more
they were Sin's prisoners, and this Deliverer purposed this
greater release also. Our Lord had been with them three and
a half years, fulfilling the Scriptures in their midst, and
now came the last and final test—would they receive him,
the Lord's Anointed, as their king ? The foreknowledge of
God, that they would reject Messiah, is shown by the
Prophet's words—" Even to-day do I declare that I will
render double unto thee."

This prophecy not only leaves no doubt about there being a double—a duplication of chastisement added to
15–B

Israel's experience because of their rejection of Messiah—but it also marks the *exact day* when it began, and makes the conclusions drawn from Jeremiah's prophecy, and fixed by our Lord's words, "Your house is left unto you desolate," doubly strong, exact and clear.

Call to mind our Lord's words at this time and in this connection—"O Jerusalem, Jerusalem, that killest the prophets and stonest them which are sent unto thee, how often would I have gathered thy children together, even as a hen gathereth her chickens under her wings, and ye would not. Behold! *your house is left unto you desolate ;* for I say unto you, Ye shall not see me henceforth till ye shall say [from the heart], Blessed is he that cometh in the name of the Lord." (Matt. 23 : 37–39.) Also we read that on the last day of their test, " when he was come near [riding on the ass], he beheld the city and wept over it, saying, If thou hadst known, even thou, at least in this thy day, the things which belong unto thy peace ! But now [henceforth] they are *hid from thine eyes.*" (Luke 19:41, 42.) Thank God, now that their " double " is complete, we can see that their blindness is beginning to be turned away. And this gives joy to the saints on their own account, too, for they realize that the glorification of the Body of Christ draweth nigh.

But our loving Father, who evidently wished to settle and to establish our hearts beyond doubt, upon the small point which decides and proves so much, has sent us word concerning Israel's "*double*" by another of his most honored servants—the Prophet Isaiah.

This prophet takes his standpoint down at this end, at the time when the "double" (*mishneh*) has been fulfilled —A. D. 1878; and, addressing us who now live, he gives us God's message, saying : "Comfort ye, comfort ye my people, saith your God. Speak ye comfortably to Jerusalem, and cry unto her that her *appointed time is accomplished,* that her iniquity is pardoned; for she hath received of the Lord's hand DOUBLE * for all her sins."—Isa. 40 : 1, 2. See marginal reading.

The student of prophecy should notice that the prophets vary their standpoints of utterance, sometimes speaking of future things as future, and sometimes assuming a position future and speaking from that assumed standpoint; as, for instance, Isaiah, speaking of our Lord's birth, assumes to stand by the manger where the babe Jesus lay, when he says, "Unto us a child *is* born, unto us a son *is* given, and the government *shall be* upon his shoulders," etc. (Isa. 9 : 6.) The Book of Psalms cannot be read intelligently unless this principle be recognized. No better illustration of this principle of different prophetic standpoints can be given than the three prophecies relating to Israel's "double" already noticed. Jeremiah foretold that the days *would come* when God would scatter them among all nations, and that, when they have received "DOUBLE," he would gather them again by a more mighty display of power on their behalf than when they came out of Egyptian bondage. Zechariah speaks as though living at the time of Christ's offering himself to Israel as their king, and tells us that there, in that *very day*, their "double" began to count. Isaiah stands beside us in A. D. 1878, and calls our attention to the fact that God had a fixed or *appointed time* for favoring Israel already arranged, and that this fixed time was after a *double*, or counterpart, of their previous favor; and he tells us that we should now give to Israel this comforting message that her *double* is complete—her appointed time accomplished. It would be difficult indeed to decide which of these three prophecies is strongest or most important. They are each important, and each would be strong alone; but combined they are a three-

---

* The Hebrew word here translated "double" is *kephel*, which signifies *double*, in the sense of a thing having been folded in the middle.

fold cord of wonderful strength to the humble, studious, trustful children of God.

The force of these prophetic utterances is increased when we remember that these prophets not only lived and wrote hundreds of years apart, but that they wrote things entirely contrary to Jewish expectation.   Surely faithless and *slow of heart* to believe all that God has spoken by the prophets are those who cannot see in this clear and harmonious testimony the finger and dealings of God.

If any should object, that the Berlin Congress and its actions were not a sufficiently marked beginning of God's returning favor to Israel, we reply that it was a far more marked return of favor than was our Lord's action upon riding into Jerusalem a mark of disfavor.   Neither, at the time of its occurrence, was recognized as a fulfilment of prophecy.   And to-day there are thousands more who know of the fulfilment of the double than up to Pentecost knew that the double *began* back there.   Thus we see that the child that Simeon said was set for the *fall* and *rising again* of many in Israel (Luke 2 : 34) proved the *fall* or stone of stumbling to Fleshly Israel as a nation ; and we have seen how, as the Head and Captain of Spiritual Israel, he is to be the Deliverer, to raise up again the fleshly house, and to restore all things after their "appointed time," their "double," is complete ; and now we see the double complete and favor to Israel beginning.   As we note these fulfilments of our Father's Word, our hearts may well sing,

> " How firm a foundation, ye saints of the Lord,
>   Is laid for your faith in his excellent Word."

While thus noting Israel's fall from favor and their consequent loss, and the cause of all this, let us not forget that in this also they foreshadowed nominal Spiritual Israel, and that the same prophets have foretold the stumbling and fall of *both* the houses of Israel—" He shall be for a stone of stumbling and for a rock of offence to *both* the houses of Israel.''—Isa. 8 : 14.

Just as truly as there was a casting off and fall of nominal Fleshly Israel, as we have seen, there is also to be a casting off and fall of nominal Spiritual Israel, the nominal Gospel Church, and for similar reasons. The casting off and fall of the one are just as vividly portrayed in the Scriptures as those of the other. And just as surely, also, as a remnant of Fleshly Israel was saved from the blindness and fall through meekness and faith, even so also a similar remnant of nominal Spiritual Israel shall be saved from the blindness and fall of the nominal mass in the ''harvest'' or close of this age. Thus the last members of the true Church, the body of Christ, are to be separated from the nominal church—to be joined to the Head, glorified. These (the remnant selected from Fleshly Israel at its fall, and the faithful few of the Gospel age, including the living remnant at its close) alone constitute the true ''Israel of God.'' These are the Elect —justified by faith in Christ's redemptive work, called to joint-sacrifice and joint-heirship with Christ, chosen through belief of the truth and sanctification by the spirit of truth, and faithful even unto death. With the completion of the selection of this company, in the harvest of this age, quite a commotion may be expected among the wheat and tares; for many divine favors, specially granted because of the *faithful few*, will be withdrawn from the nominal mass, when the little flock, for whose development they were granted, has been completed.

We should expect that the order here would be, as in the typical Jewish harvest, a separating work, fulfilling the words of the Prophet, ''Gather *my saints* together unto me, those that have made a covenant with me by sacrifice.'' (Psa. 50 : 5.) And as A. D. 33 marked the giving over of the *nominal* Jewish house, as a system, to disfavor, disruption and overthrow, so the corresponding date, A. D. 1878, marked the beginning of the disfavor, disruption and overthrow of the *nominal* Spiritual Israel, of which we shall have more to say in succeeding chapters.

MATHEMATICAL DEMONSTRATION.

Assuming that the foregoing evidence is conclusive and satisfactory, we now proceed to demonstrate chronologically : First, that the Jewish age, from the death of Jacob to where their house was left desolate when their *double* or second part began to count, was eighteen hundred and forty-five (1845) years long ; and second, that the *double* ended in A. D. 1878, and favor was due to begin there —proving thus the close of the Gospel age favors.

The second point really requires no demonstration ; for it being a fact that our Lord died in A. D. 33, it becomes an easy matter to add eighteen hundred and forty-five years to A. D. 33, and find the year A. D. 1878 to be the year in which favor to Israel was due to begin, provided we can prove our first proposition, that the period of Israel's waiting for the fulfilment of God's promises *under his favor* was a period of eighteen hundred and forty-five years.

The length of this period is fully set forth in the chapter on Chronology except one item, namely, the period from the death of Jacob to the coming out of Egypt. This period was rather peculiarly hidden, or covered, until recently ; until it was noticed the length of the Jewish age was not known ; and without it the double of it could not have been measured, even if the prophecies regarding the double had been noticed and understood. The Chronology runs smoothly until Jacob's death, but from that date until the coming out of Egypt, there is no full record. Various snatches here and there are given, but no connected thread by which we could surely know. It was for this reason that at this point in the table of Chronology we were compelled to look to the New Testament. There we received aid from the inspired Apostle, who gave us the connecting link. We thus learned that it was a period of four hundred and thirty (430) years from the Covenant, at the death of Terah, Abraham's father, to Israel's exodus from Egypt.

We find the hidden period between the death of Jacob and Israel's coming out of Egypt, exactly, by first calculating the period from the death of Terah to the death of Jacob, and then deducting that number of years from the four hundred and thirty years, the period from Terah's death to the exodus from Egypt. Thus:—

Abraham was seventy-five (75) years old when the Covenant was made with him, at the death of Terah (Gen. 12 : 4), and Isaac was born twenty-five (25) years after. (Gen. 21 : 5.) Hence—

From the Covenant to the birth of Isaac, .	25 years.
From Isaac's to Jacob's birth (Gen. 25 : 26), .	60 "
From Jacob's birth to his death (Gen. 47 : 28), .	147 "
Total years from the Abrahamic Covenant to Jacob's death, ...	232 "
From the Covenant to the day Israel left Egypt (Exod. 12 : 41), at the Passover, . .	430 "
From this deduct the period from the Covenant to Jacob's death, ...	232 "
The period from Jacob's death to the Exodus, therefore, was	198 "

Thus all difficulty relative to the length of Israel's national existence is cleared away. The hidden period from Jacob's death to the Exodus was no doubt purposely concealed, until due to be seen. To this we now add the periods presented in the Chronological Table, as follows:—

Period from Jacob's death to the Exodus,	198 years.
Israel in the wilderness, ...	40 "
To the division of Canaan, ...	6 "
Period of the Judges, ...	450 "
" " Kings, ...	513 "
" " Desolation, . . .	70 "
From the the first year of Cyrus to A. D. 1,	536 "
Total years from Jacob's death to our Anno	—— "
Domini, ...	1813 "
From A. D. 1 to the crucifixion, at the Pass-over in the spring of A. D. 33—full years, Jewish ecclesiastical time, * . . .	32 "
Total period of Israel's waiting for the king-dom, under divine favor and recognition,	—— 1845 years.

To find the measure of their *double,* when favor was due and began toward them, and when therefore it began to depart from the *nominal* Spiritual Israel, we count eighteen hundred and forty-five (1845) years from the Spring of A. D. 33, and obtain the date of the Passover, A. D. 1878. Their rising again from A. D. 1878 *to* A. D. 1915 (the closing of Gentile Times), under the favor of the King whom they rejected, and whom by that time they will recognize, corresponds in length with their thirty-seven years of falling, from the day their house was left *desolate,* A. D. 33, until their utter overthrow as a people, A. D. 70.

We have already examined many striking parallels between the Jewish age shadow, or type, and the Gospel age substance, or antitype, and here we have just proved another : *The length of the two ages corresponds exactly*—the Gospel Church being called *during* Israel's "*mishneh*" or double of *disfavor.* And while other correspondencies are

---

* The Jewish ecclesiastical year dated from the Spring; and the Passover occurred on the 15th day of the first month of each new (ecclesiastical) year.

striking, especially so are the closing features of the two ages—their "harvests," their reapers, their work and the time devoted, all serve to give us clear outlines of the closing work to be accomplished in the harvest which is the end of this age. Notice carefully the correspondencies of these two harvests, as we shall briefly recapitulate :—

REVIEW OF HARVEST PARALLELS.

The Jewish age ended with a "harvest," our Lord and the apostles doing the work of reaping fruit, the seed of which had been sown by Moses and the prophets. "Lift up your eyes (said Jesus), and look on the fields, for they are white already to harvest." "I send you forth to reap that whereon ye have bestowed no labor : other men labored, and ye are entered into their labors." (John 4 : 35–38.) The end of the Gospel age is also called a harvest—"The harvest is the end of the world" (age). "In the time of harvest, I will say to the reapers, Gather first the tares and bind them in bundles, . . . but gather the wheat into my barn."—Matt. 13 : 39, 30.

John foretold the work and effect of the Jewish harvest, saying (Matt. 3 : 12), "Whose fan is in his hand, and he will thoroughly purge his floor, and gather his wheat [Israelites indeed] into the garner [the Christian Church]; but he will burn up the chaff [the refuse of the nation] with unquenchable fire"—(a trouble which consumed them nationally). Here was the baptism of the holy Spirit and of fire—the holy Spirit coming upon the "Israelites indeed" at Pentecost, and the fire of trouble upon all others, during the thirty-seven years following their rejection. (Matt. 3 : 11.) In that trouble Israel *as a nation* was destroyed, but not as individuals. The Revelator tells of the harvesting of this age with the sharp sickle of truth, because the *time to reap* is come, and shows a double work, part of which relates to the vine of the earth, as distinguished from the true vine of the Father's planting, Christ Jesus and his members or branches. (John 15 : 1-6.) The harvest of this age is said to be of wheat and tares (Matt. 13 : 24-30, 36-39): that of the Jewish age was called one of wheat and chaff. And as the chaff predominated largely there, the analogy and parallelism so marked in every other feature implies that the tares will be much more abundant than the wheat in this harvest.

The Jewish harvest, in all a period of forty years, began with our Lord's ministry and ended with nominal Israel's rejection and overthrow, and the destruction of their city, accomplished by the Romans, A. D. 70. And the harvest of this age began with the presence of our Lord at the beginning of Earth's Great Jubilee, in 1874, as shown in chapter vi., and ends with the overthrow of Gentile power— A. D. 1914, likewise a period of forty years—another of the wonderful parallels of the two ages.

While the Jewish harvest began with our Lord's ministry, and God's favor departed from their nominal system three and a half years later, and was followed by thirty-seven years of trouble upon that system, yet special favor continued to individuals of that nation, and the call to the high position of joint-heirship with Christ was given to them exclusively for three and a half years after our Lord's rejection by them and of them—thus verifying the promise to Daniel (Dan. 9 : 27), that favor would be shown to his people to the full end of the seventieth week, in the midst of which Messiah was cut off. This promise was fulfilled to all the true wheat, while the *system* which held that wheat was condemned and cast off in the midst of the week. The harvesting of the wheat of the Jewish age lasted for several years, beginning with our Lord's ministry, though all the special favor ceased three and a half years after the

death of Christ. The trouble (fire) upon that nation began to kindle early, but did not reach its terrible fury until the wheat of that nation had been about all garnered.

Similar periods are marked in the harvest of this age now closing, corresponding to the features of that harvest. The fall of A. D. 1874, where the Jubilee cycles point out that our Lord was due to be present, corresponds to the time of his baptism and anointing by the holy Spirit when he became Messiah the Prince (Dan. 9 : 25), and began his work of reaping the Jewish harvest. The Spring of A. D. 1878 (three and a half years after) corresponds to the date at which our Lord assumed the office of King, rode on the ass, cleansed the temple of its money-changers, and wept over and gave up to desolation that nominal church or kingdom ; and it marks the date when the nominal church systems were "spewed out" (Rev. 3 : 16), and from which time (A. D. 1878) they are not the mouth-pieces of God, nor in any degree recognized by him. And the three and a half years following the Spring of A. D. 1878, which ended October, A. D. 1881, correspond to the three and a half years of continued favor to individual Jews in the last half of their seventieth week of favor. As in the type that date—three and a half years after the death of Christ—marked the end of all special favor to the Jew and the beginning of favor to the Gentiles, so we recognize A. D. 1881 as marking the close of the special favor to Gentiles—the close of the "high calling," or invitation to the blessings peculiar to this age—to become joint-heirs with Christ and partakers of the divine nature. And, as we have seen, this marks a great movement among the Jewish people toward Christianity, known as the "Kishenev Movement." And now trouble is impending over nominal Christendom, but the storm is stayed until the wheat is garnered, until God's messengers seal his servants in their foreheads (intellects) with the truth.—Rev. 7 : 3.

The features of this harvest corresponding to those of the Jewish harvest have been very marked also as regards the preaching done. In the first three and a half years of the Jewish harvest, the Lord and the disciples had for their special text *time*, and the fact of Messiah's *presence.* Their proclamation was, "The time is fulfilled," the Deliverer has come. (Mark 1:15; Matt. 10:7.) So it was in this harvest also: up to A. D. 1878 the time prophecies and the fact of the Lord's presence, substantially as here presented, though less clearly, was our message. Since then the work has widened, and the view of other truths has become brighter and clearer; but the same facts and scriptures, teaching the same *time* and *presence,* stand unchallenged and incontrovertible. As the favor which was continued to individual Israelites, after their house nominal was cut off from favor, was not intended to convert and reform their *nominal church system,* nor granted in hope of changing their chaff into wheat, but was intended merely to separate and garner every grain of ripe wheat, so in this harvest the object of the continued and abounding favor (of the light of truth) of the present is not designed to convert whole sects or to work national reforms, but on the contrary to separate completely the wheat class from the tare class. They have grown together side by side for centuries, and a *pure,* all-wheat sect has been unknown; but now in the harvest the separation must come, and the strain will be terrible. It will mean, in many instances, the uprooting of earthly friendships and the sundering of many tender ties; and the *truth* will do the separating. The Lord's prediction as to the "harvest" at the first advent will be true again in the present harvest. (See Matt. 10:35–38; Luke 12:51–53.) As there the truth set the father against the son, the daughter against the mother, and the mother-in-law against the daughter-in-law, so again, a man's foes shall oftenest be they of his own household. This cannot be avoided. They who love peace more than the truth will be tested, and they who love truth supremely will be accepted and approved as the "overcomers"—just as in the Jewish "harvest."

In the Jewish "harvest" the messengers chosen and sent forth as heralds of the King and of the Kingdom at hand were humble, untitled men, and those who opposed the message were the Chief Priests, Scribes, Pharisees and Doctors of Divinity; and as we should expect we find it here: the blindest are the leaders of the blind, who, like their Jewish types, "*Know not the time* of their visitation."—Luke 19:44.

The *presence* was one of the main points of testing there, and the *cross* was the other. John the Baptizer cried to them, "There standeth one *among you* whom ye know not." Yet only the Israelites indeed were able to realize the fact of Messiah's presence; and of these many stumbled over the cross; for though willing to accept Messiah as a Deliverer, their pride made them unwilling to receive him as *Redeemer*, also. So here, likewise, the *presence* of Christ, the "harvest" in progress, and the rejection of the nominal mass of professors, stumble many; and the great Deliverer, for whose coming and kingdom many have prayed (as did the Jews), they are unready to acknowledge. Again it is true, "There standeth one among you whom ye know not." And again the *cross* of Christ becomes a test and a stone of stumbling or trial as none could have expected; and many, many are now falling over it, saying, We will accept Christ as our *Deliverer*, but reject him as our Redeemer or Ransomer.

Surely all who will consider the matter carefully must acknowledge that the evidence that our Lord is now present (a spirit being, and hence invisible) is greater and clearer than the evidence which the Jew had of his presence in the flesh at the first advent. And not only are the prophetic evidences of the Lord's presence now more full, complete and numerous, but the signs of the times everywhere about us, showing the harvest work in progress, are much more apparent and convincing, to those whose eyes are anointed (Rev. 3 : 18), than were the circumstances of the first advent, when our Lord Jesus, with a handful of followers, through much opposition and under many unfavorable conditions, announced, "The *time* IS FULFILLED ; repent and believe the good tidings "—Messiah has come, the Messenger of the great Jehovah, to fulfil to you all the promises made to the fathers.   What wonder that only the humble minded ones could accept of the humble Nazarene as the great Deliverer, or of the humble, untitled men with him as part of his chosen cabinet—as those who were to be princes under him.   Only the few could see in the one who rode on the ass and wept over Jerusalem the great King of whom Zechariah had prophesied that Zion would receive him as King with shoutings of joy.

At his first advent he humbled himself, taking the form and nature of man (Heb. 2 : 9, 15), thereby to accomplish our redemption by giving himself as our ransom price.   He is now highly exalted, and dieth no more ; and at his second advent, clothed with all power (Phil. 2 : 9), he will exalt his "body," and then *bestow* upon the world the blessing of restitution which he *purchased* for them at his first advent with his own precious blood.   Remember, he is no longer flesh, but a spirit being, and will shortly change, and glorify as his members and joint-heirs, all his faithful followers.

To the Jewish house Jesus presented himself in three characters—as Bridegroom (John 3 : 29), Reaper (John 4 : 35, 38) and King (Matt. 21 : 5, 9, 4).   To the Christian house he presents himself in the same three characters. (2 Cor. 11 : 2 ; Rev. 14 : 14, 15 ; 27 : 14.)   To the Jewish house he came as Bridegroom and Reaper in the beginning of their harvest (the beginning of his ministry); and just before his crucifixion he presented himself as their King, exercising kingly authority in pronouncing judgment against them, in leaving their house desolate, and in the typical act of cleansing their temple. (Luke 19 : 41–46 ; Mark 11:15–17.) Just so it has been in this harvest : Our Lord's presence as Bridegroom and Reaper was recognized during the first three and a half years, from A. D. 1874 to A. D. 1878. Since that time it has been emphatically manifest that the time had come in A. D. 1878 when kingly judgment should begin at the house of God. It is here that Rev. 14 : 14–20 applies, and our Lord is brought to view as the Reaper *crowned*. The year A. D. 1878, being the parallel of his assuming power and authority in the type, clearly *marks the time* for the actual assuming of power as King of kings, by our present, spiritual, invisible Lord—the time of his taking to himself his great power to reign, which in the prophecy is closely associated with the resurrection of his faithful, and the beginning of the trouble and wrath upon the nations. (Rev. 11 : 17, 18.) Here, as in the type, judgment begins with the nominal church, in condemning to destruction the nominal *systems* (not the people), outwardly representing the true Church—"the body." Here also is the cleansing of the true temple, the true Church, the body of Christ—the consecrated class. (1 Cor. 3 : 16; Rev. 3 : 12.) This consecrated or *temple* class in the nominal church stands related to the nominal church, as a whole, as the literal temple stood related to the holy city Jerusalem, as a whole. After the city was given up the temple was *cleansed:* so now the temple class must be cleansed : every selfish, carnal thought and all worldliness must be cast out, that the temple may be clean, the dwelling place of God's holy Spirit—the temple of the living God.

The special work since A. D. 1878 has been the proclamation of the King's command, " Come out of her [Babylon], my people, that ye be not partakers of her sins, and that ye receive not of her plagues." (Rev. 18 :4.) "Depart ye, depart ye; go ye out from thence; touch no unclean thing; go ye out of the midst of her; be ye [the royal Priesthood] clean, that bear the vessels of the Lord."—Isa. 52 : 11.

Another marked point of similarity accompanying the first and second advents is the prevailing sense of the need of a deliverer, and a wide-spread impression among the nations that deliverance must in some way soon come— the ideas of some even approximating the truth of the matter.   But in each case only a few are able to recognize the Deliverer and enlist under his banner in the service of the truth.   In the Jewish harvest, there was a going forth of many to meet the Lord when all men " were in expecta-tion " of him (Luke 3 : 15), at the time of his birth, thirty years before his anointing as Messiah at the beginning of his ministry; and so there was a corresponding expectation and movement on the part of many (afterward called Ad-ventists) led mainly by a Baptist brother named William Miller, in this country, and by Mr. Wolff and others in Europe and Asia.   This culminated in the year A. D. 1844, just thirty years before A. D. 1874, when Christ the Bridegroom and Reaper actually came, as shown by the Jubilee's teaching. In this we find another striking time-parallel between these ages; for those thirty years corresponded exactly to the thirty years from the birth of the babe Jesus unto Messiah the Anointed—baptized, and introduced as Bridegroom and Reaper, at the age of thirty.—Matt. 3 : 11 ; John 3 : 29.

In both cases there was a disappointment and a tarrying-time of thirty years, during which all slumbered, and only a few in each case awakened at the *proper* time to a realiza-tion of Messiah's presence.   The great nominal mass in both houses fail to recognize the visitation, because over-charged and lukewarm, neglecting the command to take heed and watch. Thus will be fulfilled the prediction by the Prophet—"He shall be for a stone of stumbling and for a rock of offence to *both* the houses of Israel." (Isa. 8 : 14.) The fleshly house stumbled because they had made void the law of God through giving attention to traditions (Mark 7 : 9, 13), and so had not a proper conception of the manner and object of the first advent. For that reason they were unprepared to receive him in the way he did come, and so stumbled over him and his work of sacrifice. The mass of nominal spiritual Israel are now stumbling over the same rock, and for the same reason. They are blinded by the tra-ditions of men and sectarian prejudices which hinder a prop-er enlightenment by the Word of God ; consequently they have not a proper conception of the manner or object of the Lord's second advent. And here also the cross of Christ, the doctrine of the ransom, is becoming a test to all. It is worthy of careful notice, too, that neither house would stumble or fall over a rock not present. The Rock is now present, and nominal systems are stumbling, falling and being broken to pieces ; while now, as at the first advent, the "Israelites indeed" are individually recognizing and ac-cepting the Rock, and by climbing upon this truth are being lifted spiritually far above the stumbling, rejecting masses.

Those who have the eyes of their understanding enlight-ened do not stumble ; but as they climb upon the Rock, from its higher standpoint they see much more clearly both the past and the future of the divine plan—some things not possible to utter, relative to the coming glory of the Church and the gala-day of earth. They who put their trust in the Lord shall never be confounded.

The full force of this parallelism is not obtained unless it is noticed that the Jubilee cycles and the Gentile Times mark the periods which correspond so exactly with these in the Jewish parallels. It is not an imagination that the Jewish and Christian ages are type and antitype—the apostles and prophets testify to their correspondency. Nor do we rely merely on the parallels in proof of the harvest work of the Christian dispensation now in progress: this harvest, as already shown, is otherwise marked—both its beginning and its close. The Jubilee cycles prove that our Lord Jesus was due to be present and begin the restitution work in the fall of 1874 A. D. And the parallelism above referred to shows that date (1874) to correspond exactly with the anointing of Jesus as the Messiah, at the beginning of the Jewish "harvest," at the first advent. The "Gentile Times" prove that the present governments must all be overturned about the close of A. D. 1914; and the Parallelism above shows that this period corresponds exactly with the year A. D 70, which witnessed the completion of the downfall of the Jewish polity. A reasonable question, then, in view of all this, is, Are these time-correspondencies mere accidents, or are they of the same divine ordering which we have seen arranged the other affairs of the fleshly house as shadows of the realities of this dispensation?

No, they are not accidental: undoubtedly the same all-wise One who taught us through the Chronology that six thousand years from Adam's creation ended with A. D. 1872, and that the seventh thousand, the Millennial age, began there; who through the Jubilee cycles taught us that the Lord would be present and the Times of Restitution begin in the fall of 1874; and who through the Times of the Gentiles showed us that we must not expect these things to be done in haste, but by seemingly natural means covering a period of forty years, has in these Parallel Dispensations marked by Israel's "double" given us evidence which not only itself teaches clearly the Lord's presence, the harvest

and the restitution (beginning with favor to fleshly Israel), but at the same time furnishes a *proof* of the correctness of the other prophetic evidences and of the Chronology. For be it distinctly noticed that if the Chronology, or any of these time-periods, be changed but one year, the beauty and force of this parallelism are destroyed. For instance, if the Chronology be altered but one year, more or less— if we add one year, say to the period of the Kings or the Judges, or if we make it one year less—it would spoil the parallelism. If we should add one year it would make the first of Israel's periods 1846 years long, and the double or other half of it would thus be thrown *one year later*, while, on the contrary, by such a change of the Chronology the Jubilee cycles would be thrown one year earlier, *i. e.*, A. D. 1873 ; and it would make the 6000 years end in A. D. 1871, while the Gentile Times would not be affected by it at all. All can see that the harmony or parallelism would thus be utterly destroyed. Or, if one year should be deducted from the Chronological reckoning the confusion would be just as great, the changes to the several periods being in an opposite direction. Thus these various time-prophecies corroborate each other, while the parallelism of the two dispensations clinches their testimony.

It will be noticed by those at all familiar with the calculations usually made by "Second Adventists" and others, relative to the prophetic periods, etc., that this method of dealing with these subjects is very different from theirs. They usually attempt to make all prophecies end at some *one* date. Their erroneous expectations lead them to this. They expect that a few moments will witness the entire program which will really occupy a thousand years—the Lord's coming, the resurrection, and the judgment of the world. And their expectation concerning those few moments is that they close by the burning up of the world.

To appreciate and accept the prophecies which point out various dates for various steps in God's great plan, they would need first to understand the "Plan of the Ages" and the true manner of the Lord's second advent. But the great majority are too much blinded by their theories and prejudices to do this. Their attempts to apply prophecy to their false expectations often lead to twisting, stretching or whittling, according to the necessities of the case, in the endeavor to get all the prophecies to terminate at some one date. These friends should awake to their error in this direction; for one after another their expectations have failed, while we and they know that some of the prophecies they have used cannot be stretched into the future, but are in the past, and are now abandoned by them. They are fulfilled, but differently from what they expected, and they know it not.

On the contrary, the prophecies here presented, and those yet to be considered, are unstrained, and without twisting or whittling. We simply present them as we find them in God's Word; and, having correct expectations from God's great "Plan of the Ages," it is easy for those seeing it clearly to note how the various prophetic chains fit to it and measure it. They mark it, some at one important point and some at another; and to such as see this much, this parallelism of the Jewish and Christian dispensations shows and proves beyond reasonable doubt the correctness of all the others.

The statement of the time-periods of God's plan, furnished in the prophecies, is very similar to an architect's specifications; and the parallels of the Jewish dispensation resemble his outline drawings. Suppose we had an architect's specifications for a house, without any drawings, and were to sit down and make a drawing from the specifications, and afterward should receive from the architect his outline drawings of the prospective building—if a comparison of it with our own sketch, made from the specifications, showed all the angles and measures exactly alike, we should be doubly assured as to our correct understanding of the specifications. So here, the drawing, the type or shadow of the Gospel age furnished us in the Jewish age, and the correspondence of prophecies and events with those fore-shadowings, give us as strong assurance of the correctness of our conclusions as could be asked, while we still "walk by faith and not by sight."

Other prophetic testimonies yet to be examined will also be found in perfect accord with these parallels. One of them, the Days of Daniel, points out a great blessing upon the consecrated who would be living in A. D. 1875 and onward—a blessing surely being fulfilled in the grand unfolding of the truths of God's Word since that time. To him be the praise who hath called us out of darkness into his marvelous light !

Remember that the *forty years'* Jewish harvest ended October, A.D. 69, and was followed by the complete overthrow of that nation ; and that likewise the forty years of the Gospel age harvest will end October, 1914, and that likewise the overthrow of "Christendom," so-called, must be expected to immediately follow. "In one hour" judgment shall come upon her.—Rev. 18:10, 17, 19.

The reader's attention is directed to the Table of Correspondencies following, which will well repay careful study.

"BOTH THE HOUSES OF ISRAEL."

CORRESPONDENCIES OF THE

MOSAIC AND CHRISTIAN DISPENSATIONS.

ISRAEL AFTER THE FLESH.	*ISRAEL AFTER THE SPIRIT.*
A HOUSE OF SERVANTS. 1 COR. 10:18; ROM. 9:7, 8; 4:16; HEB. 3:5.	A HOUSE OF SONS. GAL. 4:5, 6, 7, 30, 31; 6:15, 16; JOHN 1:12; ROM. 8:15.
FOUNDED IN JACOB'S TWELVE SONS. 1 KINGS 18:31.	FOUNDED IN JESUS' TWELVE APOSTLES. REV. 21:14.
A KINGDOM AND PRIESTHOOD, A HOLY NATION. EXOD. 19:6.	A ROYAL PRIESTHOOD, A HOLY NATION. 1 PET. 2:5, 9.
AARON, FLESHLY HIGH-PRIEST. HEB. 9:7.	JESUS, THE SPIRITUAL HIGH-PRIEST. HEB. 9:11.
CIRCUMCISION OF THE FLESH. ROM. 2:28, 29.	CIRCUMCISION OF THE HEART. ROM. 2:28, 29.
LAW OF SIN AND DEATH. ROM. 8:2.	LAW OF THE SPIRIT OF LIFE IN CHRIST JESUS. ROM. 8:2.
EARTHLY PROMISES. GEN. 13:14-17; ACTS 7:2-5.	"BETTER PROMISES." HEB. 9:23; 11:40.
IN CAPTIVITY TO LITERAL BABYLON. 2 CHRON. 36:20.	IN CAPTIVITY TO MYSTIC BABYLON. REV. 17:5; 18:4.
LENGTH OF FAVOR 1845 YEARS, FROM JACOB'S DEATH TO ISRAEL'S REJECTION AND THE BEGINNING OF SPIRITUAL ISRAEL, A.D. 33.	LENGTH OF FAVOR 1845 YEARS, FROM JESUS' DEATH TO THE BEGINNING OF CHRIST'S REIGN AND THE REJECTION OF BABYLON, A.D. 1878.
THE NOMINAL SYSTEM CAST OFF, A.D. 33. MATT. 23:38.	THE NOMINAL SYSTEM SPEWED OUT, A.D. 1878. REV. 3:16.

37 YEARS IN FALLING, TO A.D. 1914.

THE END OF THE AGE A HARVEST OF 40 YEARS.
MATT. 13:24-30, 36-43.

SPIRITUAL PRESENCE OF CHRIST AS REAPER.
REV. 14:14,15.

OUR LORD'S PRESENCE AND THE SACRIFICIAL CHARACTER OF HIS DEATH, THE STUMBLING-STONE.

"He shall be for a stone of stumbling and for a rock of offence to *both the* [nominal] *houses of Israel.*"—Isa. 8:14.

THEY KNEW NOT THE TIME OF THEIR VISITATION.
LUKE 19:44; MATT. 24:38,39.

OUR LORD PRESENTED IN THREE CHARACTERS—AS BRIDEGROOM, REAPER AND KING.
JOHN 3:29; 4:35,38; MATT. 21:5,9,4; 2 COR. 11:2; REV. 14:14,15; 17:14.

AN ADVENT MOVEMENT IN 1844, THIRTY YEARS PRIOR TO THE ACTUAL TIME OF HIS PRESENCE, TO AWAKEN AND TEST THE CHURCH.
MATT. 25:1.

ACTUAL PRESENCE OF THE LORD AS BRIDEGROOM AND REAPER—OCTOBER, A.D. 1874.

POWER AND TITLE OF KING ASSUMED THREE AND A HALF YEARS LATER—A.D. 1878.

37 YEARS IN FALLING, TO A.D. 70.

THE END OF THE AGE A HARVEST OF 40 YEARS.
LUKE 10:2,16.

PRESENCE OF CHRIST IN THE FLESH AS REAPER.
JOHN 4:35-38.

OUR LORD'S PRESENCE AND THE SACRIFICIAL CHARACTER OF HIS DEATH, THE STUMBLING-STONE.

AN ADVENT MOVEMENT AT THE TIME OF JESUS' BIRTH, THIRTY YEARS PRIOR TO HIS ADVENT AND ANOINTING, AS MESSIAH, AT BAPTISM.
MATT. 2:1-16; ACTS 10:37,38.

ACTUAL PRESENCE OF THE LORD AS BRIDEGROOM AND REAPER—OCTOBER, A.D. 29.

POWER AND TITLE AS KING ASSUMED THREE AND A HALF YEARS LATER—A.D. 33.

FIRST WORK OF THE KING, JUDGMENT.

NOMINAL JEWISH HOUSE REJECTED; LITERAL TEMPLE CLEANSED.—MATT. 20:18; 21:5-15; 23:37; 24:1.

ENTIRE DESTRUCTION OF JEWISH POLITY, ACCOMPLISHED IN 37 YEARS AFTER BEING CAST OFF—OR 40 YEARS FROM THE BEGINNING OF THE HARVEST—A.D. 70.

FIRST WORK OF THE KING, JUDGMENT.

NOMINAL CHRISTIAN HOUSE REJECTED; SPIRITUAL TEMPLE CLEANSED.—1 PET. 4:17; REV. 3:16; MAL. 3:2.

ENTIRE DESTRUCTION OF NOMINAL CHRISTENDOM, ACCOMPLISHED IN 37 YEARS AFTER BEING CAST OFF—OR 40 YEARS FROM THE BEGINNING OF THE HARVEST—A.D. 1914.

STUDY VIII.

ELIAS SHALL FIRST COME.

How This Important Prophecy Stands Related to the Second Advent.—A Partial and Typical Fulfilment in John the Baptist.—The Real Fulfilment.—The Vision on the Holy Mount.—Remarkable Correspondencies between Elijah, the Type, and the Antitypical Elijah.—The Time is at Hand.—The Outlook.—Elijah's Successor, Elisha.

"Behold, I will send you Elijah the prophet before the coming of the great and dreadful day of the Lord. And he shall turn the heart of the fathers to the children, and the heart of the children to their fathers, lest [*i. e.* or else] I come and smite the earth with a curse."—Mal. 4:**5,6.**

IN considering the evidences of the time being at hand for the establishment of Messiah's Kingdom in the earth, this prophecy, showing the priority of Elijah's coming, must not be overlooked.

The expression of our text is peculiar. The thought seems to be that Elijah's work will be to *turn* (*i. e.*, convert) parents to a humble, childlike condition, and, after making them teachable as little children, to turn their hearts from error, sin and unfaithfulness, and lead them back into harmony with their "fathers"—a name given by Hebrews to their *faithful* patriarchs and prophets.

Malachi's prophecy, the last message sent by Jehovah to Israel, seems to have deeply impressed them—especially the last two chapters, which particularly refer to Messiah's coming, and to the special trials which the day of the Lord's presence would bring with it. (See Mal. 3 : 1–3, 13–18; 4 : 1–6.) Gathering from this that the testing would be peculiar, they took comfort from the last verses

249

quoted above, which promised that Elijah the prophet, who had once converted the entire nation from the worship of Baal back to the worship of God, would come again to prepare them, before this severe testing time which Messiah's coming would bring.

This prophecy was not *fulfilled* at the first advent of our Lord—neither the portion which relates to Messiah nor that which refers to Elijah. The reference of the prophecy is evidently to the second advent; to the coming of the "Messenger of the Covenant" in glory and power; and to the testing and great trouble of the Day of the Lord at that time. However, Christ's presentation to typical Israel, and the great trouble which came upon them as a nation when they rejected him, was, as God had foreseen and intended, another shadow which further illustrated in many particulars the things presented in this prophecy. John the Immerser, in the spirit of Elijah, did a work for Israel similar to that of the Elijah promised, but failed of success; and, as a result, trouble (a curse) upon that nation followed. The real Elijah referred to by the prophet was to do a great work for the whole "earth," to prepare all mankind for the second advent; and he will for a time also fail of success, and as a result the great time of trouble (the curse) will smite the whole earth.

The coming of Elijah mentioned by the prophet is "*before*" this "great and dreadful Day of Jehovah."* And since, as we have just shown, the great Day of Jehovah began in A. D. 1874, will continue forty years, and will end with the expiration of Gentile Times in the complete overthrow of worldly and Satanic dominion in the earth, and the full investiture of Immanuel—Christ Jesus and his saints—with all power and dominion, it is important for us to show here that *Elijah has come*. He has failed to turn

---

* See Vol. I., Chapter xv.

the hearts of the world to childlikeness and to the [true] wisdom of the just; and therefore the great time of trouble comes, as God foresaw and foretold. In it, God will teach mankind by severe and bitter experiences lessons they need to learn thoroughly, to prepare them to gratefully accept the Christ,—Jehovah's Messenger of the New Covenant— with all the just arrangements, laws, etc., of that covenant.

At the first advent, as we have just seen, many of God's promises and plans were carried out on a small scale with one nation, Israel, as an illustration of the greater, grander realities to be accomplished at Christ's second coming. And as the miracles, cures, etc., represented the greater works of the Millennial age, and our Lord's riding on the ass as King represented his assuming the greater power, majesty and honor at the second advent as King of kings and Lord of lords, so "the *man* Christ Jesus" and his little band of disciples represented the Lord of Glory highly exalted, associated with the saints, his bride and co-heirs, at the second advent. And *thus* John the Baptist and his disciples engaged in the same work with and under him, in attempting to convert Israel and to prepare them to receive Messiah, *represented the real Elijah* (the true Christian church), whose work has been to *attempt* the conversion of the world before the coming of Messiah to the world—the spiritual Lord of glory and King of kings. John the Immerser, in the spirit and power of Elijah, failed to reform Israel, and, as a consequence (Matt. 27:12), Israel rejected Jesus in the flesh, and brought upon themselves a great "*day of vengeance*," trouble and wrath. (Luke 21:22.) So, likewise, only on the larger scale, the *real and greater Elijah* has failed to convert and prepare the world to receive the King of Glory, and now, consequently, the great day of wrath must come upon the world, to melt and mellow and humble and prepare all to cry out from the heart

—Hosannah! Blessed is he that cometh in the name of Jehovah!

It is thus seen that the *Church in the flesh* (the Christ in the flesh, Head and body) is the Elijah or forerunner of the *Church in glory*, Jehovah's Anointed. Not the nominal church, but the really consecrated Church, which on the other side of the tomb will be the great Anointed Deliverer, —these constitute the Elijah. Their mission is to reprove error and sin, and to point to the coming Kingdom of glory. Our Lord Jesus and the Apostles, and all the faithful in Christ Jesus since, are of this great antitypical Elijah, prophet or teacher—the same class (Head and body) which shall shortly compose the King of Glory. The work in which the Church is now engaged is merely preliminary to its future work, so far as the reforming of the world is concerned. In its kingly office the Church shall accomplish for the world what it fails to do as the Elijah teacher.

Let us not be misunderstood: We have heretofore shown that God's plan does not extend to the converting of the world during the Gospel age. He did not intend it to do so, but merely designed the selection and trial of the Church now, and the blessing of the world through the Church, the Christ, in an age to follow this. We do not contradict this when we say that the Elijah (Christ in the flesh) *has tried* to convert the world and failed, except in bringing about partial reforms; for though God knew and foretold that our mission to the world would be largely a failure, except in selecting a choice little flock, yet, knowing that the effort would react favorably upon ourselves, his commission to us through our Lord was to *try* to convert the world, when he said, "Go ye into all the world and preach the good tidings to every creature." Seeing that he foretold our present failure, but our future success, when he shall glorify and endue us with divine power, we are enabled to rejoice even while viewing the comparative failure of the past eighteen centuries, realizing that the labor of the true Elijah class has not been in vain, but has served the divine purpose in developing the true Church while bearing witness before the world—which will profit it in due time.

John the Baptist was not actually Elijah returned to earth, neither is the Church; but as it was true of John, that he did an Elijah work to Israel (Luke 1 : 17) to prepare them, and introduced the Lord in the flesh, so it is true of the Church—it does the predicted Elijah work "in the spirit and power of Elijah" to the world, and announces our Lord's second advent in almost the same words which John used at the first advent: "There standeth one among you whom ye know not. * * * He it is who, coming after me, is superior to me."—John 1 : 26, 27.

All could not receive John's testimony nor realize that he was forerunner to the King in the flesh. Had they done so, they would have been prepared thereby to receive Jesus as their Messiah. To as many of them as could and did accept John's message and receive Christ, to these John *did do* the Elijah work. As our Lord said to them of John (Matt. 11 : 14), "If ye will *receive it*, this is the Elias which was to come;" though John and his work did not complete the prediction concerning Elijah, even as our Lord in the *flesh* did not fulfil all that was predicted of Messiah. He was, to all who could receive it, Jehovah's Anointed, even before he had finished his work of sacrifice, or had been glorified, or had come again in the exercise of the great office of Messiah or Deliverer. John, at the first advent, was really a finishing out, in a measure, of the type begun in the person and work of Elijah; and John's work at the first advent foreshadowed the closing work of the Church at the second advent. These, the feet of Christ in the flesh—the feet of Elijah—announce the Kingdom. (Isa. 52 : 7.) To those who "*can* receive it" we announce, as at hand, the reign of the Christ glorified; and likewise *to those who "can receive it"* we have pointed out the foretold antitypical Elijah. Some, probably, will not "receive it," but will still look for some one man to fulfil Malachi's predictions, and will "know not the time of their visitation" until the great day of trouble is burning as an oven.

It will be seen, then, that the failure of the Elijah (the Christ in the flesh) to convert and restore the world was as much a foreseen result as was John's failure to convert Israel. Nevertheless it will be the same Elijah class, only glorified and empowered, which will during the Millennial age bless and teach the world and restore all things, as promised by the mouth of all the holy prophets (Acts 3:19–21); only in the name and likeness the Elijah type ceases with our earthly career. In harmony with this were our Lord's words in reply to his disciples who asked, "Why then say the scribes that Elijah must first come?" Our Lord's answer does not attempt a full explanation of Elijah's being a type and John a continuation of the same while at the same time a shadowy fulfilment of it, etc.— things which the disciples were not then prepared to understand, and which moreover were not then due to be understood; and hence, while pointing out John's *failure* as a partial fulfilment of the prophecy, our Lord adds, "Elijah truly shall * come, and *restore all things*." (Matt. 17:11.) Evidently he had in mind his own glorious work of the coming age, associated with his glorified "body" which the Gospel age would select and test. He was looking beyond the vail to the Millennial age, and seeing the Elijah class caught up in the chariots of fire in power and great glory—spiritual exaltation.

---

* Oldest Manuscripts omit *first*.

A *woman* is the figure used when the **Church** alone is referred to, separate from her Lord and Head. Separate and distinct from her Lord, the Bridegroom, she is an espoused virgin. But in this instance a man, Elijah, is the figure used, because the work prefigured is not the work of the Church separate from her Lord, but the one work of both. Our Lord was the Head and Forerunner of the Church in the flesh (the Elijah), as truly as he is Head of the Church triumphant—the Christ. Other instances in which a man is the figure used, when a *joint* work of Christ Jesus and his body, the Church, is typified, are numerous: for instance, Aaron and all his successors in the office of Chief Priest represented the Lord and the under priests, members of his body; Melchisedec similarly represented the *whole body* in glory; so did Moses, David and Solomon. Hence the use of Elijah as a figure, in representing a *united* work of Christ and the Church, is in harmony with the Scripture usage.

In view of the class which Elijah represented, how forcibly eloquent was that *"vision"* which the Lord showed to the three disciples on the mount of transfiguration. (Matt. 17 : 1–9.) It was a vision of the coming Kingdom, Peter tells us. (2 Pet. 1 : 16–18.) Our Lord, transfigured, appeared radiant before their eyes, while a figure of Moses represented the Mosaic or Law Dispensation and a figure of Elijah represented the Gospel or Christian Dispensation. Both dispensations look toward and point out and speak of the sacrifice and sufferings of Christ and the glory to follow.

Before leaving this subject we will point out some features and incidents in the life of the Prophet Elijah, the type, comparing them with the history of the Church, the antitypical Elijah, which will certainly astonish all who have not noticed them heretofore. That the comparison may be readily seen, we will place these in parallel columns.

ELIJAH.	THE CHURCH.
Elijah was persecuted for fidelity to truth and righteousness.	The Church was persecuted for fidelity to truth and righteousness.
His principal persecutor was Jezebel, the wicked queen of Israel, who is mentioned by name as the type of the enemy of the saints.—Rev. 2 : 20.	The principal persecutor was the apostate Church of Rome, which claims to be a " queen " and ruler over spiritual Israel.—Rev. 18:7.
Jezebel's persecuting power was exercised through her husband, Ahab, the king.	Papacy's persecuting power was exercised through the Roman Empire, to which she was joined.
Elijah fled from Jezebel and Ahab, into the wilderness, to a place prepared of God, where he was miraculously nourished.—1 Kings 17 : 5-9.	The true Church fled into the symbolic wilderness—or condition of isolation—to her place, prepared of God, where she was sustained.—Rev. 12 : 6, 16.
Elijah was "three years and six months" in the wilderness, and during that time there was no rain, and a great famine was in the land. —James 5 : 17; 1 Kings 17:7; 18 : 2.	The Church was three and a half symbolic years (a day for a year—1260 literal years) in the wilderness condition, during which there was a spiritual famine because of the lack of truth—the living water.—Comp. Rev. 12 : 6; 11 : 3; Amos 8 : 11.
After the three and a half years, 1260 days, when Elijah returned from the wilderness, the errors of Jezebel's priests were manifested, the true God was honored, and copious rains followed.—1 Kings 18 : 41-45.	At the end of the 1260 years the power of the truth and its witnesses was manifested (A. D. 1799) ; and since then the truth has flowed at the rate of millions of Bibles every year, refreshing the world and bringing forth fruit.
The king and the people at first rejoiced, and Elijah and his God were honored; but the spirit of Jezebel was unchanged. She still sought Elijah's life, and he was again compelled to flee into the wilderness.—1 Kings 18 : 40, 45, 46; 19 : 1-4.	The Bible has brought such blessings that the empires of earth recognize the Lord's hand; yet the *principles* of Papacy — Jezebel — in so-called Protestant sects compel the saints again to flee into the wilderness condition.
Elijah's career ended by his being taken from the earth.	The saints will be changed from earthly to heavenly conditions.

These are striking coincidences, and are not accidental. And the fact that Elijah was to come before the great day, and that *now* we have found in the Church the antitypical Elijah to whom Malachi the prophet referred and whom John the Baptist further typified, should be esteemed *another* evidence that the time is at hand—that the great Day of the Lord has come. But, beyond this, there are in this type suggestions, supported by other scriptures, designed to guide and to prepare the saints to act well their part, and to strengthen and sustain them in the stormy day just upon us.

We have no desire to draw before the mind a dark picture: we would prefer to think of and point out the glory to follow the great day of wrath, and the joys of the incoming Millennial Day, rather than the afflictions and discouragements of the nearer future which precedes full sunrise. But it is necessary that the saints should be at least in some measure forewarned of impending events, that when such come to pass they may not be alarmed or disheartened, but being fore-armed may know how to meet them; and also that they may more fully appreciate the blessings of the present, so as diligently to "work while it is *called* day; for the night [a much darker time in comparison with the present, *called* day] cometh, *wherein no man* CAN WORK."

The present little season, before the storm-cloud bursts upon the world, is a most favorable time for the work of the Elijah class, and corresponds to the successful days of both Elijah and John. It is favorable for personal growth in grace and knowledge, and also for the spread of the truth— the most favorable time that has ever been known. How the early truth-seekers, the Bereans, for instance, would have rejoiced at such students'-helps as we now possess, in the way of complete and printed Reference Bibles, Concordances, Histories, Cyclopædias, Dictionaries and other valuable works of reference, at prices within the reach of all, and ac-

17–B

cessible to all without price in the public libraries of even moderate-sized towns ; and in addition to all these, the increasing light of the dawning Millennial day, and the ability of all classes to read and think intelligently for themselves. With such helps more can be learned of God's Word and plan in a day than it was possible to learn in a year in less favored times. Nor has there ever been a time so favorable for Christian effort, or so spurring to Christian zeal and activity, as this time of the glorious harvest message of the Lord's presence and the glad tidings of the approaching kingdom.

If we would travel from place to place, to meet with believers, we can do as much traveling in a week as Paul could do in a month or more, and with much more comfort. If we would preach by voice, we can do so with none to molest or make us afraid ; and we live at a time when the masses of the people can read and write, which only the very few could do in times past, and when the printed gospel is cheap, convenient, and often more effective than oral sermons. The willing heart can do far more thus than Aquila and Priscilla could do in their way and time with the same amount of effort. We can preach with both the printed and the written page through the agency of the wonderful mail systems of our day, to friends and strangers the world over, and at almost no cost.

But the Apostle, referring to the nominal Church in the last days, asserts that " the time will come when they *will not endure* sound doctrine." (2 Tim. 4: 3.) While this is true now, in the same sense that it has been true for centuries, it is to have a more forcible and clear fulfilment future. It is true now that the Church nominal will not endure preachers who ignore their creeds and " preach the Word," the " whole counsel [plan] of God;" but having " itching ears " they love human speculations on evolution, and philosophies falsely so called, rather than the Word of God.

And yet, because they cannot hinder it, they endure the sound doctrine to some extent—to an extent far beyond what Rome in her palmy days would have endured.

Just before the words we have here cited, the Apostle refers directly to the perilous times of the last days of this age (2 Tim. 3 : 1–13), pointing out its high-minded, pleasure-loving and good-despising characteristics, with its formalism, covetousness, pride and unthankfulness; and he declares that (*in the Church*) evil men and leaders-astray [from the truth] shall grow worse and worse, deceiving others, and being deceived themselves by their sophistries. And since the Apostle was thinking and writing specially about the last days, and not about the middle ages, we are surely justified in querying whether a time may not be but a short distance before us, in these "last days," when sound doctrine will not be *endured* or permitted to any degree.

While it is true now, to a large extent, that none are permitted to buy or sell [trade in the truth] in the common marts or synagogues, except those who have the mark of the beast or the number of his name (Rev. 13 : 17), yet the fully consecrated have learned that magnificent temples of fashion, called churches, are no more necessary to the preaching of the gospel now than they were in the days of the Apostles, and that grand organs and trained choirs are not necessary accompaniments to attract the attention of the people ; for now, as in the early days, the common people hear the gospel gladly on the street corners, in the market places, through the mails and from the printed page. The question is, May not this statement of the Revelator mean still more than is at present experienced? and, like the Apostle Paul's statement, may it not imply that a time will come, in the last days, when sound doctrine will not be *endured at all*? May not ours in this respect correspond somewhat to the experience of John the Baptist (the

type), who was shut up in prison? In other words, What may
we expect between the present comparatively favorable time
—though it is not without its difficulties—and the coming
blessed time of unhindered righteousness? Will it continue
to be as favorable as the present for labor in the vineyard—
or more so, or less so? Let us notice what these types indicate; for since our Lord has directed our attention to
them, whatever we find in the life and experience of either
Elijah or John which seems to fit well to the experience
of the Church, and to the testimony regarding her future
earthly course, we are justified in recognizing as typical.

Elijah was separated from earthly scenes by a chariot of
fire, representative of the spiritual glory and exaltation
awaiting, at the end of the earthly race-course, those of the
Church alive and remaining to the last days. But we should
also remember that it was by a whirlwind or storm that he
was taken away; and a storm is the symbol of trouble, as
much as the fiery chariot is a figure of victory and glorious
escape from that trouble.

John the Baptist's closing experiences are still more
clearly marked by the trouble feature. Though he was not
obeyed by the people (Matt. 17:12), they for a short time
recognized him as a servant and prophet of God (John 5:35);
yet when he had announced the presence of Messiah his
influence soon began to wane, as he had testified it would
do, saying of Christ, "He must increase, but I must decrease." So it must be in the end of this age: the work
of the John class (the Elijah class) closes with the announcement that the Kingdom of Heaven is at hand, and
that the King is present. This is now being done; and the
exact words of John's testimony apply with equal force at
this time of the Lord's second advent: "There standeth
one *among you* [present] whom ye know not," " whose fan
is in his hand, and he will thoroughly purge [cleanse] his

[threshing] floor, and gather his wheat into the garner; but he will burn up the chaff with unquenchable fire"—the great time of trouble.—John 1:26; Matt. 3:12.

As John decreased—his special work being accomplished when his message was delivered—so the Church in the flesh must decrease when its last message is given, until the last member has laid down his consecrated life, and passed beyond the veil into "glory," thenceforth to be a member of the glorious, reigning Christ. As John said that Jesus must increase, so now that the real kingdom is about to be established we can confidently say that the King is present, and that his kingdom must increase until it fills the earth. And John's announcement of the "harvest" work —the gathering of the wheat, and the trouble coming upon the chaff—also finds its parallel in the present time.

John's liberty was restrained soon after the delivery of his message, announcing the *present One* and the work before him; and he was cast into prison because he had reproved the king of improper union with a woman (Matt. 14:4). And though the faithful children of God have often pointed out that union between the Church and the civil power is out of order, being in the Scriptures termed harlotry (Rev. 17:5), and though in a great measure the world has withdrawn from the churches, the union still exists, and the Scriptures seem to point out that, in the time of trouble approaching, the nominal churches, professedly virgins of Christ, will be on the side of the kings of the earth, and united to them; and the true Church, like its type, John the Baptist, will be unpopular and restrained of liberty, because of faithfulness in opposing and condemning error.

In John's case as well as in Elijah's it was a woman that persecuted,—a king acting as her agent and tool: with the true Church it has been in the past that which these symbolize, and doubtless will be so in the future—the nominal church represented by a woman and civil government by a king. Not only does prophecy point out a closer union between these than at present exists, but any close observer can see that the principal *lever* by which the royal aristocracy rules the masses is the superstition that God appointed these "great men," though often both weak and vicious, to rule over them ; and that to rebel against tyranny and injustice, and to claim justice, liberty and equal rights, is to oppose God's will. Hence the tendency of governments and churches is toward open or secret union for their mutual welfare in the coming storm.

Not only so, but the coming struggle between the aristocracy and the masses of every civilized land will be so peculiar, so unlike any former experience, that moderate, conservative, religiously-inclined people, fearing the utter wreck of society in chaos and anarchy, will naturally prefer monarchy, oppression and bondage to anything certain to be worse. Hence such will affiliate with church and empire, with wealth and aristocracy, in the general effort to repress and prevent that irrepressible conflict —"The battle of the great day of God Almighty."

Eventually, probably the only exceptions to this course, among the lovers of peace and true religion, will be those to whom the King of kings is pleased, through his Word, to reveal his plans (John 16 : 13), and who have full confidence in his wisdom and love, as well as in his power to make all things work out according to his promises. Only such, among the conservative, order-loving people, as see the part which the coming social revolution *must* play in God's plan, in removing effete systems whose day is past, and in preparing the world, by a great leveling process, for the Millennial reign of righteousness, will be able to comprehend the situation and to act accordingly. But these will be misunderstood, and their endeavors to point out the true state of the case, and the real and only remedy, will probably be interfered with by those who do not see the grand outcome, and who, because unwilling to submit their own wills, ideas and plans, are unable to see God's plans. When repressive, restrictive and coercive measures are thought to be necessary, such measures will probably include not only labor organizations and the publications which advocate their rights and wrongs, but also such others as point out the plan of God, and the real cause and only remedy for the great distress of the nations. Yes, the time is probably not many years distant, when repressive measures may be brought to bear against every effort of the saints to spread the good news of the coming kingdom, all on the plea that the general interests and the public welfare demand such a course.

Thus would be fulfilled the predictions of the Second Psalm, and probably in the end with more bitterness than can now well be imagined, though it has been partially fulfilled already upon the Head of the body.—Acts 4: 25–29.

The same necessity for restricting liberty on political and social questions will probably be supposed to apply equally to freedom of expression on religious questions, which really lie at the foundation of all liberty. It would not be surprising if a "strong government," a monarchy, would some day replace this present Great Republic; and it is entirely probable that one common standard of religious belief will be deemed expedient and will be promulgated, to teach outside of which will be treated and punished as a political offense. Such a persecution would not only furnish, in the end or harvest of this age, another parallel to the harvest of the Jewish age (Acts 4: 10–13, 23–30; 5: 29–41; 11: 19), but would also give a wider and deeper significance to the words of the Apostles Paul and John (2 Tim. 4:3; Rev. 13: 17), and to the typical illustrations of the close of the earthly career of the true Church, as represented in Elijah's whirlwind departure and John the Baptist's imprisonment and beheading.

Two lessons we may draw from this to advantage, whether future developments shall prove that we have read the prophetic testimony correctly or incorrectly; and they are these: First, we should be so prepared, so armed and so thoroughly furnished with the invincible truth, that persecution would move us only to greater zeal, and not lead us through surprise or fear to lower our standard, nor to surrender when the kings of the earth stand up, and, with the religious rulers of the people, are gathered against us, and against the truths to which God has granted us the privilege of witnessing, as his servants and ambassadors. (1 John 3:1.) Second, such reflections relative to the future, contrasted with the privileges of the present, should serve to stimulate every consecrated child of God to make diligent use of the present grand harvest opportunities and privileges, remembering that "he that reapeth receiveth wages," as truly as he that planted and watered, and that now is pre-eminently a time for *gathering fruit* unto eternal life. The little quiet of the present favorable time, with its greater liberties and advantages in every way, is divinely arranged in order to the sealing of the true servants of God in their foreheads (intellectually, with the truth).—Rev. 7:3.

> "Let the 'little while' between
> In its golden light be seen."

The Master saith: "Work while it is *called* day; for the night cometh, when no man can work." "Labor not for the meat that perisheth, but for that which endureth unto everlasting life."

So, then, in the present due time, we see that Elijah the prophet came, as foretold, before the great and notable day of the Lord. And we hear his closing testimony, like that ot John, saying, "There standeth one among you whom ye know not"—whose fan is in his hand, and he will thoroughly cleanse his threshing-floor: he will gather his wheat into the garner, and burn up the tares [as tares—not as men] with unquenchable fire in the great time of trouble—the curse, which must needs come to prepare the way of the Great King of kings. He must increase, but the Elijah must decrease and finally be entirely restrained. Not only do we hear this testimony from a few of the Elijah class now, but every one who is of the Elijah class will ere long be found proclaiming this message and engaging in the Elijah work. Such only as are thus faithful will be of the glorified Elijah, and permitted to share in the work of restitution of all things which, during the Millennium, will be a grand success. A depth of significance is found in the meaning of the name *Elijah*. It signifies *God* [mighty-one] *of Jehovah*. It is thus a fitting name for the Lord's Anointed, whose grand work will be to restore all things which God hath spoken by the mouth of all his holy prophets since the world began.

Concluding this subject, we notice briefly the fact that in the close of the Prophet Elijah's career he called Elisha, who, after sacrificing, left all and followed with Elijah, and became his successor as prophet when Elijah was taken away in the whirlwind—receiving his mantle of authority and a large degree of his spirit and power. (1 Kings 19: 16.) And since Elijah represented the Body of Christ in the flesh—the overcoming Church, a company, a number —it is but reasonable that we should conclude that Elisha represented a class also; a class which will come into deep sympathy with the Elijah class, and follow the Lord's leading with it; and yet a class which will not be expecting to be glorified. These will be separated, by the "whirlwind" of trouble, from the Elijah class, yet nevertheless will retain an interest and will receive a blessing. After Elijah was gone, Elisha became bold and powerful, so that the theologians of that day ("sons of the prophets") said, The spirit of Elijah rests upon Elisha now!

The meaning of the name *Elisha* is *mighty deliverer*, and the career of Elisha was one of restitution work. This doubtless foreshadows a work by a class which in the future will be the active agents among men in carrying on the restitution work in the power of the then glorified Church. Among other wonderful works, Elisha healed the waters, so that there should not be thence any more death or barren land; he increased the poor widow's oil to cancel her debt; he raised the Shunamite's son to life; and when there was famine in the land, and the mess of pottage for the theologians ("sons of the prophets") was found to be poisoned, so that none could eat of it, Elisha healed it and made it wholesome for food. He caused bread sufficient for only a few to more than supply a large number. He healed the leprosy of Naaman. He was also God's agent in the anointing of Jehu, at whose hands, according to the word of the Lord by Elijah, the royal family of Ahab, including Jezebel, was entirely cut off, and all her priests as well.—2 Kings 2 : 19–22 ; 4 : 1–7, 18–44 ; 5 : 1–10 ; 9 : 1–37 ; 10 : 28.

It is not difficult to trace in these works of Elisha what bears a close resemblance to the very restitution work which may be expected ere long, when the waters of truth shall no longer be brackish with error, being healed at the very spring by a clearer understanding of the Word of God; when the poor shall be helped to secure the oil of joy for the spirit of heaviness; when the dead shall be restored; when in the famine the food (truth) shall be made wholesome and plentiful; and when the powers and systems represented by Ahab and Jezebel, and all who unite with them against the Lord, shall be fully and finally overthrown.

STUDY IX.

THE MAN OF SIN—ANTICHRIST.

Antichrist Must be Developed, Revealed and Smitten Before the Day of the Lord.—A Contrary View of This Subject Considered.—Prophetic Delineation.—Antichrist's Birth.—His Rapid Development.—The Historic Picture and the Bible Description Agree.—His Kingdom a Counterfeit.—His Head and Mouth Notable.—His Great Swelling Words of Blasphemy.—His Blasphemous Teachings.—His Wearing Out of the Saints of the Most High.—His Millennial Reign.—Antichrist Smitten with the Sword of the Spirit.—His Final Struggle and End.

"Let no man deceive you by any means; for that day shall not come, except there come a falling away first, and that Man of Sin be revealed, the Son of Perdition."— 2 Thes. 2 : 3.

IN VIEW of these pointed words of the Apostle Paul, showing that a character which he designates "The Man of Sin must precede the coming of the Day of the Lord, which we have proved has already begun to dawn, it is important that we look about, to see if such a character has yet appeared. For if such a character as Paul and the other apostles so carefully describe has not yet come, the above words should be understood as Paul's veto to all the other testimony concerning the Lord's presence and the setting up of his Kingdom *now*. And that veto must stand as an unanswerable argument until this Man of Sin shall be recognized, corresponding in every particular to the prophetic description.

It is clearly stated, not only that this Man of Sin must first rise, but that he must develop and prosper, before the

Day of the Lord comes.   *Before* Christ's day the prosperity
and influence of this power will have reached their climax
and will be on the decline ; and it is to be by the bright
shining of the Lord's *presence* at his second advent that
this Man of Sin shall be utterly destroyed.   These foretold circumstances we must observe, in order to see whether
this caution to the Church in Paul's day is still applicable
in our day.   Now, after eighteen centuries, the claim is
again made that the day of Christ has come ; and the important question arises, Does anything which Paul said in
correcting the error of the Thessalonians stand as an objection to this claim now ?

From the Apostle's exhortations to the Church, to watch
for the Lord's return, taking heed to the sure word of prophecy, and from his care in pointing out the signs of Christ's
presence, the character of his work at that time, etc., it is
evident that he was quite as anxious that the Church
should be able to recognize the Lord's presence when he
should come, as that they should not be deceived into the
error that he had come, before the time of his presence.
A fall into the latter error, in the early part of the age,
exposed those who embraced it to the deceptions of the
Antichrist *principle* which was even then working ; while a
failure to recognize the Day of the Lord, and his presence
in the day when his presence is due, exposes those failing
to recognize him to the continued deceptions and false
doctrines of Antichrist, and blinds them to the grand
truths and special privileges of this day.   Hence the Apostle's anxiety for the Church at both ends of the age, and
his warning —"Let no man deceive you by any means."
Hence also the exact description of the Man of Sin, in
order that he might be recognized in his time.

While Christians in this end of the age are inclined to
forget even the promise of the Lord's return, and, when

they do remember it, to think of it only with dread and fearful forebodings, the early Church looked for it anxiously, and with joyful anticipation, as the fruition of all its hopes, the reward of all its faithfulness and the end of all its sorrows. Consequently, the believers of that day were ready to hearken diligently to any teaching which claimed that the Day of the Lord was either very near or present; and hence they were in danger of being deceived on this point unless they were careful students of the teachings of the apostles on the subject.

The Church at Thessalonica, impressed with the erroneous teachings of some, to the effect that the Lord had come again, and that they were living in his day, evidently supposed that the idea was in harmony with Paul's teaching in his first epistle to them, wherein he said (1 Thes. 5:1–5) that the Day of the Lord would steal on quietly and unobservedly, as a thief in the night, and that, though others would be in it unawares, the saints would be in the light concerning it. Learning of the serious error into which they had fallen, of supposing the day of the Lord's presence to have already come, Paul wrote them a second epistle, the central thought of which was the correction of this error. He says:—"Now we beseech you, brethren, concerning the coming of our Lord Jesus Christ and our gathering together unto him, that ye be not readily agitated in mind nor troubled; neither by spirit, neither by word, neither by letter as from us, as though the Day of the Lord [*enestemi*] *is present.* Let no man delude you, by any means; because the falling away [apostasy] *must first come,* and there must be revealed that Man of Sin, the Son of Destruction, the Opposer, exalting himself above all, being called a god [mighty ruler] or that receives homage—so as to seat himself in the Temple of God, openly displaying himself that he is a god. Remember ye not that while I was yet with you I told you these things? And now ye know what interposes, in order that he [Christ] may be revealed in his own [due] season. But insubordination [to Christ] is already working, only as a secret thing, until the now hindering one shall be out of the way; and *then* shall that insubordinate one be revealed, whom the Lord shall kill with the spirit of his mouth and annihilate by the bright shining of his [*parousia*] *presence.*" Paul could write thus positively of the development of the Man of Sin before the Day of the Lord, because of his study of Daniel's prophecy, to which our Lord also referred (Matt. 24: 15); and probably because Paul himself, in his "visions and revelations," had been shown the great havoc which this character would work in the Church.

It should be observed that Paul did not use arguments such as some to-day are disposed to use against the claim that the day of the Lord has begun. He did not say, O foolish Thessalonians, do ye not know that when Christ comes your eyes shall behold him, and your ears shall hear a dreadful sound of the trump of God? and that you will have further proof of it in the reeling tombstones and the rising saints? Is it not evident that if such a criticism had been proper, Paul would have been quick to avail himself of an argument so simple and so easily grasped? And moreover, is not the fact that he did not use this argument a proof that such an argument is not, and could not be, founded on the truth?

From the fact that Paul, in his energetic effort to correct their error, offered but this one objection to their claim, he thereby evidently endorsed as correct their general ideas of the Day of the Lord—that it could be commenced while many might be in ignorance of it, that it could come without outward demonstration to mark it. But the only ground of his objection was, that there must *first* come a falling away, and, in consequence of that falling away, the development of the Man of Sin—which, whatever it may be (whether a single individual, or a great Antichrist system which he thus personifies), must rise, flourish and begin to decline—*before* the day of the Lord's presence. So, then, if this one objection which Paul offered be no longer in the way—if we can clearly see a character in actual existence whose history corresponds in every particular to the prophetic description of the Man of Sin, from the beginning of his existence down to the present time—then Paul's objection, which was well taken in his day, and his only one, is no longer a valid objection against the present claim that we are living in the Day of the Lord, the day of the Lord's presence. And, further, if the Man of Sin can be readily distinguished, if his rise, development and decline are clearly seen, then this fact becomes another corroborative proof of the teaching of the preceding chapters, which show that we are now in the Day of the Lord.

HIS PROPHETIC DELINEATION.

The student of prophecy will find that the Man of Sin is distinctly noted throughout the sacred writings, not only by giving a clear description of his character, but also by showing the times and places of his beginning, prosperity and decline.

This character is very forcibly delineated even in the names applied to it by the inspired writers. Paul calls it "That Wicked One," "The Man of Sin," "The Mystery of Iniquity," "The Antichrist," and "The Son of Perdition;" the Prophet Daniel calls it "The Abomination that maketh desolate" (Dan. 11 : 31 ; 12 : 11) ; and our Lord refers to the same character as "The Abomination of Desolation, spoken of by Daniel the prophet" (Matt. 24 : 15), and again as a "Beast" (Rev. 13 : 1–8). This same char-after was also prefigured by a little horn, or power, out of a terrible beast that Daniel saw in his prophetic vision, which had eyes, and a mouth that spoke great things, and which prospered and made war with the saints, and prevailed against them. (Dan. 7 : 8, 21.) John also saw and warned the Church against this character, saying, "Ye have heard that Antichrist shall come." He then advises how to escape Antichrist's influence. (1 John 2 :18–27.) The book of Revelation, too, is in large part a detailed symbolic prophecy concerning this same Antichrist—though this we shall merely glance at here, leaving its more particular examination for a succeeding volume.

These various appellations and brief descriptions indicate a base, subtle, hypocritical, deceptive, tyrannical and cruel character, developed in the midst of the Christian Church ; at first creeping in and up very gradually, then rapidly ascending in power and influence until it reaches the very pinnacle of earthly power, wealth and glory—meanwhile exerting its influence against the truth, and against the saints, and for its own aggrandizement, claiming, to the last, peculiar sanctity and authority and power from God.

In this chapter we purpose to show that this Man of Sin is a system, and not a single individual, as many seem to infer ; that as the Christ consists of the true Lord and the true Church, so Antichrist is a counterfeit system consisting of a false lord and an apostate church, which for a time is permitted to misrepresent the truth, to practice deceit and to *counterfeit* the authority and future reign of the true Lord and his Church, and to intoxicate the nations with false claims and assumptions.

We hope to prove, to the satisfaction of every conscientious reader, that this great apostasy or falling away mentioned by Paul has come, and that this Man of Sin has been developed, has sat "in the temple of God" (the real, not the typical), has fulfilled all the predictions of the apostles and prophets concerning his character, work, etc., has been revealed, and now, since A. D. 1799, is being consumed by the spirit of the Lord's mouth (the truth), and will be *utterly destroyed* during this day of the Lord's wrath and revelation with flaming fire of retribution, already beginning.

Without any desire to treat lightly the opinions of others, we nevertheless feel it necessary to point out to the reader a few of the absurdities connected with the common view concerning Antichrist, that thereby the dignity and reasonableness of the truth on this subject may be properly estimated, in contrast with the narrow claim that all which the Scriptures predict concerning this character will be accomplished by some one literal *man*. This man, it is claimed, will so charm the whole world that in a few short years he will secure to himself the homage and *worship* of all men, who will be so easily imposed upon as to suppose this man to be God, and, in a rebuilt Jewish temple, to worship him as the Almighty Jehovah. All this is to be done at lightning speed,—three and a half years, say they, misinterpreting the symbolic time, even as they misinterpret the symbolic "man."

Tales of fiction and the most absurd imaginations of childhood furnish no parallel to the extreme views of some of God's dear children who are stumbling over a *literal* interpretation of Paul's language, and thereby blinding themselves and others to many precious truths, which, because of error on this subject, they are unprepared to see in an unprejudiced light. No matter how much we may sympathize with them, their "blind faith" forces a smile as they seriously tell over the various symbols of Revelation which they do not understand, misapplying them literally to their *wonderful man*. In this, the most skeptical age the world has ever known, he will, they claim, in the short space of

18–B

three and a half years, have the whole world at his feet, worshiping him as God, while the Cæsars, Alexander, Napoleon, Mahomet and others sailed through bloody seas and spent many times three and a half years, without accomplishing the one thousandth part of what is claimed for this *man*.

And yet those conquerors had all the advantages of dense ignorance and superstition to aid them, while to-day we live under conditions most unfavorable to such a development of deceit and fraud : in a day when every *hidden* thing is being manifested as never before ; in a day when fraud of the sort claimed is too preposterous and ridiculous for consideration.   Indeed, the tendency of our day is toward a lack of respect for men, no matter how good, talented and able, or what offices of trust and authority they may occupy.   To such an extent is this true, as never before, that it is a thousand times more likely that the whole world will deny that there is *any God*, than that they will ever worship a fellow human being as the Almighty God.

One great obstacle to many, in considering this subject, is the contracted idea generally entertained of the meaning of the word *god*.   They fail to note that the Greek *theos* (*god*) does not invariably refer to Jehovah.   It signifies a *mighty one*, a ruler, and especially a religious or sacerdotal ruler.   In the New Testament, *theos* is seldom used except in referring to Jehovah, because, in their discourses, the apostles spoke rarely and little of the false systems of religion, and hence seldom noticed their sacred rulers or gods ; yet in the following texts the word *god* (*theos*) is used to refer to others than the one supreme being, Jehovah—viz.: John 10:34,35 ; Acts 7:40, 43 ; 17:23 ; 1 Cor. 8:5.

Recognizing the breadth of the Greek word *theos*, it will be seen at once that the Apostle's statement concerning Antichrist—that he will seat himself in the temple of God, showing himself to be *a god*—does not of necessity mean that Antichrist will attempt to exalt himself above Jehovah, nor even that he will attempt to take Jehovah's place. It simply implies that this one will exhibit himself as a religious ruler, claiming and exercising authority over and above all other religious rulers, even to the extent of exalting himself in the Church, which is the true Temple of God, and there claiming and exercising lordly authority as its chief or authorized ruler. Wherever in the Greek the word *theos* is used in any sentence where its meaning would be ambiguous, it then is preceded by the Greek article, if it refers to Jehovah; as if in English we were to say *the* God. In the texts above, which refer to *other* gods, and in this text (2 Thes. 2:4), which refers to Antichrist, there is no such emphasis.

With this seen clearly, a great stumbling-block is removed, and the mind is prepared to look for the right things as fulfilments of this prediction: not for an Antichrist claiming to be Jehovah and demanding worship as such, but for one claiming to be the chief, supreme religious teacher in the Church; who thus attempts the usurpation of the authority of Christ, the divinely appointed Head, Lord and Teacher.

Strangely enough, too, they who take this literal view of the Man of Sin are generally those who are believers in the Lord's premillennial coming, who are looking for and expecting the Lord to come "*at any moment now.*" Why cannot all see the Apostle's meaning, when he positively declares that the Day of the Lord (the Day of his presence) cannot come and should not be expected until after the Man of Sin has been revealed? It required over forty years to build the former Jewish temple, and it would surely require at least ten to twenty years to build, with more than former magnificence, the new temple at Jerusalem, where they expect a literal Man of Sin to be installed and worshiped as God. Why then should those who believe thus expect the Lord to come *at any moment now ?* Such a view is out of harmony with reason as well as with the Apostle's prophecy. Consistency demands that they should either give up looking for the Lord at any moment, or else give up their expectation of a future Man of Sin; for the Day of the Lord's presence cannot come until the falling away (the apostasy) has taken place, and until the Man of Sin has been developed and revealed out of that apostasy.

But when we get a correct view of the Apostle's words, together with correct ideas of the *manner* of the Lord's coming, we find no such discrepancies and contradictions, but a convincing harmony and fitness. And such a view we now present. Its Scripturalness the reader must prove.

The various titles applied to this system are evidently symbolic. They do not refer as names to a single individual, but as character delineations to a corrupt religious and civil combination, developed within the nominal Christian church, which, by its subtle opposition to Christ, the Head, and his true Church, his body, well earns the name *Antichrist*. Such a *system* could fulfil all the predictions made concerning the Antichrist, or Man of Sin, though an individual could not. It is evident, moreover, that this Antichrist system is not one of the heathen systems of religion, such as Mohammedanism or Brahminism; for the Christian Church has never been under the control of any such system, nor did any of these systems originate in the Christian Church. They now are, and always have been, independent of the Christian Church.

The system which fully answers the description given by inspiration must be professedly Christian, and must contain a large majority of those who claim to be Christians. And it must be one having its start as an apostasy, or falling away from the true Christian faith—an apostasy, too, which was secret and stealthy, until circumstances favored its assumption of power. Its stealthy beginning was in the days of the apostles,—in the desire of some teachers to be greatest.

We need not look long to find a character fitting all the requirements perfectly; one whose record, written by secular historians as well as by its own deluded servants, we shall see agrees exactly with the prophetic delineations of Antichrist. But when we state that the one and only system whose history fits these prophecies is Papacy, let no one misunderstand us to mean that every Roman Catholic is a man of sin; nor that the priests, nor even the popes of the Church of Rome, are, or have been, the Antichrist. No *man* is "*the* Antichrist," "the Man of Sin," described in prophecy. Popes, bishops and others are at most only parts or members of the Antichrist system, even as all of the Royal Priests are only members of the true Christ, under Jesus their head, and in the same manner that these in their present condition are together the antitypical Elijah, though no one of them is the Elijah or the Christ foretold. Notice, further, that the Church of Rome as an ecclesiastical system only is not the "*Man* of Sin," and is never presented under any figure of a *man*. On the contrary, a *woman* is always the symbol used for a church separate from its head and lord. The true Church is symbolized by a "chaste virgin," while the apostate church, which has fallen away from primitive purity and fidelity to the Lord, is symbolically called "a harlot." As the true "virgin" Church continues to be such to the end of the age, when she is to be united to her Lord and take his name—Christ—so the apostate church was not the Antichrist, or Man of Sin, until she united with her lord and head, the pope, the claimed vicegerent of Christ, and became a religious *empire*, falsely styled Christendom,—which signifies Christ's Kingdom.

Papacy is the name of this false kingdom; and it was built upon a misapplied truth—the truth that the Church is called to be kings and priests unto God and to reign on the earth. But the time for reigning had not yet come: the Gospel age was not appointed for that purpose, but for the selection, development, discipline, humiliation and sacrifice of the Church, following in the foot-prints of her Lord and patiently waiting and enduring until the time appointed for the promised exaltation and glorious reign— the Millennial age.

The Lord foresaw that nominal Christianity would spread over the world, and that, becoming popular, it would be embraced by many who would appreciate the form without entering into the spirit of its institution. He foresaw that as numbers of this sort would identify themselves with the Church, the worldly spirit, which is the opposite of the spirit of self-denial and self-sacrifice, would come in with them; that selfishness and a desire to be great and to rule, thus coming in, would not have long to wait until they could seize an opportunity; and that thus the Church would seek to dominate the world before the time—or, rather, that the worldly element which would enter the Church would make its influence felt, and *in the name* of the true Church would grasp the civil power of earth which God had given over to the Gentiles, and which cannot pass fully into the hands of the true Church until the close of the Times of the Gentiles, A. D. 1914.

And thus it actually transpired: the nominal church began to fall away as it increased in numbers under the teaching and example of ambitious men whose ideas grew more and more favorable to the power and worldly influence which numbers and wealth brought with them. Gradually the spirit of the Church became worldly, and the things of the world were coveted. The suggestion of ambition was,— "If the great Roman Empire, with all its power and influence, its armies and wealth, were only to support the

Church, how honorable and noble it would then be to be a Christian! How speedily then would heathen persecutions cease! Then it would be in our power not only to overawe them, but to compel their adherence to the Church and cross and name of Christ. It evidently is not God's design that the Church should forever be subject to the world and persecuted by it: the Apostle's words, 'Know ye not that the saints shall judge the world?' as well as our Lord's promises that we shall reign with him, and the many prophecies which refer to the reign of the Church, indicate clearly that such is God's plan. True, the Apostle wrote that our Lord would first return and exalt the Church, and exhorted that we should *"wait"* for the Lord; but several centuries are now past, and we see no sign of the Lord's coming. We must understand that the apostles were to some extent in error. To us it seems clear that we can and should use every means to obtain a hold upon civil government and conquer the world for the Lord. It must be, too, that the Church should have a *head*—one to represent the absent Lord and to represent the Church before the world—one who would receive the homage of the world, exercise the authority of Christ, and rule the world with a rod of iron, as the Prophet David predicted." Thus gradually by a slow process of reasoning covering centuries, the real hope of the Church for exaltation to rule and bless the world—namely, the second coming of the Lord —was lost sight of, and a new hope took its place: the hope of success without the Lord, under the headship and lead of a line of popes. And thus, by collusion, intriguing and exchange of favors with the world, the hope of the Church became a false hope, a delusive snare by which Satan led from one evil and error to another, both of doctrine and of practice.

The point at which the apostasy developed into the "Man of Sin" was when the Papal hierarchy exalted itself under the headship of an arranged line of popes, and claimed and attempted the rulership of earth in the name of, and pretending to be, Christ's Millennial Kingdom. It was a false, fraudulent claim, no matter how thoroughly some of its supporters believed it. It was a fraudulent, counterfeit kingdom, no matter how sincere some of its organizers and supporters may have been. It was Antichrist's, no matter how much they claimed and believed it to be the true Christ's glory and kingdom and power upon earth. It is a mistake to suppose that to be conscientious is always to be right. Every system of error doubtless has as many conscientiously deluded votaries as it has hypocrites, or more. Conscientiousness is moral honesty, and it is not dependent upon knowledge. The heathen, misinformed, conscientiously worship and sacrifice to idols; Saul, misinformed, conscientiously persecuted the saints; and so, too, many papists, misinformed, conscientiously did violence to the prophecies, persecuted the true saints and organized the great system of Antichrist. For hundreds of years Papacy has not only deceived the kings of the earth as to its power and claimed divine authority, and ruled over them, but even in the Church, God's Temple, where Christ alone should be recognized as Head and Teacher, it has seated itself and claimed to be the only teacher and lawgiver; and here it has deceived all, except the few, by its phenomenal success and boastful claims. "All the world wondered"— were astonished, deceived, bewildered—"whose names were not written in the Lamb's book of life," and many whose names are written as saints of God were seriously perplexed. And this deception is the stronger because of the very gradual formation of these ambitious designs and their yet more gradual realization. It extended over centuries, and, as an ambition, was already secretly at work in Paul's day. It was a process of little by little adding error to error,—the supplementing of one man's ambitious declarations by those of another and another farther down the stream of time. Thus, insidiously, did Satan plant and water the seeds of error, and develop the greatest and most influential system the world has ever known—Antichrist.

The name "Antichrist" has a twofold significance. The first is *against* (*i. e.*, in opposition to) Christ: the second significance is *instead* (*i. e.*, a counterfeit) of Christ. In the first sense the expression is a general one, which would apply to any enemy opposing Christ. In this sense Saul (afterward called Paul), and every Jew, and every Mohammedan, and all the Pagan emperors and people of Rome, were antichrists—opposers of Christ. (Acts 9:4.) But it is not in this sense of the word that the Scriptures use the name *Antichrist*. They pass over all such enemies, and apply the term *Antichrist* in the sense given above, as now its secondary meaning, viz.,—as *against*, in the sense of misrepresenting, counterfeiting, *taking the place of* the true Christ. Thus John remarks, "Ye have heard that *the* Antichrist shall come. Even now there are many antichrists." (1 John 2:18, 19.) [The Greek distinguishes between *the* special Antichrist and the numerous lesser ones.] And John's subsequent remarks show that he does not refer to all opposers of Christ and the Church, but to a certain class who, still professing to be of the Christ body, the Church, had left the foundation principles of the truth, and were therefore not only misrepresenting the truth, but were, in the eyes of the world, taking the place and name of the true Church—hence really counterfeiting the true saints. John says of these, "They went out from us, but they were not of us:" they do not represent us, even though they may deceive themselves and the world on this subject. In the same epistle John declares that those he mentions as many antichrists have the spirit of *the* Antichrist.

Here, then, is what we should expect, and what we do find in Papacy: not an opposition to the *name* of Christ, but an enemy or opponent of Christ in that it falsely bears his name, counterfeits his kingdom and authority, and misrepresents his character and plans and doctrines before the world—a most baneful enemy and opponent indeed—worse far than an outspoken foe. And this is true, be it remembered, even though some of those connected with that system are conscientiously astray—"deceiving and being deceived."

With these intimations as to the identity and characteristics of the Man of Sin, and when, and where, and under what circumstances, to look for him, we shall proceed to an examination of some of the historic evidences, proving, we think beyond reasonable question, that every prediction concerning the Antichrist has been fulfilled in the Papal system, in a manner and to an extent which, with the enlightenment of this day taken into account, all must admit could never be repeated. Space obliges us here to confine ourselves to a mere outline of the great mass of historic testimony. We have also confined ourselves to historians of recognized accuracy, in many instances going to Roman Catholic writers for their testimony or admissions.

THE CIRCUMSTANCES WHICH GAVE BIRTH TO THE MAN OF SIN.

A GREAT FALLING AWAY.—We first inquire, Does history record a fulfilment of Paul's prophecy of a great falling away from the original simplicity and purity of the doctrines and life of the Christian Church, and of the secret working of an iniquitous, ambitious influence in the Church, prior to the development of Papacy, the Man of Sin—*i. e.*, prior to the recognition of a pope as the head of the Church?

Yes, very clearly: The Papal Hierarchy did not come into existence for several centuries after the Lord and the Apostles had founded the Church. And of the interval between, we read*:—

"As the church grew in numbers and wealth, costly edifices were constructed for worship; the services became more elaborate; sculpture and painting were enlisted in the work of providing aids to devotion. Relics of saints and martyrs were cherished as sacred possessions; religious observances were multiplied; and the church under the Christian emperors [in the fourth century], with its array of clergy and of imposing ceremonies, assumed much of the stateliness and visible splendor that belonged to the heathen system which it had supplanted."

Says another,† "Contemporaneously with the establishment [of Christianity as the religion of the empire in the fourth century] was the progress of a *great* and *general corruption which had arisen two centuries before.* Superstition and ignorance invested the ecclesiastics with a power which they exerted to their own aggrandizement."

Rapin observes that, "In the fifth century Christianity was debased by a vast number of human inventions; the simplicity of its government and discipline was reduced to a system of clerical power; and its worship was polluted with ceremonies borrowed from the heathen."

Mosheim, in his "*History of Christianity*," traces the falling away of the Church from its original simplicity and purity, step by step, down to its deep degradation which culminated in the development of the "Man of Sin." Whether or not he recognized the Antichrist does not appear, but in a masterly way he has traced the workings of the "Mystery of Iniquity," in the Church, down to the

---

* Fisher's Universal History, page 193.

† White's Universal History, page 156.

beginning of the fourth century—when his work was suddenly cut short by death. From his excellent and voluminous work our space does not here permit quotations, but we commend the work entire as highly instructive in its bearing on the subject.

We quote, from Lord's "*Old Roman World,*" a brief and pointed sketch of the Church's history during the first four centuries, which shows clearly and concisely its gradual decline, and its rapid degeneracy after the hindrance referred to by the Apostle was removed. He says:—

"*In the First Century* not many wise or noble were called. No great names have been handed down to us; no philosophers, or statesmen, or nobles, or generals, or governors, or judges, or magistrates. In the first century the Christians were not of sufficient importance to be generally persecuted by the government. They had not even arrested public attention. Nobody wrote against them, not even Greek philosophers. We do not read of protests or apologies from the Christians themselves. They had no great men in their ranks, either for learning, or talents, or wealth, or social position. Nothing in history is more barren than the annals of the Church in the first century, so far as great names are concerned. Yet in this century converts were multiplied in every city, and traditions point to the martyrdoms of those who were prominent, including nearly all of the apostles.

"*In the Second Century* there are no greater names than Polycarp, Ignatius, Justin Martyr, Clement, Melito and Apollonius, quiet bishops or intrepid martyrs, who addressed their flocks in upper chambers, and who held no worldly rank, famous only for their sanctity or simplicity of character, and only mentioned for their sufferings and faith. We read of martyrs, some of whom wrote valuable treatises and apologies; but among them we find no people of rank. It was a disgrace to be a Christian in the eye of fashion or power. The early Christian literature is chiefly apologetic, and the doctrinal character is simple and practical. There were controversies *in* the Church, an intense religious life, great activities, great virtues, but no outward conflicts, no secular history. They had not as yet assailed the government or the great social institutions of the empire. It was a small body of pure and blameless men, who did not aspire to *control society*. But they had attracted the notice of the government and were of sufficient consequence to be persecuted. They were looked upon as fanatics who sought to destroy a reverence for existing institutions."

[ORGANIZED FOR POWER.]

"In this century the polity of the Church was *quietly organized*. There was an organized fellowship among the members; bishops had become influential, not in society, but among the Christians; dioceses and parishes were established; there was a distinction between city and rural bishops; delegates of churches assembled to discuss points of faith or suppress nascent heresies; the diocesan system was developed, and ecclesiastical centralization commenced; deacons began to be reckoned among the higher clergy; the weapons of excommunication were forged; missionary efforts were carried on; the festivals of the church were created; Gnosticism was embraced by many leading minds; catechetical schools taught the faith systematically; the formulas of baptism and the sacraments became of great importance; and monachism became popular. The Church was thus *laying the foundation of its future polity and power*.

"*The Third Century* saw the Church more powerful as an institution. Regular synods had assembled in the great cities of the empire; the metropolitan system was matured; the canons of the Church were definitely enumerated; great schools of theology attracted inquiring minds; the doctrines were *systematized* [*i. e.*, defined, limited, and formulated into creeds and confessions of faith]. Christianity had spread so extensively that it must needs be either persecuted or legalized; great bishops ruled the growing church; great doctors [of divinity] speculated on the questions [philosophy and science falsely so called] which had agitated the Grecian schools; church edifices were enlarged, and banquets instituted in honor of the martyrs. The Church was rapidly advancing to a position which extorted the attention of mankind

"*It was not till the Fourth Century*—when imperial persecution had stopped; when [the Roman Emperor] Constantine was converted; *when the Church was allied with the State;* when the early faith was itself corrupted; when superstition and vain philosophy had entered the ranks of the faithful; when bishops became courtiers; when churches became both rich and splendid; when synods were brought under political influence; when monachists [monks] had established a false principle of virtue; when politics and dogmatics went hand in hand, and emperors enforced the decrees of [church] councils—that *men of rank* entered the Church. When Christianity became the religion of the court and of the fashionable classes, it was used to support the very evils against which it originally protested. The Church was not only impregnated with the errors of Pagan philosophy, but it adopted many of the ceremonies of oriental worship, which were both minute and magnificent. The churches became, in the fourth century, as imposing as the old temples of idolatry. Festivals became frequent and imposing. The people clung to them because they obtained excitement and a cessation from labor. Veneration for martyrs ripened into the introduction of images— a future source of popular idolatry. Christianity was emblazoned in pompous ceremonies. The veneration for saints approximated to their deification, and superstition exalted the mother of our Lord into an object of absolute worship. Communion tables became imposing altars typical of Jewish sacrifices, and the relics of martyrs were preserved as sacred amulets. Monastic life also ripened into a grand system of penance and expiatory rites. Armies of monks retired to gloomy and isolated places, and abandoned themselves to rhapsodies and fastings and self-expiation. They were a dismal and fanatical set of men, overlooking the practical aims of life.

"The clergy, ambitious and worldly, sought rank and distinction. They even thronged the courts of princes and aspired to temporal honors. They were no longer supported by the voluntary contributions of the faithful, but by revenues supplied by government, or property inherited from the old [pagan] temples. Great legacies were made to the Church by the rich, and these the clergy controlled.

These bequests became sources of inexhaustible wealth. As wealth increased and was intrusted to the clergy, they became indifferent to the wants of the people,—no longer supported by them. They became lazy, arrogant and independent. The people were shut out of the government of the Church. The bishop became a grand personage who controlled and appointed his clergy. *The Church was allied with the State*, and religious dogmas were enforced by the sword of the magistrate.

"AN IMPOSING HIERARCHY WAS ESTABLISHED, OF VARIOUS GRADES, WHICH CULMINATED IN THE BISHOP OF ROME.

"The Emperor decided points of faith, and the clergy were exempted from the burdens of the state. There was a great flocking to the priestly offices when the clergy wielded so much power and became so rich; and men were elevated to great sees [bishoprics], not because of their piety or talents, but their influence with the great. *The mission of the Church was lost sight of in a degrading alliance with the State.* Christianity was a pageant, a ritualism, an arm of the State, a vain philosophy, a superstition, a formula."

Thus the great falling away from the faith, predicted by the Apostle Paul, is an established fact of history. All historians bear witness to it, even those who approve the assumption of power and eulogize the chief actors in the scheme. We regret that our space limits our quotations to some of the most pointed expressions. The falling away, covering a period of centuries, was so gradual as to be much less noticeable to those who then lived in its midst than to us who see it as a whole; and the more deceiving was it because every step of organization, and every advance toward influence and authority in the Church and over the world, was taken *in the name of Christ*, and professedly to glorify him and fulfil his plans recorded in Scripture. Thus was the great Antichrist developed—the most dangerous, most subtle and most persistent opponent of true Christianity, and the most fiendish persecutor of the true saints.

THE HINDRANCE REMOVED.

The Apostle Paul foretold that this iniquitous principle would work secretly for a time, while some opposing thing stood in the way, until, the hindrance being removed, it could have a free course, and progress rapidly to the development of the Antichrist. He says, "Only he that now hindereth will hinder, until he be taken out of the way." (2 Thes. 2:7.) What does history have to show in fulfilment of this prediction? It shows that the thing which hindered a rapid development of Antichrist was the fact that the place aspired to was already filled by another. The Roman empire had not only conquered the world and given it politics and laws, but, recognizing religious superstitions to be the strongest chains by which to hold and control a people, it had adopted a scheme which had its origin in Babylon, in the time of her greatness as ruler of the world. That plan was, that the emperor should be esteemed the director and ruler in religious as well as in civil affairs. In support of this, it was claimed that the emperor was a demigod, in some sense descended from their heathen deities. As such he was worshiped and his statues adored; and as such he was styled *Pontifex Maximus—i. e.*, Chief Priest or Greatest Religious Ruler. And this is the very title claimed by and given to the pontiffs or popes of the Roman Hierarchy since this Antichrist obtained "the power and seat and great authority" of the former ruler of Rome.—Rev. 13:2.

But ancient pagan Rome and Babylon had only a mere skeleton of sacerdotal power as compared with the complex and elaborate machinery and contrivances of doctrine and practice of Papal Rome, the triumphant successor to their scheme, who now, after centuries of cunning and skill, has its power so intrenched that even to-day, when its power is outwardly broken and it is shorn of civil dominion, it rules the world and controls kingdoms secretly, under cover, more thoroughly than the Roman emperors ever ruled the kings subordinate to them.

To their credit be it recorded that not one of the Roman emperors, as Pontifex Maximus or Chief Religious Ruler, ever exercised the tyranny of some of their successors on the Papal throne. On this point Gibbon says:* "It must be allowed that the number of Protestants who were executed in a single province and a single reign, *far exceeded* that of the primitive martyrs in the space of three centuries and of the [entire] Roman empire." According to the custom of their day they did favor the most popular gods, but wherever their armies went, the gods and worship of the conquered people were generally respected. This was illustrated in Palestine, in which, though under Roman control, religious liberty and freedom of conscience were generally respected by the imperial *Pontifex Maximus*, who as religious ruler thus showed his clemency toward the people, and his harmony with all the popular gods.

So, then, we see that what hindered the early development of Antichrist was the fact that the coveted seat of spiritual supremacy was filled by the representatives of the strongest empire the world had yet known; and that for any to have attempted an open display of ambition in this direction would have exposed them to the wrath of the masters of the world. Hence this iniquitous ambition at first worked secretly, disclaiming any intent to gain power or authority, until a favorable opportunity was presented—after the nominal Church had become large and influential and the imperial power was shattered by political dissensions and was beginning to decay.

The power of Rome was rapidly failing, and its strength and unity were divided among six claimants to the imperial

---

* Vol. II., page 85.

19-B

honors, when Constantine became emperor. And that, in part at least, he adopted Christianity to strengthen and unify his empire, is a reasonable supposition. On this point history says:—

"Whether Constantine embraced it [Christianity] from conviction of its truth, or from policy, is matter of dispute. Certain it is, that this religion, though receiving from the Roman power only silent obloquy, or active persecution, had extended among the people, so that Constantine strengthened himself in the affection of the soldiers by adopting it. . . . Worldly ambition pointed to the course which the emperor pursued in declaring himself a Christian, and not the spirit of Christ, who said, My kingdom is not of this world. Constantine made it the religion of the empire, and thenceforth we find its influence sullied with earthly things. . . . No particular bishop was regarded as head of the whole Church, but the emperor was such in point of fact. In this capacity he called the *Council of Nice*, having in the controversy between Athanasius and Arius taken sides against the latter. *The council agreed with the emperor.*"*

"Whatever advantages might be derived from the acquisition of an imperial proselyte, he was distinguished by the splendor of the purple, rather than the superiority of wisdom or virtue, from the many thousands of his subjects who had embraced the doctrines of Christianity . . . The same year of his reign in which he convened the Council of Nice was polluted by the execution of his eldest son. The gratitude of the Church has exalted the virtues and excused the failings of a generous patron who seated Christianity on the throne of the Roman world."†

Here, then, under Constantine's reign, the opposition of the empire to Christianity gave way to favor, and the Imperial Pontifex Maximus became the patron of the *professed* but really apostate Church of Christ; and, taking her by the hand, he assisted her to a place of popularity and splen-

* Willard's Universal History, page 163.

† Gibbon, Vol. II., page 269.

dor from which she was able afterward, as the imperial power grew weak, to put her own representatives upon the religious throne of the world as Chief Religious Ruler—*Pontifex Maximus*.

But it is a mistake to suppose, as many do, that the Church at this time was a pure (virgin) church, suddenly lifted into a dignity and power which became her snare. Quite the contrary is true. As already stated, a great falling away had occurred, from primitive purity and simplicity and freedom into creed-bound, ambitious factions, whose errors and ceremonies, resembling those of the pagan philosophies, garnished with some truths and enforced and clinched with the doctrine of everlasting torment, had drawn into the church a vast horde, whose numbers and influence became *valuable* to Constantine and were respected and used accordingly. No such worldly man ever thought seriously of espousing the cause of the humble, Christ-like "little flock,"—the truly consecrated Church, whose names are written in heaven. The popularity with his soldiers, mentioned by the historians, is very different from popularity with real soldiers of the cross.

In proof of this let us here quote from history, regarding the state of religious society under Diocletian, the predecessor of Constantine, who, toward the close of his reign, believing that Christians had attempted to destroy his life, became embittered against them and persecuted them by ordering the destruction of Bibles, the banishing of bishops, and finally by decreeing the death of such as opposed these enactments. Gibbon * says of this era:—

"Diocletian and his colleagues frequently conferred the most important offices on those persons who avowed their abhorrence for the worship of the gods, but who displayed abilities proper for the service of the state. The bishops held an honorable rank in their respective provinces, and

* Vol. II., pages 53 and 57.

were treated with distinction and respect, not only by the people, but by the magistrates themselves. Almost in every city, the ancient churches were found insufficient to contain the increasing number of proselytes; and in their place more stately and capacious edifices were erected for the public worship of the faithful. The corruption of manners and principles, so forcibly lamented by Eusebius, may be considered as not only a consequence but a proof of the liberty which the Christians enjoyed and abused under the reign of Diocletian. Prosperity had relaxed the nerves of discipline. Fraud, envy and malice prevailed in every congregation. The proselytes aspired to the episcopal office, which every day became an object more worthy of their ambition. The bishops, who contended with each other for ecclesiastical pre-eminence, appeared by their conduct to claim a secular and tyrannical power in the church; and the lively *faith* which still distinguished the Christians from the Gentiles was shown much less in their lives than in their controversial writings.

"The story of Paul of Samosata, who filled the metropolitan see [bishopric] of Antioch while the East was in the hands of Odenatus and Zenobia, may serve to illustrate the condition and character of the times. [A. D. 270.] Paul considered the service of the church a very lucrative profession. His ecclesiastical jurisdiction was venal and rapacious: he extorted frequent contributions from the most opulent of the faithful, and converted to his own use a considerable part of the public revenues. [It is claimed by critics, says Gibbon, that Paul held the office of Imperial *Ducenarius*, or procurator, with an annual salary of two hundred *Sestertia*,—$77,000.] By his pride and luxury, the Christian religion was rendered odious in the eyes of the Gentiles. His council chamber, and his throne, the splendor with which he appeared in public, the suppliant crowd who solicited his attention, the multitude of letters and petitions to which he dictated his answers, and the perpetual hurry of business in which he was involved, were circumstances much better suited to the state of a civil magistrate than to the humility of a primitive bishop. When he harangued his people from the pulpit, Paul affected the figurative style and the theatrical gestures of an

Asiatic sophist, while the cathedral resounded with the most extravagant acclamations in the praise of his divine eloquence. Against those who resisted his power, or refused to flatter his vanity, the prelate of Antioch was arrogant, rigid and inexorable, but he relaxed the discipline and lavished the treasures of the church on his dependent clergy.''

Thus under Constantine's reign all hindrance was finally removed, and, as we shall find, the organization of Papacy —the church nominal under the headship of the bishop of Rome as pope—was speedily effected.

RAPID DEVELOPMENT OF ANTICHRIST.

The rapid development of the Papal Hierarchy after the accession of Constantine is a very remarkable feature of its history. ''The prince of this world'' was true to his promise to give power and dominion as a reward for worshiping and obeying him. (Matt. 4:8, 9.) By the edict of Milan, Constantine gave legal security to the possessions of the Church, and Christians recovered lands formerly forfeited. A second edict, A. D. 321, granted the liberty of bequeathing property to the Church, while Constantine himself set an example of liberality and lavished wealth upon the Christian clergy unsparingly. This example of the Emperor was followed by thousands of his subjects, whose offerings during life and whose bequests in the hour of death flowed into the ecclesiastical treasury. White says: *

''The church of Rome began early to assume authority over the others [over the churches of other cities and countries,] as well from the numbers and wealth of its converts as from its position in the capital city. Many circumstances concurred to augment the influence of its bishop, although his usurpation and ambition were for a time vigorously repelled. The transference of the seat of power [by Constantine, from Rome to Constantinople, A. D. 334] increased the power of the western church by conferring the chief magistracy on the bishop. To this must be added

* White's Universal History, page 155.

the sanction given by Gratian and Valentinian to the custom of appeals to Rome, and the frequent pilgrimages to the tombs of St. Peter and St. Paul and other martyrs.''

After the death of Constantine the varied fortunes of the Roman Empire seemed to co-operate for the advancement of the apostate church and the development of Antichrist; for a union under one head or pope, esteemed the representative or vicegerent of Christ, had not yet been effected. The emperors succeeding Constantine, down to Theodosius, continued to regard themselves as the heads of the Church, in whom centered divine authority. Though no one of the eighteen hundred bishops of the empire was yet prepared to *demand recognition* as the head, or pope, several had their eyes on that prize, and the emperors were shown the shallowness of their claims to the title *Pontifex Maximus*, in the argument that since they worshiped dead saints they owed a similar respect to their living representatives —the bishops. Nevertheless, the emperors in their edicts repeatedly referred to the empire as a *divine hierarchy* and to themselves as divine personages.*

The power and headship of the bishop of Rome came on apace: within fifty years from the time Christianity was legally established, his wealth and dignity, as the bishop of the capital and chief city of the world, were very great. Ammianus, a contemporary historian, describing his wealth and ostentation, says, ''He surpassed kings in splendor and magnificence, rode in the stateliest chariots, was arrayed in the finest attire, and was distinguished by his luxury and pride.'' The removal of the seat of empire to Constantinople, the exposure of the city of Rome to the invasion of the barbarians from the north, the continual changes of generals and governors in the now fast falling empire, left the bishop of the church at Rome the most

---

* See Gibbon, Vol. II., page 108.

permanent and most honored official there; and his gradually increasing prestige was heightened as well by the removal of the rival splendors of the imperial court to Constantinople as by the reverence attaching to the very name of Rome, among all the peoples of the world.

As an illustration of this, we note that when, in A. D. 455, the city of Rome was invaded and plundered by the Vandals, and all around was distress and desolation, Leo, the bishop of Rome, improved the opportunity for impressing upon all, both barbarians and Romans, his claim of spiritual power. To the rude and superstitious barbarians, already greatly impressed by what they saw about them, of Rome's greatness and wealth, Leo, arrayed in his pontifical robes, exclaimed: "Beware! I am the successor of St. Peter, to whom God has given the keys of the kingdom of heaven and against whose church the gates of hell cannot prevail; I am the living representative of divine power on the earth; I am Cæsar, a Christian Cæsar, ruling in love, to whom all Christians owe allegiance; I hold in my hands the curses of hell and the benedictions of heaven; I absolve all subjects from allegiance to kings; I give and take away, by divine right, all thrones and principalities of Christendom. Beware how you desecrate the patrimony given me by your invisible king; yea, bow down your necks to me and pray that the anger of God may be averted."

The veneration for the place and name was actively taken advantage of by the bishop of Rome, who soon claimed a superiority to all other bishops, governors and rulers. Soon he claimed not only ecclesiastical dominion of the world, but also civil dominion: that the right to crown and uncrown, to make and degrade any and all rulers of the old Roman Empire was the right and inheritance of the Church of Rome, which, it was claimed, God had thus invested with the dominion of earth. These claims were made repeatedly, and repeatedly denied by opposing bishops, so that to fix an exact year as the date of its beginning would be impossible. As for itself, Papacy claims that it was organized in the days of the apostles, and that Peter was the first pope; but this is not only without proof, but is most positively contradicted by all history, which shows that though the *iniquity of ambition* worked secretly for a long time, it was hindered from developing into Antichrist, and from making such open claims, until the Roman Empire began to disintegrate.

Henceforth we deal with the Antichrist, whose gradual *development* and *organization* from secretly working ambition are a fitting prelude to the terrible character displayed after the coveted power had been grasped—from 539 A. D. to 1799 A. D., 1260 years. Of this period the first three hundred years mark the rise of this temporal power; the last three mark its waning under the influences of the Reformation and civilization; and the intermediate period of seven centuries embraces Papacy's glory-time and the "dark ages" of the world, full of frauds and deceptions in the name of Christ and true religion.

A Roman Catholic writer fully corroborates our findings on this subject, and we present his words regardless of their gloss, as corroborative testimony. Giving, with glowing enthusiasm, a description of the rise of the Papacy to temporal power, describing it as a plant of heavenly origin, and therefore of rapid growth and high exaltation in the world, he says:—

"The rise of the temporal power of the Popes presents to the mind one of the most extraordinary phenomena which the annals of the human race offer to our wonder and admiration. By a singular combination of concurring circumstances a new power and a new dominion grew up, silently and steadily, on the ruins of that Roman Empire which had extended its sway over, or made itself respected by, nearly all the nations, peoples and races that lived in the period of its strength and glory; and that new power, of lowly origin, struck a deeper root, and soon exercised a wider authority, than the empire whose gigantic ruins it saw shivered into fragments and mouldering in dust. In Rome itself the power of the successor of Peter grew side by side with, and under the protecting shadow of, that of the emperor; and such was the increasing influence of the popes, that the majesty of the supreme Pontiff was likely ere long to dim the splendor of the purple.

"The removal by Constantine of the seat of empire from the West to the East, from the historic banks of the Tiber to the beautiful shores of the Bosphorus, laid the broad foundation *of a sovereignty which in reality commences from that momentous change.* Practically, almost from that day, Rome, which had witnessed the birth, the youth, the splendor, and the decay, of the mighty race by whom her name had been carried with her eagles to the remotest regions of the then known world, was gradually abandoned by the inheritors of her renown; and its people, deserted by the emperors, and an easy prey to the ravages of the barbarians whom they had no longer the courage to resist, beheld in the bishop of Rome their guardian, their protector, their father. Year by year the temporal authority of the popes grew into shape and hardened into strength, without violence, without bloodshed, without fraud, by the force of overwhelming circumstances, fashioned, as if visibly, by the hand of God."

While Roman Catholics thus represent the rise of the Papacy on the ruins of Pagan Rome as a triumph of Christianity, those who are acquainted with the true spirit of Christianity look in vain to see any trace of that spirit in the prostitution of the Church and her unholy alliance with the world. Neither can the true Christian see in the advantages furnished by ignorance, superstition, calamities, and the various circumstances of the times of which the Church of Rome took advantage, any evidence of divine interposition in her favor. Nor yet can they discover, in the exaltation of the Church of Rome to earthly power and glory, any verification of the Lord's promise to the true Church, to exalt her *in due time*—after the Antichrist has come and gone; for the exaltation of the true Church is not to be to a blood-stained and crime-polluted throne, such as the throne of the Papacy has been from its very beginning: neither will the true Christ ever need to call upon earthly kings to establish or defend his power.   The marks which distinguish the counterfeit from the real kingdom of Christ are easily recognizable by those acquainted, through the Scriptures, with the real Christ and his body, the true Church, with the principles upon which his kingdom is to be established, and with the object for which it is to be set up.

But let no one suppose that the real Church of Christ, even in those corrupt times, was either extinguished or lost sight of.   "The Lord knoweth them that are his" in every age and under every condition.   As wheat they were permitted to grow in the midst of a field overrun with tares; as gold they were in the furnace, being tried and purified and "made meet for the inheritance of the saints in light." True, the course of the multitude, who called themselves Christians, occupies the most prominent place on the pages of history; but undoubtedly a faithful few through all the persecutions, and in the midst of all the deceptive arts of the Mystery of Iniquity, walked worthy of their high calling, were laid to rest and recorded of God as heirs to the crown that fadeth not away, reserved in heaven for them.

Thus, clearly, on the pages of history, the fact is pointed out that this Man of Sin, Antichrist, was born in Rome; and, though at first opposed, he gradually raised himself up to power; or, as expressed in Daniel's prophecy, as "a little horn," it came up out of the head of that old Roman beast, that "great and terrible beast," for which Daniel could find no name, which had such power to hurt and to destroy.

And, as we proceed, we shall find that Antichrist's history corresponds exactly, not only with Daniel's prophecy, but with all the prophecies recorded concerning him.

ANTICHRIST'S CHARACTER IN HISTORY.

Having located Antichrist, we next proceed to compare the character of Papacy with the prophecies recorded, descriptive of the character and deeds of the Antichrist or Man of Sin.

Some may query whether it be right to pass over the emperors of Rome (who claimed to be Supreme religious rulers), without calling their system Antichrist, and to apply that title complete and entire to the organized Papal system. We answer, This is certainly right ; and we refer the reader again to the definition of Antichrist already given, as used in the Scriptures, viz., *in the place of, instead of,* i.e., to be a spiritual empire: it must claim to rule the kingdoms of earth by this spiritual authority ; it must thus be not only an antagonist but a counterfeit, misrepresenting and pretending to be Christ's kingdom, and exercising what will in God's due time be the authority of the true Christ, the church glorified and complete under the only true Head and Lord,—the real *Pontifex Maximus.*

Not only does Papacy claim to be the glorified kingdom of Christ promised by the Lord, the apostles and the prophets, but it applies to itself and its successive heads (the popes, who, it claims, take the place of Christ, as Pontiff, Chief or King of this kingdom) all those passages of the prophets which describe the Millennial glory of the Christ. And, " deceiving [others] and being deceived" themselves (by their false theories, developed slowly by sinful ambition for greatness, during centuries), the popes have piece by piece arranged the titles of all associated in the hierarchy, their gorgeous clothing, their imposing ceremonials, their grand cathedrals with solemn, awe-inspiring services, on a scale to correspond as nearly as possible with their claims—the gorgeous surroundings and clothing and ceremonies match-ing, as best they can make them match, the glories and grandeur portrayed by the prophets.

For instance, Psalm 2:12 reads, "Kiss the Son, O ye kings of the earth, lest he be angry, and ye perish by the way, when his anger is kindled but a little." This is not a command to kiss literally, but to yield willing, cheerful submission to our Lord, and applies to the present hour, when, preparatory to the great and true Millennial reign of the true Christ, the kings or great ones of earth, politically, socially, financially and ecclesiastically, are being tested by their willingness or unwillingness to bow to the righteous regulations now due to go into operation. Those who re-sist righteousness resist the scepter of this King of glory, and all such shall be overthrown in the great time of trouble which ushers in the Millennial reign of the new King: all who would not have him reign shall be slain. (Luke 19:27.) "His enemies shall lick the dust"—be vanquished.

Misapplying this prophecy to his counterfeit kingdom, Antichrist's representative head, the pope, in the palmy days of his prosperity caused kings and emperors to bow before him, as before Christ, and to kiss his great toe—ap-plying the same as the fulfilment of this prophecy,

Claims like these are very generally passed over lightly by prophetic students and writers, while they search out and specially notice immoralities; but herein they greatly err, for criminalities have been plentiful enough in every age, and would need no such special, prophetic delin-eations as are given of Antichrist. Could it be proved that those connected with the papal system have been very models of morality, it would be none the less identical with the character noted in Scripture as the great Antichrist—the counterfeit which has arrogated to itself the titles, privileges, powers and reverence belonging to the Lord's Anointed. As a counterfeit, it has also misrepresented the plan of God with reference to the selection of a "little flock," or Church, in the present time; and it has entirely set aside the real hope of the Church, and the Lord's provision for the blessing of the world during the Millennial reign of Christ—which it represents as fulfilled in its own reign.

The ill effects of such perversion and misrepresentation of God's plan can scarcely be estimated. They have been the direct source from which sprang all the corrupt doctrines which, one after another, were introduced to support the claims and add to the dignity of Antichrist. And though the Reformation, three centuries ago, ushered in an era of Bible study and liberty of thought, and led to the rejection of many evils and errors, yet the counterfeit was on so elaborate a scale, so complete in all its parts and arrangements, and had so thoroughly deceived the whole world that, even after Luther and many others had recognized Papacy as the outcome of the great falling away—the Antichrist of prophecy—they, while denouncing it as a system, held firmly to the false theory which led to its peculiar errors of doctrine and practice. To this day the great majority of Protestants of all denominations support the theory of Antichrist, that Christ's Kingdom *has been set up.* Some have endeavored to do as Papacy did—to organize their church under some one person as its head—while others supply the place of this head with a council or synod; but all are under the delusion imposed by the false and misleading interpretations of Scripture doctrines started by Antichrist—that now, and not at a future time, is the *reign of Christ's Kingdom;* and, denying the coming age, as the

Antichrist does, they, like that system, are careless of the full development of holiness among believers and are zealous rather for the accomplishment now of the work of the next age (the conversion of the world)—so much so, that they are often willing to misrepresent God's plan and Word, and to invent theories to frighten and drive the world into a profession of godliness; and willing also to resort to questionable and worldly methods to add to their attractions, to make their various systems the more enticing to the *unconverted*, whom they, like Antichrist, are willing to count in for pride's sake and to make a good showing.

Such find it difficult to see that Papacy is Antichrist. How could they, while faith is not yet free from the poison, and reason is still greatly blinded by the very essence of Antichrist's error. The greatness, the grandeur and the necessity of Christ's Millennial Kingdom and its work of blessing all the families of the earth must be seen, before the greatness of the Antichrist counterfeit can be appreciated, or its havoc to the truth and its desolating and defiling influence in the nominal church or temple of God can be rightly estimated.

None need be surprised at the completeness of this counterfeit, when we reflect that it is *Satan's workmanship*, and has been patterned after the types and illustrations of future glory presented in the Scriptures. Seeing that the time for the selection of the Church had come, and that the truths planted by the Lord and the apostles had gained rapid headway against all the heathen religions, seeking out the meek wherever it went, the great adversary sought to destroy the purity of the Church and to turn into other and false channels that which he could not stop. Thus the triumph of Antichrist, as well as its present power, has really been Satan's success. But here we behold the wisdom of God; for while the success of Antichrist seemed to presage

THE CHURCH OF GOD,

THE ROYAL PRIESTHOOD.

THE REALITY
DURING
THE MILLENNIUM.

TRUE TYPE.		COUNTERFEIT.
AARON— and successors—Chief or High Priest, head and representative and mouthpiece.	CHRIST JESUS, our Lord and Head and representative; the High-Priest of our profession or order.	THE POPES, in turn, High-Priests of the Papal Hierarchy; its lord, head and mouthpiece.
Under-Priests, deriving their official dignity and rights and privileges of service through Aaron, whose body they represented, typified the Church of Christ.	The Church glorified, the Body of Christ, sharers of his glory, majesty, and office of ruler: whose offices will differ, as star differeth from star in glory.	The Church of Rome consists of the bishops and prelates, who share the dignities of the hierarchy, though differing in degrees of honor— cardinals, bishops, etc.

Subject to the Hierarchy are assistants, as follows :—

The Levites, who did services connected with the typical Tabernacle—teaching, etc., etc. An inferior order of priests not permitted to enter the Most Holy Sanctuary (typical of the spiritual nature), neither to look therein.	The earthly phase of the Kingdom of God; through whom the glorified Church will have more direct contact with the world, in teaching, governing, etc., and who also will have closest communion with the spiritual Church in glory.	The under-priests of Papacy, not parts or members of *the* church or hierarchy, but called "Brothers" and "Sisters." Of these are the teachers, nurses, etc., in direct contact with the *people* as well as with the hierarchy.
All Israel was taught and directed by the above described hierarchy. And in Moses, who was a type of the complete Christ, they had prophet, priest and king united, typical of Christ's Millennial authority.—Acts 3:22.	The World will be taught, directed, ruled and helped by the above described Kingdom of God and its earthly representatives, which will have all power, and must be obeyed; and all who obey not will be "cut off."—Acts 3:23.	Papacy *claims* the obedience of the World to its rule and teachings —as being the Kingdom of God. The lower priesthood is its agent. When in power, it attempted to enforce its laws, and to "cut off" those who obeyed not.

the defeat of God's plan it was really, though unwittingly, co-operating to insure the success of his plan; for by no other means could the *truly consecrated* have been so thoroughly tried, and their faithfulness to God's Word so thoroughly tested, as by the permission of this great counterfeit.

The accompanying table will serve to show how complete has been the counterfeit of the future organization of Christ's kingdom in Papacy, and how it was drawn from the Jewish typical priesthood.

Mosheim, explaining the rise of the hierarchical system in the Church, very clearly shows this counterfeiting, in these words, Vol. I., p. 337 :—

"Whilst the least probability remained that Jerusalem might at one time or other again rear its head from the dust, the Christian teachers and elders assumed to themselves no titles or distinctions, at least none but the most modest and humble ones; but when the fate of that city had been sealed by Hadrian [A. D. 135], and not the most distant hope could any longer be entertained by the Jews, of seeing their ancient government re-established, these same pastors and ministers *conceived a wish to have it believed by their flocks that they themselves had succeeded to the rights of the Jewish priesthood.* The bishops, therefore, made it their business to inculcate the notion that they were invested with a character resembling that of the great High Priest of the Jews, and were *consequently possessed of all those rights which had been recognized as belonging to the Jewish Pontiff.* The functions of the ordinary Jewish priest were, in like manner, stated to have devolved, though under a more perfect form, on the presbyters of the Christian Church: and finally the deacons were placed on a parallel with the Levites, or inferior ministers."

THE HEAD AND MOUTH OF ANTICHRIST.

HIS GREAT SWELLING WORDS.

The pope (each pope in his turn) is the *head* of the false church, which is his body, even as Christ Jesus is the *head* of the true Church, which is his body. Since the head is the representative of the body, and its *mouth* speaks for the body, we find, as we should expect, this feature of Antichrist prominently referred to in the Scriptures. In Daniel 7:8, 11, 25, and Rev. 13:5, 6, the mouth of Antichrist is brought specially to our notice as a leading characteristic. Daniel says this horn had "eyes like the eyes of man,"—symbolic of intelligence and a far-sighted policy. This *"horn"* was to be different from all the other powers; it was to be more wise, more cunning, than other empires which attempted to rule the world; its power was to be that of its mouth (utterance) guided by its eyes (knowledge), rather than that of physical force. And no one acquainted with the history of Papacy can deny that the figures used to illustrate its power and methods are strikingly good.

"And there was given unto him a mouth speaking great things. And he opened his mouth in blasphemy against God, to blaspheme his name, and his tabernacle, and them that dwell in heaven." "And he shall speak great words against the Most High."—Rev. 13:5,6; Dan. 7:8, 25.

It should not be forgotten that these are figurative expressions descriptive of the character and claims of a symbolic "beast" (government) and "horn" (power) out of the old Roman beast or empire. In some respects, Papacy was a new government ("beast"), distinct from the old Roman empire; and in others, it was a horn or power among others out of that empire, which for a time held superior control over the other horns or powers. It is presented in symbol from both these standpoints so as most thoroughly to locate and designate it.

Antichrist's great swelling words, or blasphemies, cover the whole period of his long career. The expression, "blasphemy," in our day, is usually given only a coarse meaning,

20–B

as if it related to the most vulgar forms of cursing and pro-
fanity only. But, in its true significance, the word "blasphemy" is applicable to *any indignity* offered to God. *Bou-
vier* defines it thus: "*Blasphemy* is to attribute to God
that which is contrary to his nature, and does not belong to
him,—and to deny what does."—See Webster's Unabridged
Dictionary under heads of *Blasphemy* and *Blasphemously.*
And in evidence that this is the sense in which the word
"blasphemy" is used in the Scriptures, notice the manner
in which our Lord and the Pharisees used it: "The Jews
answered, For a good work we stone thee not, but for
blasphemy; and because thou, being a man, makest thyself
God." Jesus answered them, "Say ye of him whom the
Father hath sanctified, and sent into the world, Thou blas-
phemest, *because I said*, I am the Son of God?"—John
10:33, 36. See also Mark 14:61–64.

With this, the proper definition of "blasphemy," before
us, how evident it must be to the simplest minds that Papacy's great swelling words and boastful claims have, one
and all, been blasphemies. The establishment of a counterfeit Kingdom of God was a libel upon God's government,
a gross blasphemy, and a misrepresentation of his character
and plan and word. God's character, *i. e.*, his "*name,*"
was blasphemed in the thousand monstrous edicts, bulls and
decretals issued in his name, by the long line of those who
claimed, as vice-gerents, to represent his Son ; and God's
tabernacle, the *true* Church, was blasphemed by the false
system which claimed to take its place—which claimed that
its faithful were the true and only tabernacle or Church of
God. But we must let history tell us of these great swelling words, these blasphemous assumptions, which successive
popes, as the head of Antichrist, uttered and approved.

In a work entitled, "The Pope the Vicar of Christ, the
Head of the Church," by the celebrated Roman Catholic

Monsignor Capel, is a list of no less than sixty-two blasphemous titles applied to the pope; and, be it noticed, these are not mere dead titles from the past, for they were arranged by one of Papacy's foremost living writers. We quote from the list as follows:—

"Most Divine of all Heads."

"Holy Father of Fathers."

"Pontiff Supreme over all Prelates."

"Overseer of the Christian Religion."

"The Chief Pastor—Pastor of Pastors."

"Christ by Unction."

"Abraham by Patriarchate."

"Melchisedec in Order."

"Moses in Authority."

"Samuel in the Judicial Office."

"High Priest, Supreme Bishop."

"Prince of Bishops."

"Heir of the Apostles; Peter in Power."

"Key-bearer of the Kingdom of Heaven."

"Pontiff Appointed with Plenitude of Power."

"Vicar of Christ."

"Sovereign Priest."

"Head of all the Holy Churches."

"Chief of the Universal Church."

"Bishop of Bishops, that is, Sovereign Pontiff."

"Ruler of the House of the Lord."

"Apostolic Lord and Father of Fathers."

"Chief Pastor and Teacher."

"Physician of Souls."

"Rock against which the proud gates of hell prevail not."

"Infallible Pope."

"Head of all the Holy Priests of God."

In addition to the long list of titles of which the above are instances, the author gives the following quotations from a letter which St. Bernard, Abbott of Clairvaux, wrote to Pope Eugenius III., A. D. 1150:—

"Who art thou?—The High-Priest, the Supreme Bishop. Thou art the Prince of Bishops, thou art the Heir of the Apostles.   Thou art Abel in Primacy, Noah in government, Abraham in the patriarchal rank, in order Melchisedec, in dignity Aaron, in authority Moses, Samuel in judicial office, Peter in power, CHRIST IN UNCTION.   Thou art he to whom the keys of heaven are given, to whom the sheep are in-trusted.   There are indeed other door-keepers of heaven, and other shepherds of the flocks; but thou art the more glorious in proportion as thou hast also, in a different fash-ion, inherited before others both these names. . . . The power of others is limited by definite bounds: thine ex-tends even over those who have received authority over others.   Canst thou not, when a just reason occurs, shut up heaven against a bishop, depose him from the episcopal office, and deliver him over to Satan?   Thus thy privilege is immutable, as well in the keys committed to thee as in the sheep intrusted to thy care."

All these blasphemously flattering titles have been applied to and received by the Roman pontiffs with complacency and marked satisfaction, as rightfully belonging to them.

From Pope Boniface VIII. we have the following decree, which is still extant in the common law: "We declare, say, define, pronounce it *necessary to salvation* for every human creature to be subject to the Roman pontiff."   Pope Gregory VII., who in the year 1063 ordained that the pope should be called *father of fathers*, draws the following from Gen. 1 : 16, to support papal pretensions: "God made two great lights in the firmament of heaven; the greater light to rule the day and the less to rule the night; both great, but one the greater.   '*In the firmament of heaven*,' that is, the universal church, 'God made two great lights;' that is, he instituted two dignities, which are the pontifical author-ity and the regal power; but that which presides over the day, that is, the spiritual, is the greater; but that which presides over carnal things is the less; for as the sun differs from the moon, so do popes differ from kings." Other popes have adopted this interpretation, which has done much to enforce the idea of papal supremacy.

St. Antonius, Archbishop of Florence, after citing Psalm 8: 4–8, " Thou hast made him a little lower than the angels," etc., and applying it to Christ, transfers it to the pope in the following words : " And because he left us in his bodily presence, he left his vicar [substitute] on the earth, viz., the chief pontiff, who is called papa, which means father of fathers ; so that these words may be fitly expounded of the pope. For the pope, as Hostiensis saith, is greater than man but less than an angel, because he is mortal ; yet he is greater in authority and power. For an angel cannot consecrate the body and blood of Christ, nor absolve or bind, the highest degree of which power belongs to the pope ; nor can an angel ordain or grant indulgences. He is crowned with glory and honor ; the glory of commendation, because he is called not only blessed, but most blessed. Who shall doubt to call him blessed whom the very top of such great dignity hath exalted? He is crowned with the honor of veneration, so that the faithful may kiss his feet. A greater veneration cannot exist.—'*Adore his footstool.*' (Psa. 9:9.) He is crowned with the magnitude of authority, because he can judge all persons, but can be judged of none, unless he be found to deviate from faith [the faith of Antichrist, of course]. Hence he is crowned with a triple, golden crown, and is ' placed over all the works of his hands,' to dispose of all inferiors. He opens heaven, sends the guilty to hell, confirms empires, regulates the whole clergy."

The Council of Lateran in its first session gave to the pope the appellation of " Prince of the Universe ;" in its second session it called him " Priest and King, who is to be adored by all people, and who is very like unto God ;" and in its fifth session it referred prophecies of Christ's glorious reign to Leo X. in these terms : " Weep not, daughter of Zion, for behold, the Lion of the tribe of Judah, the root of David : behold, God hath raised thee up a savior."

From Ferraris' *Ecclesiastical Dictionary*, a standard Roman Catholic authority, we quote the following condensed outline of papal power as given under the word *papa*, article 2nd :—

"The pope is of such dignity and highness that he is not simply a man but, as it were, God, and the vicar [representative] of God. . . . Hence the pope is crowned with a triple crown, as king of heaven, of earth and of hell. Nay, the pope's excellence and power are not only about heavenly, terrestrial and infernal things, but he is also above angels, and is their superior ; so that if it were possible that angels could err from the faith, or entertain sentiments contrary thereto, they could be judged and excommunicated by the pope. . . . He is of such great dignity and power that *he occupies one and the same tribunal with Christ;* so that whatsoever the pope does seems to proceed from the mouth of God. . . . The pope is, as it were, God on earth, the only prince of the faithful of Christ, the greatest king of all kings, possessing the plenitude of power ; *to whom the government of the earthly and heavenly kingdom is entrusted.*" He further adds : " The pope is of so great authority and power that he can modify, declare or interpret the divine law." " The pope can sometimes counteract the divine law by limiting, explaining, etc."

Thus, Antichrist not only endeavored to establish the Church in power before the Lord's *time*, but it was audacious enough to attempt to " counteract" and " modify" divine *laws* to suit its own schemes. How clearly did it thus fulfil the prophecy which over a thousand years before declared—" He shall think to change *times* and *laws*."— Dan. 7:25.

In a bull, or edict, Sixtus V. declares :

" The authority given to St. Peter and his successors, by the immense power of the eternal King, excels all the power of earthly kings and princes. It passeth uncontrollable sentence upon them all. And if it find any of them resisting God's ordinance, it takes more severe vengeance on them, casting them down from their thrones, however powerful they may be, and tumbling them down to the lowest parts of the earth as the ministers of aspiring Lucifer."

A bull of Pope Pius V., entitled "The damnation and excommunication of Elizabeth, queen of England, and her adherents—with an addition of other punishments," reads as follows:—

"He that reigneth on high, to whom is given all power in heaven and in earth, committed one holy, catholic and apostolic church (out of which there is no salvation) to one alone upon earth, namely, to Peter, the Prince of the apostles, and to Peter's successor, the bishop of Rome, to be governed in fulness of power. Him alone he made prince over all people and all kingdoms, to pluck up, destroy, scatter, consume, plant and build."

St. Bernard affirms that "none except God is *like the pope*, either in heaven or on earth."

"The Emperor Constantine," says Pope Nicholas I., "conferred the appellation of God on the pope; who, therefore, being God, cannot be judged by man."

Said Pope Innocent III.—"The pope holds the place of the true God;" and the canon law, in the gloss, denominates the pope—"our Lord God."

Innocent and Jacobatius state that "the pope can do nearly all that God can do," while Decius rejects the word *nearly*, as unnecessary. Jacobatius and Durand assert that "none dare say to him any more than to God—Lord, what doest thou?" And Antonius wrote:—

"To him [the pope] it belongs to ordain those things which pertain to the public good, and remove those things which prevent this end, as vices, abuses which alienate men from God. . . . And this according to Jeremiah 1:10 [Here again appropriating to Antichrist a prophecy which belongs to Christ's Millennial reign]: 'Behold, I have placed thee over the nations and kingdoms, to root up and destroy, to scatter and disperse,' that is, as it regards vices; 'to build up and plant,' that is, as it regards virtues. . . . In regard to the power of the pope over those in hell, who are designated by the fishes in the sea (Psalm 8.)—because, as the fishes are continually agitated by the waves of the sea, so those in purgatory are continually exercised by the afflictions of punishment—God hath subjected to the pope also the fishes of the sea, that is, those who are in purgatory, to relieve them by indulgences.

"Pagans are subject to the pope, who presides in the world in the place of Christ. But Christ hath full power over every creature. The pope is the vicar of Christ, and no one can lawfully withdraw himself from his obedience, as no one can withdraw himself lawfully from obedience to God. . . . The pope can punish pagans and barbarous nations. . . . And though pagans cannot be punished with the spiritual punishment of excommunication and the like, yet they can be punished by the church with pecuniary punishment, and by princes with corporeal punishment also. . . . The church can punish, indirectly, the Jews with spiritual punishment, by excommunicating Christian princes to whom the Jews are subject, *if they neglect to punish them with temporal punishment* when they do anything against Christians. . . . If the conversion of some *should be desired*, they may be compelled by terrors and stripes, not indeed to receive faith, but that they should present no obstacle to faith by an obstinate will. For the conversion of infidels, the judgment of God ought to be imitated."

Here is an illustration of how error of doctrine produces unrighteousness. Men may speedily be led into every form of cruelty and oppression, if first they can convince themselves that in the exercise of such depravities they are the more like God—imitators of God. The wonder is that men are as kind and moderate as we find them, with all the terrible, false ideas and doctrines concerning God's plan for mankind, with which Satan has blinded and deluded them through the papal fountain of error, leading them in a course congenial to their fallen nature. Continuing, the same writer adds:—

" The power of the pope is exercised over heretics and schismatics, denoted also by oxen, because they resist the truth with the horn of pride. God hath subjected these also under the feet of the pope to be punished in a *four-fold way*, viz., by excommunication, deposition, the deprivation of temporal goods and military persecution. But then they are only to be taken for heretics when they refuse to reform their pestiferous doctrines, and are ready pertinaciously to defend them. . . . The pope can choose or elect the emperor. The emperor is the minister [servant] of the pope, in this, that he is the minister of *God, whose place the pope fills;* for God hath deputed the emperor as the minister of the pope. . . . I suppose it to be said as a truth, that the pope, the vicar of Christ, hath universal jurisdiction of spiritual and temporal things, in the whole world, *in the place of the living God.*"

The following utterances of the popes, culled from Fox's " Acts and Monuments," by H. G. Guinness, an English writer of note, deserves a place of prominence ; and we can sympathize heartily with this writer's comment on the system whose mouth gives forth such utterances, when he says— " If ' he that exalteth himself shall be abased,' what degradation can be commensurate with such self-exaltation as this ?"

" Wherefore, seeing such power is given to Peter, and to me in Peter, being his successor, who is he then in all the world that ought not to be subject to my decrees, which have such power in heaven, in hell, in earth, with the quick and also the dead. . . . By the jurisdiction of which key the fulness of my power is so great that, whereas all others are subjects—yea, and emperors themselves ought to subdue their executions to me—only I am subject to no creature, no, not to myself; so my Papal majesty ever remaineth undiminished ; superior to all men, whom all persons ought to obey and follow, whom no man must judge or accuse of any crime, no man depose but I myself. No man can excommunicate me, yea, though I commune with the excommunicated ; for no canon bindeth me : whom no man must lie to, for he that lieth to me is a heretic, and an excommunicated person. Thus, then, it appeareth that the great-

ness of priesthood began in Melchisedec, was solemnized in
Aaron, perfectionated in Christ, represented in Peter, *exalted in the universal jurisdiction, and manifested in the
Pope*. So that through this *pre-eminence of my priesthood*,
having all things subject to me, it may seem well verified
in me, that was spoken of Christ, 'Thou hast subdued all
things under his feet.'

"And, likewise, it is to be presumed that the bishop of
that church is always good and holy. Yea, though he fall
into homicide or adultery, he may sin, but yet he cannot be
accused, but rather excused by the murders of Samson, the
thefts of the Hebrews, etc. All the earth is my diocese, and I
am the ordinary of all men, having the authority of the King
of all kings upon subjects. I am all in all, and above all, so
that God himself, and I, the vicar of God, have both one
consistory, and I am able to do almost all that God can do.
In all things that I list my will is to stand for reason, for I am
able by the law to dispense above the law, and of wrong
to make justice in correcting laws and changing them.
Wherefore, if those things that I do be said not to be done
of man, but of God—WHAT CAN YOU MAKE ME BUT GOD?
Again, if prelates of the church be called and counted of
Constantine for Gods, I then, being above all prelates,
seem by this reason to be ABOVE ALL GODS. Wherefore, no
marvel if it be in my power to change time and times, to
alter and abrogate laws, to dispense with all things, *yea,
with the precepts of Christ;* for where Christ biddeth Peter
put up his sword, and admonishes his disciples not to use
any outward force in revenging themselves, do not I, Pope
Nicholas, writing to the bishops of France, exhort them to
draw out their material swords? . . . And whereas Christ was
present himself at the marriage in Cana of Galilee, do not
I, Pope Martin, in my distinction, inhibit the spiritual
clergy to be present at marriage-feasts, and also to marry?
Moreover, where Christ biddeth us lend without hope of
gain, do not I, Pope Martin, give dispensation for the same?
What should I speak of murder, making it to be no murder
or homicide to slay them that be excommunicated? Likewise, against the law of nature, item against the apostles,
also against the canons of the apostles, I can and do dispense; for where they, in their canon, command a priest

for fornication to be deposed, I, through the authority of Sylvester, do alter the rigor of that constitution, considering the minds and bodies also of men now to be weaker than they were then. . . . If ye list briefly to hear the whole number of all such cases as properly do appertain to my Papal dispensation, which come to the number of one-and-fifty points, that no man may meddle with but only I myself alone, I will recite them. [Here follows the list.]

"After that I have now sufficiently declared my power in earth, in heaven, in purgatory, how great it is, and what is the fulness thereof in binding, loosing, commanding, permitting, electing, confirming, dispensing, doing and undoing, etc., I will speak now a little of my riches and of my great possessions, that every man may see my wealth and abundance of all things—rents, tithes, tributes; my silks, my purple mitres, crowns, gold, silver, pearls and gems, lands and lordships. For to me pertaineth first the imperial city of Rome; the palace of Lateran; the kingdom of Sicily is proper to me; Apula and Capua be mine. Also the kingdoms of England and Ireland, be they not, or ought they not to be, tributaries to me? To these I adjoin also, besides other provinces and countries, in both the Occident and the Orient, from the north to the south, these dominions by name. [Here follows a long list.] What should I speak here of my daily revenues, of my first-fruits, annates, palls, indulgences, bulls, confessionals, indults and rescripts, testaments, dispensations, privileges, elections, prebends, religious houses, and such like, which come to no small mass of money? . . . whereby what vantage cometh to my coffers it may partly be conjectured. . . . But what should I speak of Germany, when the whole world is my diocese, as my canonists do say, and all men are bound to believe. Wherefore, as I began, so I conclude, commanding, declaring, and pronouncing, to stand *upon necessity of salvation, for every human creature to be subject to me.*"

It is presumed by many to-day that these boastings of the Papacy belong only to the distant past, and that a great change has come over that system in later times; but a little reflection and observation prove that these sentiments of the Papacy are still unchanged. We should bear in mind, too, that the constant claim of Papacy is that its doctrines are unchangeable: that the decrees of its popes and councils are *infallible;* and that those decrees, breathing out blasphemy against God, and persecution against his saints, are still held sacred by the Roman Catholic Church of the present day. The change in Papacy is merely the loss of power brought about by the awakening of the Reformation. The will is still possessed, but the power to do is curtailed by the increase of knowledge and liberty in which the Bible has been the principal factor. Antichrist is being gradually "rendered powerless" by the true Christ— by the "spirit of his mouth"—his Word. Soon the bright shining of Immanuel's *presence* will utterly destroy the vainglorious counterfeit, and wholly free the world from the chains of its delusive claims and errors.

For an illustration of latter time assumptions, note the fact that the present pope, upon ascending the papal throne, took the title of Leo. XIII, and shortly after subscribed himself *"Leo de tribus Juda"*—*i.e.,* "The Lion of the tribe of Judah";—one of the titles of the true Head. Surely in presumptuous claims, therefore, he is not behind those who held the same office during the dark ages.

The following, called *The Adoration,* is still a part of the ceremony connected with the installation of a new pope. The new pope, clad in white, studded with many brilliant gems, and wearing red shoes with large gold crosses for buckles, is conducted to the altar, where he kneels. Then,—"The pope rises, and, wearing his mitre, is lifted up by the cardinals and placed by them upon the altar-throne to sit there. One of the bishops kneels, and the singing of *Te Deum* [We praise thee, O God] begins. Meantime the cardinals kiss the feet and hands and face of the pope." A coin representing this ceremony, struck in the Papal mint, bears the words, "Whom they create, they adore."

Cardinal Manning, Papacy's chief representative in England, endorses and draws public attention to the following clause of the Catholic faith:—

"We declare, affirm, define, and pronounce it necessary to salvation, for every human creature to be subject to the Roman Pontiff." And in a published discourse he represents the pope as saying, " I claim to be the Supreme Judge and Director of the consciences of men ; of the peasant that tills the field, and the prince that sits on the throne ; of the household that lives in the shade of privacy, and the Legislature that makes laws for kingdoms. I am the sole, last, Supreme Judge of what is right and wrong."

Surely, too, in observing modern instances of Papacy's " great swelling words of vanity," we should not overlook the notable decree of the Ecumenical Council, held in Rome in A. D. 1870, declaring the infallibility of the Pope. True, it had been claimed now and then in the past, by supercilious popes, that they were infallible ; and bishops and princes desirous of flattering their pride had virtually so pronounced them, in the declaration, "Thou art another god, *on earth;*" but it remained for a Papal Council in this enlightened nineteenth century to coolly and deliberately inform the world how great this " god on earth" is,—that he is *almost* as perfect as the other God, in heaven ; that he cannot err more than the other ; that in his *ex cathedra* utterances the pope is *infallible*—unerring.

The vote of the council was taken July 13th, 1870, and on the 18th the decree was formally promulgated, with ceremony, at the great St. Peter's Cathedral in Rome. The following description of the event, by Dr. J. Cummings, of London, will be read with interest. He says:—

" The Pope had a grand throne erected in front of the eastern window in St. Peter's, and arrayed himself in a perfect blaze of precious stones, and surrounded himself with cardinals and patriarchs and bishops in gorgeous apparel, for a magnificent spectacular scene. He had chosen the early morning hour and the eastern window,—that the rising sun should flash its beams full upon his magnificence, and by it his diamonds, rubies and emeralds be so refracted and reflected that he should appear to be not a man, but what the decree proclaimed him, one having all the glory of God. . . . The pope posted himself at an early hour at the eastern window, . . . but the sun refused to . . . shine. The dismal dawn darkened rapidly to a deeper and deeper gloom. The dazzle of glory could not be produced. The aged eyes of the would-be God could not see to read by daylight, and he had to send for candles. Candle-light strained his nerves of vision too much, and he handed the reading over to a cardinal. The cardinal began to read amid an ever blackening gloom, but had not read many lines before such a glare of lurid fire and such a crash burst from the inky heavens as was never equaled at Rome before. Terror fell upon all. The reading ceased. One cardinal jumped trembling from his chair, and exclaimed, ' It is the voice of God speaking, the thunders of Sinai.' ''

Among the blasphemous pretentions of Antichrist should be remembered several of its doctrines, particularly the doctrine of the Mass, which we will notice in a subsequent volume. Passing over the worshiping of saints and of Mary, we note some of the still more grievous errors.

Church Infallibility was one of the first, and paved the way to others. It was claimed before the office of Pope was acknowledged. It has been a most serious error, and has barred the way against the rectifying of errors when afterward discovered. It has placed the decrees of church councils beyond contradiction or questioning, either by reason or Scripture, and has made human ignorance and weaknesses and misconceptions the *standards of faith* instead of God's word—the Bible ; for, once conceded that the voice of the church council was *infallible* (unerring), everything must be forced to conform thereto ; and each council felt bound to render no decisions contrary to preceding councils ; and those which did otherwise were liable to be repudiated. So an error once affirmed could not be denied nor even dropped, and the Bible and reason had to be interpreted and twisted to match the *infallible* decrees of fallible men. No wonder it was found that it required a very expert theologian to interpret the Scriptures so as to make them agree with the so-called infallible decrees. No wonder either that, from expediency, Antichrist—

Proscribed the Bible. The history of Papacy shows clearly that, while professing to reverence the Bible as the Word of God, it has kept it in the background and its own *infallible words* in the front. Not only so, but it has proscribed God's Word entirely, as unfit to be read and dangerous to the people, that its own infallible word might have full control. It well knew that the Bible was dangerous to its power, and a constant denouncement of its blasphemous pretensions.

In the days of Papal power, the possession or reading of the Bible by the people was treated as a criminal offence. The art of printing and the general revival of learning resulting therefrom, about the sixteenth century, secured the resurrection of the Bible from the sepulcher of dead languages where Antichrist had long kept it hidden, forbidding the translating of it under severe penalties. And when an awakening spirit of independence began to scatter it in living languages among the people, Bible-burning was no uncommon thing; and long and loud were the merciless curses that issued from the Vatican against the presumptuous sinners who dared to translate, publish or read the Word of God.

When Wickliffe published his translation, Pope Gregory sent a bull to the Oxford University condemning the translator as "run into a detestable kind of wickedness." Tyndale's translation was also condemned; and when Luther published his German translation, Pope Leo. X. issued a bull against him. Nevertheless, the work went grandly and steadily forward : the Bible was to have a complete resurrection, and was destined to shed light upon men of every nation and language. Slowly the Church of Rome came to realize this, and resolved, therefore, to permit the translation of the Scriptures into modern languages, by Catholic translators, accompanied with Catholic notes. These, however, were not to be given to the people, except where there was danger of their receiving the Protestant translations. The Rhemish translation declares this.

The following show the character of some of the *Notes* of the Rhemish translation—which, however, is in recent years being superseded by the *Douay* translation, very similar, but with less pointed notes. A note on Matt. 3 reads: " Heretics may be punished and suppressed ; and may, and ought, by public authority, either spiritual or temporal, to be chastised or executed.'' One on Gal. 1 :8 reads: "Catholics should not spare their own parents, if heretics.'' On Heb. 5 :7 the note reads : "The translators of the Protestant Bible ought to be translated to the depths of hell.'' And on Rev. 17 :6 the comment reads : " But the blood of Protestants is not called the blood of saints, no more than the blood of thieves, man-killers, and other malefactors, for the shedding of which, by the order of justice, no commonwealth shall answer.''

The following are some of the restrictions imposed when it was found that the reading of the Bible could not be entirely prevented. The fourth rule of the *Index Expurgatoris* says :

" If any shall have the presumption to read or possess the Bible without written permission, he shall not receive absolution until he have first delivered up such Bible to the ordinary. Book-sellers who shall sell or otherwise dispose of Bibles in the vulgar tongue, to any person not having such permission, shall forfeit the value of the books, . . . and be subjected by the bishop to such other penalties as the bishop shall judge proper, according to the quality of the offence.''

Said the Council of Trent, in its session A. D. 1546:—

'' In order to restrain petulant minds, the council decrees that in matters of faith and morals, and whatever relates to the maintenance of Christian doctrine, no one, confiding in his own judgment shall dare to wrest the sacred Scriptures to his own sense of them, contrary to that which hath been held, and still is held, by the holy mother church, whose right it is to judge of the true meaning.''

From the bull of Pius VII., against Bible Societies, issued June 29, 1816, to the Primate of Poland, we quote:—

''We have been truly shocked at this most crafty device, by which the very foundations of religion are undermined; and having, because of the great importance of the subject, conferred in council with our venerable brethren, the cardinals of the holy Roman Church, we have, with the utmost care and attention, deliberated upon the measures proper to be adopted by our pontifical authority, in order to remedy and abolish *this pestilence* as far as possible. . . . Of your own accord you have already shown an ardent desire to detect and overthrow the impious machinations of these innovators; yet, in conformity with our office, we again and again exhort you that whatever you can achieve by *power*, provide by *counsel*, or effect by *authority*, you will daily execute with the utmost earnestness. . . . The Bible printed by heretics is to be numbered among other prohibited books, conformably to the rules of the Index.''

The same pope, in the year 1819, issued a bull against the use of the Scriptures in the schools of Ireland. From it we quote:—

'' Information has reached the ears of the sacred congregation that Bible Schools, supported by the funds of the heterodox, have been established in almost every part of Ireland ; in which the inexperienced of both sexes are invested with the fatal poison of depraved doctrines. . . . Every possible exertion must therefore be made, to keep the youth away from these destructive schools. . . . Do you labor with all your might to keep the orthodox youth from being corrupted by them—an object which will, I hope, be easily effected by the establishment of Catholic schools throughout your diocese.''

Here we have a candid admission of the real object of the establishment of Catholic parochial schools in Great Britain and North America, viz.: to protect their lines. Antichrist has no other object in offering education to the common people. Ignorance and superstition are Papacy's bulwarks; and the centuries of its power, including what is known as the " dark ages," prove this. The education of the clergy under " restrictions" was not neglected; but, that no provision was made for the education of the people, the dense ignorance of all old Roman Catholic countries is strong proof. Schools and Bibles have ever been Antichrist's unendurable enemies, and would not be tolerated, except as they became necessities—upon which a false light must be thrown for the preservation of Antichrist's existence.

From a bull by Leo XII. to the Roman Catholic clergy of Ireland, A. D. 1825, we quote:—

" It is no secret to you, venerable brethren, that a certain society, vulgarly called the Bible Society, is audaciously dispreading itself through the whole world. After despising the traditions of the holy fathers, and in opposition to the well known decree of the Council of Trent, this society has collected all its forces, and directs every means to one object :—to the translation, or rather to the perversion, of the Bible into the vernacular languages of all nations.''

Even the late Pope Pius IX. expressed his anguish of heart at the triumph on every hand of this great enemy of Antichrist—the Bible. He said, " Accursed be those very crafty and deceitful societies called Bible Societies, which thrust the Bible into the hands of the inexperienced youth.''

True, it was decreed at the Roman Catholic Plenary Council of Baltimore, A. D. 1886, that an approved Bible shall be permitted in Catholic schools of the United States. This, however, betokens no change in the real sentiment of Antichrist; it is but another stroke of its far-sighted policy, in deference to the spirit of liberty in this country, which abhors such restraints. They well knew, however, that the *liberty* and not the *Bible* was wanted; and inquiry discovers that now, two years after, the Bible is not to be found in Catholic schools hereabouts.

The doctrine of the natural, inherent immortality of man (that a human existence once begun can never cease) was another fruitful error, borrowed from Grecian philosophy. And, being admitted, it led naturally to the conclusion that if existence *must continue* forever, then the Bible expressions concerning the destruction of finally wilful sinners, the second death, etc., must be construed to *mean* the opposite of what they *say*, viz.: everlasting life, in some condition. Next, it was easy to decree that to the wicked it must be a life of suffering; and the torments were frequently pictured upon the walls of the churches as well as by the words of zealous priests and monks. This error was the more easily impressed upon converts because the Greek philosophers (then the leaders of the world in matters of science, religion and philosophy—whose ideas, as Josephus shows, had even begun to tincture Judaism) had long held and taught a punishment for the wicked in death. To their credit, however, be it noted that they never descended to the horrible *blasphemies* of God's character and government taught to the world by Antichrist. Next, it was in order to fix a place for this torment and call it hell, and to seek passages of Scripture referring to *sheol* and *hades* and *gehenna* which describe the real wages of sin—the first and second deaths—and dextrously to apply these and the parables of our Lord and the symbols of Revelation, so as to delude themselves and the whole world on this subject and most grievously to malign and blaspheme the character and plan of God, our all-wise and gracious Heavenly Father.

Purgatory was brought in, to relieve and make endurable

this terrible dose of doctrine, and withal to give Antichrist a firmer hold upon the people. It claimed to hold the keys of heaven and hell and to have power to remit the pains of purgatory: not only the Adamic penalty, and the weaknesses inherited thereby, but also the penalties of wilful, deliberate sins. What a leverage of power this gave, over an ignorant people, can be easily imagined—especially when the emperors and chief men of earth acknowledged and bowed before the deceiver.

Masses for the dead followed; and rich and poor alike felt it a duty to pay, and liberally, too, to have these. The efficacy of masses, for the relief of purgatorial sufferings, is claimed to be omnipotent—so that not even Jehovah or Christ could interfere with it. This became a source of great income to Antichrist; for the priests were not slow to remind the dying, if wealthy, of the propriety of leaving liberal bequests for masses for themselves—lest those who inherited their wealth should neglect the matter. And, indeed, within the present year warnings of a similar kind have appeared in Roman Catholic journals, urging that less money be spent upon funeral flowers, that the more might be spent for masses for the dead.

Indulgences came in, some time before the " Crusades": we know that indulgences were offered, as a bounty, to secure volunteers for these " Crusades" or " Holy Wars." By Papal edict, whoever would engage in these holy wars would not only have forgiveness for sins past, but also merit to offset sins future; and thus be guaranteed against certain purgatorial sufferings. These indulgences, Roman Catholics tell us, are not designed to be licenses to commit sins, but are rewards of merit which offset or *cancel* a certain number of days or years of purgatorial anguish: so that if a man's sins made him liable to one thousand years of suffering, and he, at one time, or at various times, secured indulgences to the amount of one thousand years, either for money, or for services rendered to Papacy, or by penances done, he would go free; if he had to his credit nine hundred years indulgence, he would have to endure one hundred years of suffering; and if indulgences were reckoned to much overbalance his penalties, he would probably be accounted a saint, of special influence in heaven, to be prayed to and adored. Of this order Louis, king of France, the Crusader, would be an example. He was canonized, and is now adored and prayed to as Saint Louis.

There is indeed a difference between this view of Indulgences and a license to commit sins; and yet it is very slight; for Papacy affixed to various common sins a certain amount of suffering, and not only could sins past be thus offset and cancelled, but those who had reason to think that they might commit certain sins, in the future, could thus provide beforehand merit to cancel them. Besides this, some, called "*plenary* [complete, entire] indulgences," are certainly understood to cover all sins, past and future.

The practice even at the present day seems scarcely credible. Romanists have certain prayers, a repetition of which constitutes a ground for indulgence for a limited period; and many added together, they claim, will protect from wrath a long time. Thus, those who say the "*Hail, Holy Queen*" are granted forty days of indulgence, while for saying the "*Litany of the Blessed Virgin*" there is an indulgence of two hundred days; and for those who say the "*Blessed be the Holy, Immaculate and Most Pure Conception of the Virgin Mary*" one hundred years indulgence is granted, etc., etc. In the "darker ages," when indulgences were freely offered for money and for services in the persecution of infidels and heretics, it may readily be imagined to what corruption this blasphemous doctrine led.

To crimes generally committed by the rich, who *could* pay liberally, enormous penalties were affixed, while the basest violations of justice, more common among the poorer classes, were lightly excused. Thus, marriage with a first cousin cost $5000, while wife-murder or parricide cost only $20. Spanheim says: "The institution of Indulgence was the mint which coined money for the Roman Church; the gold mines for the profligate nephews and natural children of the popes; the nerves of the Papal wars; the means of liquidating debt, and the inexhaustible fountain of luxury to the popes."

To regulate this traffic a graded scale of penalties was affixed to various sins—so many days or years in purgatory for each; and a scale of prices was also arranged to correspond, so that those obtaining indulgence for a murder or a theft, for infanticide, or adultery, or perjury, or other sins, could be charged at different rates. By this means penances were canceled and the torments of purgatory mitigated or ended, at the pleasure of Antichrist's agents. We cannot wonder that the people speedily got to understand that so much money paid for so much sin.

To such an extent was crime increased by these indulgences, that the indignation of the better classes of society was roused to rebellion against the church. Men's eyes began to be opened, and they saw the clergy, from the highest dignitaries of the church down to the lowest orders of officials, steeped in iniquity.

As the darkest hour precedes the storm, so just before the great Reformation movement was, morally, the darkest hour of Antichrist's dark reign. There the open and shameful traffic in indulgences produced nausea, and led Luther and other zealous papists to question and examine the entire system, both in its moral, and afterward in its doctrinal, aspects. Finally, Luther struck the true idea—that Papacy was indeed the Antichrist. And, having discovered this, he fearlessly pointed out some of the symbols of

Revelation, and showed their applicability and partial fulfilment in the Papal Hierarchy.

On this subject we quote the following from the pen of the well known clergyman, Lyman Abbott. He says:—

"Among other conditions, for which indulgences were formerly granted more than now, was the contribution of money to the church. This traffic reached its height in the beginning of the sixteenth century, under Leo X., who published indulgences to all who would contribute toward the erection of St. Peter's [Cathedral] at Rome. His chief agent for the sale of indulgences in Germany was one John Tetzel. The notorious vices of Tetzel did not prevent him from being selected as the bearer of these pardons to other purer souls, and no extravagance seemed to him too great, so that it brought money to his coffers. He declared that the red cross, which accompanied him wherever he went, had as great efficacy as the cross of Christ—that there was no sin so great that he could not remit it. 'Indulgences save not the living alone, they also save the dead. The very moment that the money chinks against the bottom of the chest, the soul escapes from Purgatory and flies free to heaven.' Such were some of his blasphemous declarations. A regular scale of prices was established. 'Polygamy cost six ducats; sacrilege and perjury, nine; murder, eight; witchcraft, two.' It was this open and shameless traffic which, more than anything else, led to the Reformation. Indulgences continued to be granted, not only for acts of worship, but also for contributions in money to the church; but the public and open sale of indulgences is now banished, for the most part, from the Church of Rome."

Another writer quotes Tetzel's language further, thus:—

"Draw near and I will give you letters duly sealed, by which even the sins you shall hereafter desire to commit shall be all forgiven you. There is no sin so great that indulgence cannot remit. Pay, only pay largely and you shall be forgiven. Ye priests, ye nobles, ye tradesmen, ye wives, ye maidens, ye young men, hearken to your departed parents and friends, who call to you from the bottomless abyss, 'We are enduring horrible torment; a small alms would de-

liver us. You can give it, Will you not?' With ten gro-
schen you can deliver your father from purgatory. Our
Lord God no longer deals with us as God—He has given
all power to the Pope.''

The following is handed down as a copy of the blanks
used by Tetzel—filled out with the name of the purchaser,
his sins, etc. :—

'' Our Lord Jesus Christ have mercy on thee. . . .,
and absolve thee by the merits of his most holy sufferings.
I, in virtue of the Apostolic power committed to me, absolve
thee from all. . . . excesses, sins and crimes that thou
mayest have committed, however great and enormous they
may be, and of whatever kind, . . . I remit the pains
thou wouldst have had to endure in purgatory, . . .
I restore thee to the innocence and purity of thy baptism,
so that, at the moment of death, the gates of the place of
torment shall be shut against thee, and the gates of paradise
open to thee. And if thou shouldst live long, this grace
continueth unchangeable till the time of thy end. In the
name of the Father, and of the Son, and of the Holy Ghost,
Amen. The brother, John Tetzel, commissary, hath signed
this with his own hand. ———.''

As to the immediate present we cannot say, but we know
that, only a few years since, printed indulgences with prices
affixed were kept on sale, at tables, in some of the large
Roman Catholic churches of Mexico and Cuba.

"IT WAS GIVEN HIM TO MAKE WAR WITH THE SAINTS AND TO OVERCOME THEM"—TO "WEAR OUT THE SAINTS OF THE MOST HIGH."

Did the papal counterfeit kingdom hold and exercise
power over the truly consecrated children of God, and overcome them,—'' wear them out'' by a long period of oppression, or *crushing*, as the Hebrew text implies? We answer,
Yes: every means that could be thought of was employed
to crush out the very spirit of true Christianity (John 8:36;
Gal. 5:1; 2 Cor. 3:17), and to substitute the spirit, doc-

trines and forms of Antichrist. It was at first less of an open attack on the faithful than of a slow, persistent, *crushing* oppression, dealing more particularly with opposing teachers ; and wearing out the patience and also the faith of many. This persistent worrying, and wearing out, are well illustrated in the institution of the Confessional, in which Antichrist not only took cognizance of every criticism and every word of objection to that system, uttered in the hearing of the confessing one, but under threat of future penalties compelled him to confess and repent of any opposing thoughts or acts of his own. This, too, was soon so backed by the civil power that to utter any protest against the church could be construed as treason against the civil power, which was upheld by papal authority.

In the first flush of papal exaltation, the people as a whole were nominally members of the church or else pagans ; and all who professed Christ were expected to conform to the usages and regulations of the gradually self-exalting hierarchy. Error, always more popular than truth, when exalted to influence and power, hunted down, proscribed and made disreputable the truth, and all who held it. This was the time when, as pictured in Revelation, the true Church (woman) fled into the wilderness—into solitude (Rev. 12:6) —an outcast because of her fidelity to the truth, and to the true Lord and Head of the Church. In this time, when apostates were being exalted as princes, the true, humble saints were experiencing what the Lord had warned them, and all who will live godly (in this present time), to expect, viz., persecution. The mother-in-law was against the daughter-in-law, father against son, and brother against brother ; and a man's foes were often indeed they of his own household. Could anything be conceived of more likely to *wear out* or *crush* the saints of the Most High than such a course, persisted in for centuries?

To gain an idea of the ferocity and relentlessness of this persecution, we must again turn to the pages of history.

The persecutions of the Christians under Pagan Rome were not worthy of comparison with those under Papal Rome, being less frequent, more limited in extent and much less severe. It is stated, on the authority of the early Christians, that the majority of the Roman magistrates who exercised in the provinces the authority of the emperor, or of the senate, and in whose hands was the power of life and death, behaved like men of polished manners and liberal education, who respected the rules of justice. They frequently declined the odious task of persecution, dismissed charges against the Christians with contempt (as Pilate and Herod attempted to do in the case of our Lord—Luke 23:14–16, 20, 22; Matt. 27:24), or suggested to accused Christians some legal evasion. When possible, they used their power much oftener for the relief than for the oppression of Christians; and the Pagan tribunals were often their surest refuge against their Jewish accusers.* The cruel persecution under the execrable tyrant Nero, who burned some of the Christians to divert public suspicion from himself, forms one of the darkest pages in the history of Pagan Rome; but his victims were *comparatively* few. The victims of Pagan persecution were not communities generally, but prominent individuals. These persecutions of leading representatives, even, were not so much a fixed, persistent determination of opposition on the part of the government as a result of uncontrollable popular clamor, awakened by superstition, which it seemed to the rulers necessary to satisfy in the interest of peace and order. Several instances illustrative of this are found in the career of the Apostle Paul, as well as of other apostles.—See Acts 19:35–41; 25:24–27; 26:2, 3, 28. Even the more general perse-

---

* Gibbon, Vol. II., pages 31–33.

cutions, under the Roman emperors, lasted for but brief periods, except that under Diocletian, which continued with varying severity for ten years. Between these persecutions were often long periods of peace and quiet. Under the emperors, though greatly harassed, Christianity was not worn out, but, as we have seen, it greatly prospered.

How different the persecutions of Papacy, which laid hold not only of prominent opposers but of all, and whose persecutions lasted not for a few months only, but incessantly! What under Pagan emperors had been a passing rage or frenzy, under the popes was reduced to a regular system, animated by religious fanaticism and scheming ambition,—and inspired with a Satanic zeal, energy and cruelty unparalleled in the annals of history. The apostate church laid aside the sword of the spirit, and, grasping the arm of the empire, turned its carnal weapons with relentless fury upon every weaker opponent that stood in the way of its ambition ; while it courted, flattered and deceived those in authority until it gained their confidence and usurped their place and power.

Both heathenism and heresy then became the subjects of persecution—especially the latter. The so-called Christian clergy, says Edgar, "misapplied the laws of the Jewish theocracy, and the transactions of the Jewish annals, for the unchristian and base purpose of awakening the demon of persecution against the mouldering remains of Grecian and Roman [heathenish] superstition. . . . They dissolved the ancient fabric of Polytheism and transferred its revenues to the use of the church, the state and the army. . . . Gentilism was expelled from the Roman territory. . . . Coercion in general was substituted for conviction, and terror for the gospel. One blushes to read of a Symmachus and a Libanius, two heathen orators, pleading for *reason* and *persuasion* in the propagation of

religion, whilst a Theodosius and an Ambrosius, a Christian
emperor and a Christian bishop, urge violence and con-
straint.''

Upon the accession of Constantine to the sovereignty of
Rome, he was inclined to tolerate all religions, as was
shown by the celebrated edict of Milan, which granted *religious freedom* to every individual of the Roman empire.
Such a measure should have been hailed with joy by the
Christian Church, which had so longed for liberty under
previous persecutions; but such was not the case. The
true spirit of Christianity had departed, and now the ambition of the church was to exalt itself as rapidly as possible
by crushing out every spark of liberty and subduing all
things to itself. Accordingly, says Gibbon,* '' His [Con-
stantine's] ecclesiastical ministers soon contrived to reduce
the impartiality of the magistrate, and to awaken the zeal
of the proselyte; . . . and he extinguished the hope
of peace and toleration, from the moment that he assembled three hundred bishops within the walls of the palace.''
The emperor was there persuaded to declare that those who
resisted the judgment of this clerical body in matters of
faith should prepare themselves for immediate exile. And
their decisions were declared to be of divine authority.
This spirit of intolerance soon ripened into bitter and relentless persecution. Constantine issued two penal laws
against heresy, and his example was followed by succeeding emperors—Valentinian, Gratian, Theodosius, Arcadius and Honorius. Theodosius published fifteen, Arcadius
twelve, and Honorius no less than eighteen of these statutes.
These are recorded in the Theodosian and in the Justinian
codes, to the disgrace of their priestly and imperial authors.

What Antichrist was pleased to call heresy (much of
which was truth and righteousness endeavoring to hold a

---

* Vol. II., page 236.

footing) was classed as worse than infidelity, and both were opposed by kings, emperors and theologians; and both were persecuted, especially the former, by the Inquisition. When, about the beginning of the thirteenth century, there came a revival of learning, and men began to awaken from the sleep and troubled dreams of the "dark ages," those from whose minds the truth had not been entirely eradicated were stimulated, and the standard of truth was raised in opposition to the grosser errors of Antichrist. Then the persecuting spirit of Antichrist was aroused to furious action, to crush out the opposition.

Kings and princes who trembled for the security of their crowns, if they to any extent incurred the pope's displeasure, and whose realms might be laid under a dreaded interdict, should they or their people refuse to render absolute obedience to the pope's commands, were sworn to *exterminate heresy*, and admonished to purify their provinces from heretical perversity, on the pain of having their dominions wrested from them; and those barons who neglected to aid in the work of persecution forfeited their estates. Kings and princes, therefore, were not tardy in their efforts to comply with the mandates of the Papacy, and the barons and their retainers were at their service, to aid in the work of destruction.

Even before this awakening, as early as the year A. D. 630, the Council of Toledo compelled the king of Spain, on his accession to the throne, to swear to tolerate no heretical subjects in the Spanish dominions; and it was declared that the sovereign who should violate such oath would "be accursed in the sight of the everlasting God, and become the fuel of eternal fire." But the awful import of such demands was much more fully realized when the awakening began, and when Antichrist had obtained the maximum of his power.

The Council of Oxford in 1160 consigned a company of Waldenses, who had emigrated from Gascony to England, to the secular arm for punishment. Accordingly, King Henry II. ordered them, men and women, to be publicly whipped, branded on the cheek with a red-hot iron, and driven, half-naked, out of the city in the dead of winter; and none were permitted to show them pity or to grant them the slightest favor.

Frederick, the emperor of Germany, A. D. 1224, sentenced heretics of every description, alive, to the flames, their property to confiscation, and their posterity, unless they became persecutors, to infamy. Louis, king of France, A. D. 1228, published laws for the extirpation of heresy, and enforced their execution. He forced Raymond, Count of Toulouse, to undertake the extermination of heresy from his dominions without sparing friend or vassal.

From the earliest encroachments of the power which by degrees developed into the papal system, resistance was made; but that resistance was offered only by a faithful few, whose influence made little impression on the overwhelming tide of worldliness that swept in upon the church. Gradually, as they discerned the error, some quietly withdrew themselves from the great apostasy, to worship God according to the dictates of conscience, even at the risk of persecution. Notable among these were some, afterward called Waldenses, Albigenses, Wycliffites and Huguenots. These, though called by several names had, so far as we can judge, a common origin and a common faith. "Waldensianism," says Rainerous (3.4), the noted Inquisitor of the thirteenth century, "is the ancientest heresy; and existed, according to some, from the days of [pope] Sylvester, and according to others, from the days of the apostles." Sylvester was pope when Constantine was emperor and confessed Christianity; and thus we see that the truth was not without its adherents from the first, who, though humble and unpopular, resolutely resisted Papacy and the papal doctrines of purgatory, image-worship, invocation of saints, worship of the Virgin Mary, prayer for the dead, transubstantiation, celibacy of the clergy, indulgences, mass, etc., and discountenanced pilgrimages, festivals, the burning of incense, sacred burial, the use of holy water, sacerdotal vestments, monachism, etc., and held that the teaching of the Sacred Scriptures should be received, in opposition to the traditions and claims of the Church of Rome. They regarded the pope as the head of all errors, and claimed that the remission of sins is obtained through the merits of the Lord Jesus, only.

The faith and works of this people were a stand for reformation, and a protest against error, long before the days of Luther; and they, and other opposers of Romanism, were hunted and hated and persecuted with pitiless fury, by papal emissaries. The Waldenses and Albigenses were the most numerous bodies of Protestants against Papacy; and when the literary awakening of the thirteenth century came, it was mainly from these that the truth shone out, though reflected and intensified in utterance by Wycliffe, Huss, Luther, and others. And their doctrines, backed by simplicity and morality, shone out with the greater luster in contrast to the pompous pride and flagrant immoralities of the then exalted Papacy.

Then it was that popes, councils, theologians, kings, crusaders and inquisitors combined their fiendish powers to exterminate every opponent, and to extinguish the faintest rays of dawning light. Pope Innocent III. first sent missionaries to the districts in which the doctrines of the Albigenses had gained foothold, to preach Romanism, work miracles, etc.; but, finding these efforts unavailing, he proclaimed a crusade against them and offered to all who would engage in it the pardon of all sins and an immediate passport to heaven without passing through purgatory. With full faith in the pope's power to bestow the promised rewards, half a million men—French, German and Italian —rallied around the standard of the cross, for the defence of Catholicism and the extinction of heresy. Then followed a series of battles and sieges covering a space of twenty years. The city of Beziers was stormed and taken in 1209, and the citizens, without regard for age or sex, perished by the sword to the number of sixty thousand, as reported by several historians. The blood of those who fled to churches, and were murdered there by the holy crusaders, drenched the altars and flowed through the streets.

Lavaur was besieged in 1211. The governor was hanged on a gibbet, and his wife was thrown into a well and crushed with stones. The citizens were without discrimination put to death, four hundred being burned alive. The flourishing country of Languedoc was devastated, its cities burned, and its inhabitants swept away by fire and sword. It is estimated that one hundred thousand Albigenses fell in one day; and their bodies were heaped together and burned.

All this rioting in blood and villainy was done in the name of religion : professedly for the glory of God and the honor of the church, but really to uphold Antichrist, sitting in the temple of God [the church], showing himself that he is a god—a powerful one—able to conquer and destroy his enemies. The clergy thanked God for the work of destruction, and a hymn of praise to God for the glorious victory at Lavaur was composed and sung. The dreadful carnage at Beziers was accounted as the "visible judgment of heaven" on the heresy of Albigensianism. The crusaders attended high mass in the morning, and proceeded throughout the day to waste the country of Languedoc and murder its inhabitants.

Be it remembered, however, that these open crusades, against the Albigenses and Waldenses, were undertaken merely because the so-called "heresy" had gained a strong hold upon large portions of these communities. It would be a great mistake to suppose that the crusades were the only persecutions: the quiet, steady *crushing* of individuals, in the aggregate numbering thousands, all over Papacy's wide domain, went steadily on—wearing out the saints of the Most High.

Charles V., Emperor of Germany and King of Spain and the Netherlands, persecuted the friends of the Reformation throughout his extensive dominions. Supported by the Diet of Worms, he proscribed Luther, his followers and his writings; and condemned all who should aid Luther or read his books, to the confiscation of their property, the ban of the empire and the penalty of high treason. In the Netherlands the men who followed Luther were to be beheaded, and the women buried alive or if obstinate to be committed to the flames. Though this wholesale law was suspended, the work of death in all its horrid forms proceeded. The Duke of Alva boasted of the execution of 18,000 Protestants in six weeks. Paolo reckons the number who in the Netherlands were executed on account of their religion at 50,000; and Grotius gives the list of the Belgic martyrs at 100,000. Charles, with his dying breath, exhorted his son, Philip II., to carry on to completion the work of persecution and extermination of heresy which he had begun—which advice Philip was not slow to follow. With fury he stimulated the spirit of persecution, consigning Protestants to the flames without discrimination or pity.

Francis and Henry, the French kings, followed the example of Charles and Philip in their zeal for Catholicism and the extermination of heresy. The massacres of Merindol, Orange and Paris are forcible illustrations of their

22–B

zeal in the cause of Antichrist. The massacre of Merindol, planned by the French king and approved by the French parliament, was committed to the president, Oppeda, for execution. The president was commissioned to slay the population, burn the towns and demolish the castles of the Waldenses, large numbers of whom resided in that section. Roman Catholic historians admit that in compliance with this commission thousands, including men, women and children, were massacred, twenty-four towns were ruined, and the country was left waste and desolate. Men, women and children fled to the woods and mountains for safety and were pursued and put to the sword. Many who remained in the towns met the same or a worse fate. Five hundred women were thrown into a barn which was set on fire, and when any leaped from the windows they were received on the points of spears. Women were violated and children were murdered in sight of their parents, who were powerless to protect them. Some were dashed over precipices and others were dragged naked through the streets.

The massacre of Orange, A. D. 1562, was of a similar character to that of Merindol, and is described with precision by Catholic historians. The Italian army sent by Pope Pius IV. was commanded to slay men, women and children ; and the command was executed with terrible cruelty. The defenseless heretics were slain with the sword, precipitated from rocks, thrown on the points of hooks and daggers, hanged, roasted over slow fires and exposed to shame and torture of every description.

The massacre in Paris on St. Bartholomew's day, August 24th, A. D. 1572, equaled in cruelty, but exceeded in extent, the massacres of Merindol and Orange. This has also been detailed by Catholic historians, one of whom, Thuanus, stigmatizes it as a " a ferocious cruelty, without a parallel in all antiquity." The tolling of the tocsin at midnight, August 23d, gave the signal of destruction, and the dreadful scenes of Merindol and Orange began to be re-enacted against the hated Huguenots. The carnival of death lasted seven days; the city flowed with human blood; the court was heaped with the slain on which the king and queen gazed with extreme satisfaction. The body of Admiral Coligny was dragged through the streets; and the river Seine was covered with floating dead bodies. Accounts of the number killed vary from 5,000 to 10,000. The work of destruction was not confined to Paris, but extended very widely through the French nation. On the preceding day special messengers were dispatched in every direction ordering a general massacre of the Huguenots. The same scenes were accordingly enacted in nearly all the provinces, and estimates of the number slain vary from 25,000 to 70,000.

In these dreadful scenes of carnage Antichrist found extreme satisfaction. The pope and his court exulted at the victory of Catholicism over Waldensianism at Merindol, and the impious Oppeda was styled "The defender of the faith and the hero of Christianity." The French king went to mass, and returned solemn thanks to God for the victory over and massacre of the Huguenots at Paris. This carnage, sanctioned by the French king and parliament and Roman Catholic subjects, was probably at the direct instigation of the pope and the Papal Hierarchy. That it was highly approved, at least, is evident from the fact that at the Papal Court the news was received with great rejoicing. The pope, Gregory XIII., went in grand procession to the church of Saint Louis to render thanks to God for the signal victory. He at once proclaimed a jubilee, and sent a nuncio to the French court, who in the pope's name praised "the exploit so long meditated and so happily executed for the good of religion." A medal was struck by the king in memory of the massacre, bearing the inscription, "*Pietas Excitavit Justitiam*"—Piety Excited Justice.

Medals commemorative of the event were also coined in the Papal mint by order of the pope. One of these is now on exhibition in Memorial Hall, Philadelphia, Pa. Its face presents a raised figure of the pope and the abbreviated inscription, "*Gregorius XIII., Pontifex Maximus Anno I.*," —the first year of his pontificate, viz., A. D. 1572. On the reverse side of this medal is a representation of a destroying angel, bearing in the left hand a cross, and in the right hand a sword, before whom, prostrate and fleeing, a band of Huguenots, men, women and children, is represented, whose faces and figures express horror and despair. Under this are the words, "*Ugonottorum Strages 1572*"—which signifies, "The slaughter of the Huguenots, 1572."

A picture of the St. Bartholomew Massacre was hung in the Vatican. It had a scroll at the top, on which was inscribed, in Latin, words signifying, "*The Pontiff approves the fate of Coligny.*" Coligny was a prominent leader of the Huguenots and one of the first to fall. After he was killed, his head was severed from his body and sent to the queen (who had it embalmed and sent as a trophy to Rome), while his body was dragged by the populace through the streets of Paris. The king was shortly afterward seized with the horrors of remorse from which he never recovered. It is recorded that to his confidential physician he said, "I know not what has happened to me, but in mind and body I am shaking as in a fever. It seems to me every moment, whether waking or sleeping, that mangled bodies present themselves to me with hideous faces and covered with blood." He died in great agony, covered with a bloody sweat.

In 1641 Antichrist proclaimed a "war of religion" in Ireland, and called on the people to massacre the Protestants by every means in their power. The deluded people heard the command as the voice of God, and were not slow to execute their commission. Protestant blood flowed freely throughout Ireland, houses were reduced to ashes, towns and villages were almost destroyed. Some were forced to murder their own relatives, and then to take their own lives—the last words that fell upon their ears being the assurances of priests, that their dying agonies were but the beginnings of eternal torment. Thousands died of cold and hunger, while endeavoring to emigrate to other lands. In Cavan, the road for twelve miles together was stained with the bloody tracks of wounded fugitives; sixty children were abandoned in the flight, by parents fiercely hunted, and it was declared that any who should in any way help these little ones should be buried by their sides. Seventeen adults were buried alive at Fermaugh, and seventy-two at Kilkenny. In the province of Ulster alone, over 154,-000 Protestants were either massacred or expelled from Ireland.

O'Niel, the primate of Ireland, pronounced this "a pious and lawful war," and the pope (Urban VIII.) issued a bull dated May 1643, granting "full and absolute remission of all their sins" to those who had taken part in "gallantly doing what in them lay, to extirpate and wholly root out the pestiferous leaven of heretical contagion."

THE INQUISITION OR "HOLY OFFICE."

To Dominic, the leading spirit in this crusade, is ascribed the honor of inventing the infernal Inquisition, though Benedict, who is zealous in ascribing to Saint Dominic the honor of being the first Inquisitor General, is doubtful as to whether the *idea* first suggested itself to Pope Innocent or to Saint Dominic. It was first established by Pope Innocent III., in A. D. 1204.

St. Dominic was a monster, devoid of every feeling of compassion, who seemed to find his chief delight in scene of torture and misery. During the crusade against the Albigenses, with a crucifix in his hand he led and encouraged the holy warriors to deeds of death and destruction. The Inquisition or Holy Office is to-day a tribunal in the Roman Catholic Church for the discovery, repression and punishment of heresy and other offences against the Church of Rome.* But in Dominic's day it had no legal tribunal, nor were the instruments of torment brought to the perfection exhibited in later days. Nevertheless, Dominic, without such machinery, found abundant means of torture, in dislocating joints, tearing nerves, and lacerating the limbs of his victims, and in burning at the stake those whose convictions were unshaken by other means, and who would not renounce their faith and liberties.

Under his commission from Pope Innocent, to punish with confiscation, banishment and death the heretics who would not receive his gospel, Dominic stimulated the civil magistracy and populace to massacre the heretical Waldenses; and he at one time committed one hundred and eighty Albigenses to the flames. It was for such faithfulness in the service of Antichrist that he was canonized a saint, and is to-day adored and prayed to by Roman Catholics. The Roman Breviary (somewhat like a Prayer Book), referring to St. Dominic, lauds " his merits and doctrines which enlightened the church, his ingenuity and virtue which overthrew the Tolossan heretics, and his many miracles which extended even to the raising of the dead." The Roman Missal (which embraces the service connected with the administration of the Lord's supper) eulogizes his merits, and prays for temporal aid through his intercession. Thus Antichrist still upholds and honors its faithful heroes.

---

* The Chair of St. Peter, page 589.

It would be impossible briefly to convey any adequate conception of the horrors of the Inquisition, or of the dreadful fear which it inspired among the people. Those not loud in their praise of Antichrist, or who ventured a criticism of his methods, were suspected of heresy; and such persons, without warning or redress, were liable to imprisonment in a dungeon for an indefinite time until a convenient season for trial—both the accuser and the accusation often being equally unknown to them. The proceedings of these trials were conducted secretly, and tortures were often employed to extort confessions. The tortures inflicted were almost too appalling to be credited in this age and land of freedom, yet their reality is confirmed by evidence which even Catholic historians cannot deny; and their fruitless attempts to apologize for them only tend to substantiate the evidence. Instruments of torture, relics of the Inquisition, are still in existence which would render denial unavailing. The "Holy Office" even employed physicians to watch the process of torture and stop it when death seemed likely to relieve the sufferer; and the victim was allowed partially to recover, that the torture might be applied a second or even a third time. These tortures were not always inflicted as punishments for the offence of heresy: they were in general for the purpose of compelling the accused to confess, retract or implicate others, as the case might be.

Even within the present century, after the Inquisition had lost many of its horrors, it was still terrible. The historian of Napoleon's wars, describing the capture of Toledo by his army, incidentally mentions the opening of the Inquisition prison, and says:—

" Graves seemed to open, and pale figures like ghosts issued from dungeons which emitted a sepulchral odor. Bushy beards hanging down over the breast, and nails grown like bird's claws, disfigured the skeletons, who with laboring bosoms inhaled, for the first time for a long series of years, the fresh air. Many of them were reduced to cripples, the head inclined forward and the arms and hands hanging down rigid and helpless. They had been confined in dens so low they could not rise up in them, and in spite of all the care of the [army] surgeons many of them expired the same day. On the following day General Lasalle minutely inspected the place, attended by several officers of his staff. The number of machines for torture thrilled even men inured to the battle field, with horror.''

"In a recess in a subterranean vault, contiguous to the private hall for examinations, stood a wooden figure made by the hands of monks and representing the Virgin Mary. A gilded glory encompassed her head, and in her right hand she held a banner. It struck all at first sight as suspicious that, notwithstanding the silken robe, descending on each side in ample folds from her shoulders, she should wear a sort of cuirass. On closer scrutiny it appeared that the fore part of the body was stuck full of extremely sharp nails and small narrow knife-blades, with the points of both turned toward the spectator. The arms and hands were jointed, and machinery behind the partition set the figure in motion. One of the servants of the Inquisition was compelled by command of the General to work the *machine* as he termed it. When the figure extended her arms, as though to press some one lovingly to her heart, the well-filled knapsack of a Polish grenadier was made to supply the place of a living victim. The statue hugged it closer and closer, and when the attendant, agreeably to orders, made the figure unclasp her arms and return to her former position, the knapsack was perforated to the depth of two or three inches, and remained hanging on the points of the nails and the knife blades.''

"Racks" of various sorts were invented, and applied as means of torture. One of the simplest methods is explained thus: The victim, stripped of all clothing, had his arms fastened behind his back with a hard cord, with which, by the action of a pully, he was raised off his feet, to which weights were attached. The sufferer was several times let fall, and raised with a jerk, which dislocated the joints of his arms and legs, while the cord by which he was suspended penetrated the quivering flesh to the very bone.

A reminder of such outrages in the name of Christ came to public notice recently. A Bible Society's printing-office in Rome being crowded for space, it rented a large room near the Vatican. A large and peculiar ring in the ceiling attracted attention, and inquiry discovered the fact that the room in which they are now busy printing the Bible,—" the sword of the spirit, which is the Word of God," by which Antichrist has already been rendered *"powerless"* to oppress and wear out the saints,—is the very room once used by the Inquisition as a torture-chamber ; the pulley-ring having probably been used to rack many a poor, gagged sufferer.

Those convicted of heresy were sometimes sentenced to what was called an "Act of Faith." The ecclesiastical authority transferred the condemned to the secular power, while the clergy, in pretense of mercy, implored the magistracy to show compassion to the condemned, and, holding up the cross, pleaded with the victim to recant and save his present and future life. The magistrates knew well their part, and showed no mercy except to recanters ; thus gaining the blessings and titles of " Defender of the Faith," and " Exterminator of Heretics." The condemned " heretic," dressed in a yellow coat variegated with pictures of dogs, serpents, flames and devils, was led to the place of execution, tied to the stake and committed to the flames.

Torquemada, another famous Inquisitor General, furnished a marked illustration of the spirit of Antichrist. Roman Catholic writers admit that he caused ten thousand two hundred and twenty (10,220) persons, men and women, to be burned alive. Llorente, who was for three years the Secretary General of the Inquisition, and had access to all the documentary evidences, in his Reports, published A. D.

1817 (4 vols.), shows that between the years 1481 and 1808, by order of this "Holy Office" *alone*, no less than 31,912 persons were burned alive, and nearly 300,000 tortured and condemned to serve penances. Every Catholic country in Europe, Asia and America had its Inquisition.

We cannot here trace Antichrist's persecutions of everything resembling reforms, liberty of conscience or political freedom. Suffice it to say, this persecution extended to every country where Papacy had a footing—to Germany, Holland, Poland, Italy, England, Ireland, Scotland, France, Spain, Portugal, Abyssinia, India, Cuba, Mexico and some South American states. Space forbids our reciting individual cases which would serve to show that many of the martyrs were truly saints and heroes, who under the most horrible sufferings had grace sufficient, and were often enabled, while dying by inches, to sing hymns of praise and thanks to the true Head of the true Church, and, like him, to pray for their enemies who, as he had foretold, persecuted them for his sake.*

Neither will we, for the same reasons, particularize all the awful, sickening, soul-harrowing tortures, inflicted upon some of the Lord's jewels because of faithfulness to their convictions. It is estimated, by those who seemingly have given the subject thorough investigation, that Papacy, during the past thirteen hundred years, has, directly or indirectly, caused the death of *fifty millions of people*. And it may safely be said that human and Satanic ingenuity were taxed to their utmost to invent new and horrible tortures, for both the political and religious opponents of Antichrist; the latter—heretics—being pursued with tenfold fury. Be-

---

*To those desiring a fuller account of these awful times and scenes we commend Macaulay's History of England; Motley's Dutch Republic; D'Aubigne's History of the Reformation; White's Eighteen Christian Centuries; Elliot on Romanism; and Fox's Book of Martyrs.

sides the common forms of persecution and death, such as racking, burning, drowning, stabbing, starving and shooting with arrows and guns, fiendish hearts meditated how the most delicate and sensitive parts of the body, capable of the most excruciating pain, could be affected; molten lead was poured into the ears; tongues were cut out and lead poured into the mouths; wheels were arranged with knife blades attached so that the victim could be slowly chopped to pieces; claws and pincers were made red hot and used upon sensitive parts of the body; eyes were gouged out; finger nails were pulled off with red hot irons; holes, by which the victim was tied up, were bored through the heels; some were forced to jump from eminences onto long spikes fixed below, where, quivering with pain, they slowly died. The mouths of some were filled with gunpowder, which, when fired, blew their heads to pieces; others were hammered to pieces on anvils; others, attached to bellows, had air pumped into them until they burst; others were choked to death with mangled pieces of their own bodies; others with urine, excrement, etc., etc.

Some of these fiendish atrocities would be quite beyond belief were they not well authenticated. They serve to show to what awful depravity the human heart can descend; and how blind to right, and every good instinct, men can become under the influence of *false, counterfeit religion.* The spirit of Antichrist degraded and debased the world as the spirit of the true Christ and the power and influence of the true Kingdom of God would have elevated and ennobled men's hearts and actions;—and as they will do, during the Millennium. This is to a slight extent illustrated by the advance in civilization, and the increase of justice and mercy, since the power of Antichrist began to wane, and the word of God began to be heard, and heeded, even slightly.

Truly, no device of which we can conceive could have been better calculated to deceive and oppress mankind. Advantage has been taken of every depraved disposition and weakness of fallen men ; every base passion has been stimulated and appealed to, and the gratification of those passions rewarded. The vicious were thus allured and enlisted as its devotees, while those of nobler cast were engaged by other means—by an outward and hypocritical show of piety, self-denial and charity manifested in its monastic institutions, but which served only to lead many such far from the paths of virtue. The gay and the frivolous found ample satisfaction in its parade and show, its pomp and ceremony ; the enterprising and chivalrous in its missions and crusades ; the profligate in its indulgences ; and the cruel bigot in its enterprises for oppressing its opponents.

In horror and wonder we ask ourselves, Why did kings, and princes, and emperors, and the people at large, permit such atrocities ? Why did they not arise long ago and smite down Antichrist ? The answer is found in the Scriptures (Rev. 18:3): The nations were *drunk* (stupefied), they lost their senses in drinking the *mixed wine* (doctrine, false and true mixed) given them by the apostate church. They were deceived by the claims of Papacy. And, truth to tell, they are only partly aroused from their stupor yet ; for though the ambassadors of kings, falling before the pope, do not as of old address him as the " Lamb of God that taketh away the sins of the world," nor think of him as " a God with power over all things on earth and in heaven," yet they are still far from realizing the truth,—that Papacy has been, and is, Satan's counterfeit of the true Kingdom.

While kings and soldiers wearied of such inhuman work, it was not so with the holy (?) hierarchy ; and we find the General Council of Sienna, A. D. 1423, declaring that the spread of heresy in different parts of the world was due to the *remissness of the Inquisitors*—to the offence of God, the injury of Catholicism and the perdition of souls. Princes were admonished, by the mercy of God, to *exterminate* heresy if they would escape divine vengeance; and plenary indulgences were granted to all who would engage in the work of destruction or provide arms for the purpose. These enactments were published in the churches every Sabbath. And Roman Catholic theologians and historians are by no means few who have wielded their pens in the unholy cause of justifying, recommending and praising the persecution of heresy. Bellarmine, for instance, declares that the apostles "abstained from calling in the secular arm only because there were in their day no Christian princes." Doctor Dens, a celebrated Roman Catholic theologian, published a work on theology in 1758, which is regarded by papists to-day as standard authority, especially in their colleges, where it ranks as Blackstone does on English civil law. This work breathes the spirit of persecution throughout. It condemns the patrons of heresy to confiscation of goods, banishment from the country, confinement in prison, infliction of death and deprivation of Christian burial.

One of the authorized curses published in the Romish Pontifical, to be used against Protestants, reads as follows:—

"May God Almighty and all his saints curse them with the curse with which the devil and his angels are cursed. Let them be destroyed out of the land of the living. Let the vilest of deaths come upon them, and let them descend alive into the pit. Let their seed be destroyed from the earth—by hunger, and thirst, and nakedness and all distress let them perish. May they have all misery and pestilence and torment. Let all they have be cursed. Always and everywhere let them be cursed. Speaking and silent let them be cursed. Within and without let them be cursed. From the crown of the head to the sole of the foot let them be cursed. Let their eyes become blind, let their ears become deaf, let their mouth become dumb, let their tongue cleave to their jaws, let not their hands handle, let not their feet walk. Let all the members of their body be cursed. Cursed let them be, standing or lying, from this time forth forever; and thus let their candle be extinguished in the presence of God, at the day of judgment. Let their burial be with dogs and asses. Let hungry wolves devour their corpses. Let the devil and his angels be their companions forever. Amen, Amen ; so be it, so let it be.''

This is the spirit of Papacy; and all who possess the spirit of the true Christ should readily recognize so base a counterfeit.

Since errors of doctrine lie at the very foundation of all these errors of conduct, it cannot be doubted that if circumstances were again favorable, the doctrines being unchanged, their bad spirit and bad fruits would shortly again appear, in similar acts of injustice, oppression, superstition, ignorance and persecution ; and any and all means conceivable would be resorted to, for restoring, upholding and extending the *counterfeit* Kingdom of God. In proof of this, let us cite a few incidents which recently chanced to come to our attention, as follows:—

In Ahuehuetitlan, Guererro, Mexico, August 7th, 1887, a native Protestant missionary, named Abraham Gomez, and two assistants, were murdered in cold blood by natives, at the instigation of a Roman Catholic priest, Father Vergara, who, when celebrating mass the day previous, is reported to have urged his people to ''make an example of the minister of Satan'' who had come among them ; adding, that they might ''kill him'' with all safety, counting upon protection from the chief of police as well as the priest. The priest's word was law to the benighted people, and to the civil authorities. The mangled body of the poor missionary, shot and hacked to pieces, was dragged through the streets, subject to all sorts of indignities, a *warning to others*. For this no redress could be obtained.

The New York *Independent* having called attention to this

bloody massacre, the following retort was made by the *Free-man*, an influential New York Roman Catholic journal :—

"They [Protestant missionaries] see honest people kneel, at the sound of the *Angelus*, in honor of the Annunciation and the Incarnation. The Bible, they say, will soon wipe out such 'superstition.' A light burns before an image of the Mother of God. 'Ha!' cries the missionary, 'We shall soon teach the benighted to break that symbol!' and so on. If the killing of a few missionaries of this kind would keep others like them at home, we should almost— we Papists are so wicked !—be inclined to say : 'On with the dance ; let joy be unconfined.'"

A minister by the name of C. G. Moule tells a painful story, which has gone the rounds of the press, of the persecution, in Madeira, of Robert Kelley and the converts resulting from his labors, who, with their children, nearly one thousand persons in all, suffered expatriation as the penalty for receiving a crumb of truth.

In "Protestant Prussia," so called, Pastor Thummel has been arrested for "insulting the Roman Catholic Church." He published a pamphlet criticising Papacy, in which one of the "insulting" remarks was to the effect that Papacy is an apostasy "built upon superstition and idolatry."

Recently the Caroline Islands were in dispute between Prussia and Spain, and the pope got himself appointed arbitrator or judge, to settle the dispute. (Much in this reminds one of his former power and policy as arbiter or supreme judge of nations.) The pope decided in favor of Spain. A man-of-war, fifty soldiers and six priests were at once dispatched by Spain ; and on their arrival Mr. Doane, an American missionary, was made a prisoner and cut off from all intercourse with his converts, without cause, except that he refused to surrender his mission work and property to the priests ; and because, the islands now belonging to Spain, and Spain belonging to the pope, none but the pope's religion could be tolerated.

A gentleman, formerly a Roman Catholic, and a friend of the writer, states that recently, when traveling in South America, he was assaulted with stones and obliged to flee for his life, because he would neither uncover his head nor kneel with the multitude, when the Romish priests bearing the crucifix and host passed along the streets. And a similar case, in which three Americans were struck by the priests, mobbed by the people and arrested by the police in the city of Madrid, Spain, for a like offence, is no doubt still fresh in the minds of many who read the daily papers.

The Converted Catholic quotes as follows from the *Watchman,* a Roman Catholic journal published at St. Louis, Mo.:

"Protestantism! We would draw and quarter it. We would impale it and hang it up for crows' nests. We would tear it with pinchers and fire it with hot irons. We would fill it with moulten lead, and sink it in hell-fire a hundred fathoms deep."

In the light of the past, it is entirely probable that with such a spirit, if the power were possessed, the Editor of the *Watchman* would soon extend his threats beyond "Protestant-*ism*" to the persons of Protestants.

In Barcelona, Spain, by order of the government, a large number of copies of the Bible were recently burned—of course at the instigation of the Church of Rome. The following, translated from the *Catholic Banner*, the organ of Papacy there, shows that they approved and appreciated the action. It said:—

"Thank God, we have at last turned toward the times when those who propagated heretical doctrines were punished with exemplary punishment. The re-establishment of the Holy Tribunal of the Inquisition must soon take place. Its reign will be more glorious and fruitful in results than in the past. Our Catholic heart overflows with faith and enthusiasm; and the immense joy we experience, as we begin to reap the fruit of our present campaign, exceeds all imagination. What a day of pleasure will that be for us, when we see Anti-clericals writhing in the flames of Inquisition !"

To encourage another crusade, the same paper says :—

"We believe it right to publish the names of those holy men under whose hands so many sinners suffered, that good Catholics may *venerate their memory:*—

"By Torquemada—

Men and women burnt alive, . . .	10,220
Burnt in effigy, ...	6,840
Condemned to other punishments, . . .	97,371

"By Diego Deza—

Men and women burnt alive, ...	2,592
Burnt in effigy, ...	829
Condemned to other punishments, . . .	32,952

"By Cardinal Jiminez de Cisneros—

Men and women burnt alive, ...	3,564
Burnt in effigy, ...	2,232
Condemned to other punishments, . .	48,059

"By Adrian de Florencia—

Men and women burnt alive, . . .	1,620
Burnt in effigy, ...	560
Condemned to other punishments, . .	21,835

"Total number of men and women burnt alive, under the ministry of 45 holy Inquisitor-Generals,	35,534
Total number burnt in effigy, . . .	18,637
Total number condemned to other punishments,	293,533
"Grand total, ...	347,704

THE PAPAL MILLENNIUM.

As the true Kingdom of the true Christ is to last a tnousand years, so the Papal counterfeit looks back upon the period of its greatest prosperity, which began A. D. 800 and closed in the dawn of the present century, as the fulfilment of the Millennial reign foretold in Rev. 20. And the period since, in which Papacy has gradually lost

23-B

all of its temporal power, suffered many indignities from nations formerly its supporters, and been greatly despoiled of territories, incomes and liberties long claimed and possessed, Romanists regard as the "little season" of Rev. 20: 3, 7, 8, at the close of the Millennium, during which Satan was to be loosed.

And the dates which mark the beginning and the close of Papacy's Millennium of ignorance, superstition and fraud are clearly shown in history. A Roman Catholic writer* thus refers to the beginning of this religious empire: "The coronation of Charlemagne as Emperor of the West, by Pope Leo., A. D. 800, was really the commencement of the Holy Roman Empire."†

Although Papacy was organized, as a religious system, long before, and was even "set up" in temporal power in A. D. 539, yet it was Charlemagne who first actually bestowed and formally recognized the *temporal dominion* of the pope. As Charlemagne was the first emperor over the "Holy Roman Empire," A. D. 800, so Francis II. was the last, and he voluntarily surrendered his title in A. D. 1806.‡ As, prior to the year 800, Papacy was rising, supported by the Roman "beast" (people) and by its "horns"

---

* The Chair of St. Peter.

† "*The Holy Roman Empire*" was the title of the great political institution of the middle ages. It had its start in Charlemagne. Fisher's Universal History, page 262, describes it thus: "In theory it was the union of the world-state and the world-church,—an undivided community under Emperor and Pope, its heaven-appointed [?] secular and spiritual heads." And, since the popes, as in Christ's stead, anointed the emperors, it follows that they were the real heads of it.

‡ "By the battle of Marengo, 1800, and of Austerlitz, 1805, Germany was twice laid prostrate at the feet of Napoleon. The main result of the latter defeat was the establishment of the Confederation of the Rhine, under the protectorate of the French ruler. *This event put an end to the old German or* [*Holy*] *Roman Empire*, after a duration of a thousand years."—*White's Universal History, page 508.*

(powers), so since 1800 it has been cast off from temporal authority over kings and peoples, and has been torn and pillaged by those who formerly gave it support. (Rev. 17:16, 17.) To-day, though still the recipient of honors, and still possessed of a wide influence over the consciences of the people, Papacy bemoans its loss of everything resembling temporal dominion.

The careful student will note four periods, more or less distinctly marked, in the development and exaltation of Antichrist, and the same number distinctly marking its fall. In its development the four dates are:—

1st. In Paul's day, about A. D. 50, a beginning of the secret working of the iniquitous ambition was the start.

2nd. Papacy, "the Man of Sin," was *organized* as a hierarchy; *i. e.*, the church came to an organized condition, and the popes came to be recognized as the Head, representing Christ, reigning in the church and over the nations, gradually, from about A. D. 300 to 494.*

3rd. The time when the popes *began* to exercise civil authority and power, as will hereafter be shown, A. D. 539. (Vol. III., Chap. iii.)

---

* The popedom struggled long for mastery as the head of the church, and gradually obtained recognition and dominion; and that this dominion was generally recognized as early as A. D. 494, is clearly shown by the Romanist writer of *The Chair of St. Peter*, page 128. After giving in detail acknowledgments of the Roman Bishop as supreme pontiff by various councils, bishops, emperors, etc., he summarizes thus:—

"These words were written as far back as the year of our Lord 494. . . . On the whole, then, it is clear, from the foregoing authentic evidence, that the primacy of the Chair of St. Peter [the Bishopric of Rome] had so far *developed itself* in the fifth century, that the pope was then universally regarded as the center of Christian unity—the Supreme Ruler and Teacher of God's church, the Prince of Bishops, the Final Arbiter of appeals in ecclesiastical causes from all parts of the world, and the Judge and Moderator of General Councils, over which he presided by his legates."

4th. The time of exaltation, A. D. 800, when, as already shown, the "Holy Roman Empire" was formed, and the pope, crowning Charlemagne emperor, was recognized as himself King of kings, Emperor of emperors, "another God, on earth."

The four periods of the fall of papal influence are as follows:—

1st. The period of the Reformation, which may be said to have had its beginning about A. D. 1400, in the writings of Wycliffe,—followed by Huss, Luther and others.

2nd. The period of Napoleon's success, the degradation of the popes, and the casting aside finally of the title "Emperor of the Holy Roman Empire," by Francis II., A. D. 1800–1806.

3rd. The final rejection of the pope as ruler over Rome and the so-called Papal States of Italy, by the pope's subjects and the King of Italy, A. D. 1870, by which Antichrist is left without the slightest temporal authority.

4th. The final extinction of this counterfeit hierarchy, near the close of the "Day of wrath" and judgment already begun—which will close, as shown by the "Times of the Gentiles," with the year A. D. 1914.

IS THERE ROOM FOR DOUBT?

We have traced Antichrist's rise, out of an apostasy or "falling away" in the Christian Church; we have heard its blasphemous claim to be Christ's Kingdom and that its pope is Vicegerent of Christ—"another God, on earth;" we have heard its great swelling words of blasphemy, arrogating to itself titles and powers belonging to the true Lord of lords and King of kings; we have seen how terribly it fulfilled the prediction, "He shall wear out the saints;" we have seen that the truth, crushed and deformed, would have been completely buried under error, superstition and priestcraft, had not the Lord, at the proper moment, prevented by raising up reformers, thus helping his saints—as it is written, "They that understand among the people shall instruct many; yet they shall fall by the sword, and by flame, by captivity, and by spoil, many days. Now when they shall fall, they shall be holpen with a little help."—Dan. 11:33, 34.

In view of all this testimony, is there room for doubt that it was concerning Papacy that the apostles and prophets were inspired to write, describing minutely as they do its prominent characteristics? We think there should remain no doubt in any unbiased mind that Papacy is the Antichrist, the Man of Sin ; and that no one man could possibly fulfil the predictions. Papacy's unparalleled success, as a counterfeit Christ, deceiving the whole world, has amply fulfilled our Master's prediction, when, after referring to his own rejection, he said, "If another shall come [boastingly] in his own name, *him ye will receive.*"—John 5:43.

It will be observed, no doubt with surprise, by many, that in our examination of the subject we have in general omitted reference to villainies, gross immoralities, on the part of the popes and other officials, and to the dark deeds of *"expediency"* practiced by the Jesuits and other secret orders, who do all sorts of detective work for Papacy. We have omitted these intentionally, not because they are untrue, for even Roman Catholic writers acknowledge many of them ; but because our line of argument does not require these evidences. We have shown that the Papal Hierarchy (even if it were composed of the most moral and upright of men—which is not the case, as all history testifies) is the Man of Sin, the Antichrist, the counterfeit and misrepresentative of Christ's Millennial Kingdom, skilfully arranged so as to deceive.

The words of Macaulay, the English historian, serve to show that some without special prophetic light can see Papacy's wonderful system ;—the *counterfeit* of the most wonderful of all systems, the Kingdom of God, yet to come.

He says :—" It is impossible to deny that the polity of the Church of Rome is *the very masterpiece of human* [we would say Satanic] *wisdom*. In truth, nothing but such a polity could, against such assaults, have borne up such doctrines. The experience of twelve hundred eventful years, the ingenuity and patient care of forty generations of statesmen, have improved that polity to such perfection, that among the contrivances of political ability it occupies the highest place."

ANTICHRIST'S FINAL END.

We have traced Papacy to the present time, to the Day of the Lord—the time of Immanuel's *presence*. This Man of Sin has been developed, has done his awful work, has been smitten with the sword of the Spirit—the Word of God. The spirit of Christ's mouth has rendered him *powerless* to persecute the saints openly and generally, no matter how strong the desire ; and now we ask, What next? What says the Apostle concerning Antichrist's end?

In 2 Thess. 2 :8–12, the Apostle Paul declares concerning Antichrist :—" Whom the Lord Jesus will *consume* with the spirit of his mouth, and annihilate with the *bright shining of his presence*." The light of truth is to penetrate every subject. By exposing rights and wrongs it will lead into the great struggle between these principles, and between the human exponents of each—causing the great time of trouble and wrath. In this struggle, wrong and evil shall fall, and right and truth shall triumph. Among other evils now to be finally and utterly destroyed is Antichrist, with which nearly every evil, of theory and practice, is more or less directly connected. And it will be this bright-shining, this sunlight from the Lord's presence, which will produce the " day of trouble," because of and in which Antichrist, with every other evil system, will be destroyed. "Whose presence is with [accompanied by or during] an energetic operation of Satan [Satanic energy and action] with all power, and signs, and lying delusions, and with every iniquitous deception for those perishing; because they did not receive the love of the truth, that they might be preserved. And for this reason God will send to them a deluding power, that they might believe the error: so that all not believing the truth, but taking pleasure in iniquity, may be judged" unworthy to share the Millennial Kingdom as joint-heirs with Christ.

We understand these words to imply that in the time of the Lord's *presence* (the present time—since 1874), through this Antichrist system (one of the principal of Satan's agencies for deceiving and controlling the world), as well as through all his other agencies, the devil will make a most desperate resistance to the new order of things about to be established. He will take advantage of every little circumstance, and all the inherited weaknesses and selfishness of the human family, to enlist their hearts and hands and pens in this final struggle against liberty and the full elucidation of truth. Prejudices will be enkindled where, if the truth were clearly seen, none would exist; and passionate zeal will be evoked, and partisan unions formed, which will deceive and mislead many. And this will be so, not because God has not made the truth clear enough to guide all the fully consecrated, but because those who will be deceived were not sufficiently in earnest in seeking out and using the truth provided as "meat in due season." And thus it will be manifested that the class misled received not the truth *in the love of it*, but rather through custom, formality or fear. And the Apostle's assurance seems to be that, in this final death-struggle of Antichrist, notwithstanding he shall seem to gain increased power in the world by new stratagems, deceptions and combinations, yet the true Lord of earth, the King of kings, in the time of his *presence*, will prevail; and shall finally, during the great time of trouble, utterly annihilate Antichrist and destroy forever his power and deceptions.

As to the exact form in which this closing struggle should be expected, we can only make suggestions, based largely upon the symbolic views of the same, given in Revelation. We anticipate the gradual formation throughout the world of two great parties—from both of which the faithful, overcoming saints will stand separate. These two great parties will be composed on the one side of Socialists, Free-thinkers, Infidels, discontents, and true liberty-lovers whose eyes are beginning to open to the facts of the case as they relate both to political and religious mis-government and despotism: on the other side will be gradually associated the opponents of human liberty and equality—Emperors, Kings, Aristocrats; and in close sympathy with these will stand the counterfeit of God's Kingdom, Antichrist, supporting and being supported by earth's civil despots. We expect, too, that Antichrist's policy will be somewhat modified and softened to seek to win back into sympathy and practical co-operation (not actual union) extremists of all Protestant denominations, who even now are panting for a nominal *union* with each other and with Rome—forgetful that the only true union is that produced and continued by the truth, and not by creeds, conventions and laws. Improbable as this co-operation of Protestants and Catholics may seem to some, we see unmistakable signs of its rapid approach. It is being hastened by the secret workings of Papacy among its people, whereby such politicians as are willing to co-operate with Papacy are assisted into prominent positions in governmental affairs.

Laws may be expected soon through which, gradually, personal liberty will be curtailed, under the plea of *neces-*

sity and the public welfare; until, one step after another being taken, it will finally be necessary to formulate some *"simple law of religion;"* and thus Church and State may be in a measure united, in governing the United States of America. These laws, simple as they can be made, to suit all so-called *"orthodox"* (*i. e.*, popular) religious views, will be calculated to repress and prevent further growth in grace, and in the knowledge now "meat in due season." The plea will probably be, the prevention of socialism, infidelity, and political eruption, of the lower and the independent classes.

Evidently, in the near future, as a part of its trouble, and even before the severity of the great trouble of this "day of wrath" has burst upon the world and wrecked the entire social fabric of earth (preparatory to the new and better one promised under the true Christ), there will be a severe hour of trial and testing of the truly consecrated Church, much as it was in the days of Papacy's triumph; only now the methods of persecution will be more refined and will comport better with the more civilized methods of the present day: the spikes and pincers and racks will have more the form of sarcasm and denunciations, restrictions of liberties, and social, financial and political boycotting. But concerning this, and the new combinations which Antichrist will form in this final struggle against the establishment of the true Millennial Kingdom, more anon.

In concluding this chapter we desire to again impress our readers with the fact that Papacy is the Antichrist, not because of its moral obliquity, but because it is the *counterfeit* of the true Christ and the true Kingdom. It is because of a failure to realize this fact that many Protestants will be deceived into co-operation with Papacy in opposition to the true King of Glory.

FAITHFUL UNTIL DEATH.

———

"Am I a soldier of the cross,
  A follower of the Lamb?
And shall I fear to own his cause,
  Or blush to speak his name?

"Must I be borne to Paradise
  On flowery beds of ease,
While others fought to win the prize,
  And sailed through bloody seas?

"Are there no foes for me to face?
  Must I not stem the flood?
Is this vain world a friend to grace,
  To help me on to God?

"Sure I must fight if I would reign.
  Increase my courage, Lord.
I'll bear the toil, endure the pain,
  Supported by thy Word.

"Thy saints in all this glorious war
  Shall conquer, though they die.
They see the triumph from afar,
  By faith they bring it nigh.

"When thine illustrious day shall rise,
  And all thy saints shall shine,
And shouts of vict'ry rend the skies,
  The glory, Lord, be th'ne."

THE TIME IS AT HAND.

THE TIME IS AT HAND for the establishment of the Redeemer's Kingdom. This is the concurrent testimony of the foregoing chapters. Nothing intervenes. We are already living in the seventh millennium—since Oct. 1872. The lease of power to the Gentile kingdoms must terminate with the year 1914. The great antitypical Jubilee, the Times of Restitution of all things, had its beginning in the year 1874, when the presence of the great Restorer was also due. The manner of his return and the character of his work up to the present time are in exact correspondence with the details of prophecy thus far. The closing features of this dispensation, now observed, are in perfect accord with those of its Jewish type. The Elias has come, and is received as foretold ; and the predicted curse—the great time of trouble—is already impending. The Man of Sin has been revealed in all his hateful deformity, and has almost run his predicted course. The establishment of the long promised Kingdom of Messiah is therefore the great event just before us. Not only so, but its establishment is now in progress. The necessary undermining and overturning of the kingdoms of this world under the prince of darkness—"the prince of this world"—are now visible to some extent even to the natural eye of the children of this world, but are much more clearly seen, as they should be, by those who look upon transpiring events through the field-glass of God's Word, which at proper focus brings distant matters and results close to view, and enables God's children to recognize the minutiæ which the natural eye cannot discern, as well as the leading features which the world's statesmen and philosophers see in but dim outline. Even the worldly-wise can discern the social trouble fomenting, as the dominance of ignorance gives place to greater general knowledge and personal independence. And though they vainly hope for some unknown and unexpected favcrable turn of affairs to occur, yet, as described in the Scriptures, their hearts are failing them for fear and for looking after the things coming upon the earth—because they see the shaking of the symbolic heavens now in progress, and perceive that with such a shaking and removal of the power of error, superstitions and religious restraints from the masses of the people, violence and anarchy must result.

But, from God's standpoint, from which the waking ones of the household of faith are privileged to look, not only the severity of the trouble is more distinct, but also the blessed results, which under God's providence it shall subserve by ushering in the Millennial Kingdom. And this is a comfort, and more than an offset for all the tribulation, even though we or our dearest ones may share it.

That we might now have the comfort of this knowledge, and not be in doubt and perplexity, was but part of the object in the giving of the time-prophecies. Another object was, that, as the representatives of that kingdom among men, we should be aware of the great dispensational changes now in progress, and able to bear testimony before the world, regarding God's plan, etc., which, though unheeded now, will greatly benefit them by and by, and help them the sooner to recognize the Lord's presence in the great day of wrath, drawing on. Another object is, that the faithful, thus armed and strengthened by God's Word, may be enabled to stand firm, when so many will be falling into infidelity and various other deceptive errors, which will soon sweep over "Christendom." Another object is, to give force and point to the entire Plan of the Ages: for it is a general experience that, while the first glimpse of God's gracious plan for blessing the whole world through the Church, during the Millennial age, fills the hearts and enlists the zeal of his faithful children to the utmost, yet as their efforts to enlighten others are coldly received, and they find that only a very few, comparatively, have "an ear to hear," the tendency is to settle down to the quiet enjoyment of the precious knowledge, in such a manner as will bring the least reproach and opposition.

Seeing this, our natural weakness, the Lord has provided time-prophecies as a spur, to quicken and awaken us fully, and keep us active in his service. Being already in the "harvest" time, harvest work should engage the time, service and thoughts of the Lord's servants, who now, like the disciples at the first advent, are to do the reaping work. (John 4: 35–38.) Let us each seek to do what our hands find to do, in obedience to the instructions of the great Chief Reaper. But, with reference more particularly to the time and order of events in this "harvest," we must refer the reader to the succeeding volume of this series, wherein the conclusions of the foregoing and other time prophecies are brought to a focus, and the various foretold signs and corroborative testimonies of the Master's presence and the progress of his work are marked, proving—that the "Time of the End" has come; that the Days of Waiting for the Kingdom are fulfilled; that the Cleansing of the Sanctuary is accomplished; that the great Harvest Work is in progress; that the Re-gathering of Israel is apparent; that the Battle of the Great Day of God Almighty is impending; and that the complete establishment of the glorious Kingdom of God at the time appointed, the end of the Times of the Gentiles, is an unquestionable certainty; and showing, further, the work of the saints during the harvest; marking the close of the "high calling," and the "change" of those saints who "are alive and remain;" and showing, also, that the Great Pyramid of Egypt is one of God's Witnesses (Isa. 19:19, 20), whose wonderful message is a full and complete corroboration of God's plan of the ages, together with its times and seasons.

MILLENNIAL DAWN.

"All things are onward moving!—Let the blessed time begin!
The Old is swiftly passing, and the New is coming in!
The golden bells are ringing, and the pageant sweeps along
Like an army that is speeding to the measure of a song.

"Dark theories now are waning: they are weak to build upon;
The light is on the hill-tops, and Truth is marching on:—
Many landmarks are but shadows, which now fade and flee away
Before the mighty forces that are coming in to-day.

"O brother, why this waiting? And sister, why so mute?
Up with the early sunshine! Watch for the golden fruit!
O poet, why this sorrow? O minstrel, why this hush?
And painter, why so long delay the heavenly tint and blush?

"Up with the larks of morning! Up with the rising sun!
Waiting not for noon-day, nor halting when begun!
For everything is moving; let the blessed time begin!
The Old is swiftly passing, and the New is coming in!

"The heavenly light is spreading,—spreading at the King's command!
It is spreading in its glory, speeding onward through the land.
Human creeds are downward tending; let them droop and fade away.
Following in the dawning sunlight, we can see a better way.

"Oh, let us all be ready for the work we have to do,—
Toiling late and early, for the laborers are few!
Reaping, as instructed, in the morning light;
Reaping in the harvest field,—toiling for the RIGHT!

"All things are onward moving! Let earth's Jubilee begin!
The Old is swiftly passing, and the New is coming in!
It is coming! Oh 'tis coming! My raptured eyes behold!
The light is on the hill-tops, the Shepherd with his Fold."

INDEX

— TO —

SCRIPTURE CITATIONS

— OF —

SCRIPTURE STUDIES, SERIES II.

367

"GO YE ALSO INTO THE VINEYARD."

" He that reapeth receiveth wages, and gathereth fruit."
—*John* 4:36.

All interested in the subject of this volume, and considering its presentations to be "meat in due season," will feel more or less constrained to become servants of the truth, and to bear the "things new and old" to yet others of the "household of faith." Your measure of zeal for such service will of course measure your activities in its service, and determine how much of time, influence, means, etc., you will devote to its spread. We are glad to coöperate with all, that those who love much may do much, and that those who love some may do something, in the name of the great Shepherd and in the interest of his sheep.

To this end we wish you to know that special provision has been made whereby you may be a co-laborer in this work, regardless of whether you have financial means to invest or not. We have quite a variety of excellent tracts, which we supply free and in large quantities for judicious circulation. We also publish twice a month a 16 page journal, THE WATCH TOWER, and desire that our list should bear your name, if you are interested. If interested in this volume you will undoubtedly be interested in the journal, which is edited by the same pen, and we are prepared to supply you with it upon your own terms; —you may have it on credit if it is not convenient to pay for it in advance, and if never able to pay for it we will, upon application, cancel the indebtedness. If you have no prospect of being able to pay for it you will be welcome to it free as one of the "Lord's poor," on application, and upon renewal of the same yearly. If you can afford to pay the price is $1 (4s.) a year.

We have various helps for Bible study, which we supply to all who are on our WATCH TOWER list at extremely low prices—these include various translations of the Bible, Concordances, etc., and especially the SCRIPTURE STUDIES series,—"THE BIBLE KEYS."

COLPORTEURING AND LOANING THE STUDIES.

Some have numbers of friends to whom they take pleasure in supplying the STUDIES *gratis;* others keep a quantity at hand which they constantly loan out amongst their friends, after the manner of a circulating library; and still others enter the Colporteur work, as being one of the most favorable opportunities to them for serving the truth to others, travelling from town to town introducing the "Bible Keys," soliciting orders and delivering the books. Our Society does all in its power to facilitate these various methods of circulating the truth, encouraging each to serve the cause to the extent of his zeal and ability, according to his own preference; assisting in the matter very materially by supplying the books at remarkably low prices. See page 2 of THE WATCH TOWER for wholesale rates to subscribers, and if the Colporteur work appeals to you, write for "Hints to Colporteurs."

We shall be glad to hear from you, and to coöperate with you, and we assure you that you will find a blessing in every sacrifice you may make on behalf of the truth. Very truly, Your fellow-servants,

INTERNATIONAL
BIBLE STUDENTS ASSOCIATION

BROOKLYN, LONDON, MELBOURNE, BARMEN-ELBERFELD,
OREBRO, CHRISTIANIA

THINGS YOU WANT TO KNOW

——— AS ———

CHRISTIAN BIBLE STUDENTS

THERE ARE EVIDENCES THAT—

—Six thousand Years from Adam ended in A. D. 1872.
—The Date of our Lord's Birth was October, B. C. 2.
—The Date of Annunciation to Mary, Dec. 25th, B. C. 3.
—The Date of our Lord's Baptism was October, A. D. 29.
—The Date of our Lord's Crucifixion, April, A. D. 33.
—The "Seventy Weeks" of Israel's favor ended A. D. 36.
—The Jewish Age "Harvest," was 40 years, A. D. 30 to 70.
—The Christian Age "Harvest," 40 years, A. D. 1874–1914.
—The Jewish Jubilees were Typical of the "Time of Restitution of all Things."—Acts 3:19–21.
—The Typical Jubilees Mark the Date of their Antitype.
—The "Times of the Gentiles" will end with A. D. 1914.
—The Jewish Age, in its Length, its Ceremonies, etc., Typified the Realities of the Christian Age and its Length.
—Elias or "Elijah the Prophet" was a Type.—How fulfilled.
—The Antichrist Has Come!—What? When? Where?

———

These subjects and many others deeply interesting to "the Household of Faith," and "Meat in due season" to all who love and study God's Word, can be had in

"The Time is at Hand"

(In English, German, Swedish, Dano-Norwegian, French and Greek.)

380 PAGES—CLOTH BOUND, 35 CENTS, POSTPAID ; DELIVERED BY COLPORTEURS, 35 CENTS.

———

ADDRESS ORDERS TO PUBLISHERS

INTERNATIONAL
BIBLE STUDENTS ASSOCIATION

BROOKLYN, LONDON, MELBOURNE, BARMEN-ELBERFELD,
OREBRO, CHRISTIANIA

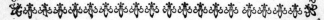

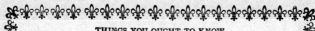

THINGS YOU OUGHT TO KNOW

—— AS ——

CHRISTIAN BIBLE STUDENTS

DO YOU KNOW THAT

—We are now living in "the Time of the End" of this Gospel age?

—Our epoch is "the Day of God's Preparation" for the Millennial age?

—The "Days of Waiting" are ended and the "Cleansing of the Sanctuary"—the Church,—the separating of its Wheat and Tares, is now in progress?

—This is the reason for the beginning of the Return of Divine Favor to Fleshly Israel—blinded for centuries—to permit the gathering of an elect class from among the Gentiles?

—This favor is gradually taking shape and known as Zionism?

—Immanuel's Kingdom is now in process of establishment?

—The Great Pyramid in Egypt is a Witness to all these events of the ages and of our day—testifying in symbols?

—The Pyramid's downward passage under "A Draconis" symbolizes the course of Sin? Its First Ascending Passage symbolizes the Jewish age? Its Grand Gallery symbolizes the Gospel age? Its Upper Step symbolizes the approaching period of tribulation and anarchy,"Judgments,"upon Christendom? Its King's Chamber the Divine Nature, etc., of the Overcoming Church—the Christ, Head and Body? Its Ante-Chamber the Correction in Righteousness of the "Great Company" etc.? Its Queen's Chamber those of Israel and the world who attain Restitution?

All these interesting topics with ten Pyramid illustrations can be had in

"Thy Kingdom Come"

(In English, German, Swedish, Dano-Norwegian and Greek,)

380 PAGES—CLOTH BOUND 35 CENTS, POSTPAID; DELIVERED BY COLPORTEURS, 35 CENTS.

ADDRESS ORDERS TO PUBLISHERS

INTERNATIONAL BIBLE STUDENTS ASSOCIATION

BROOKLYN, LONDON, MELBOURNE, BARMEN-ELBERFELD, OREBRO, CHRISTIANIA

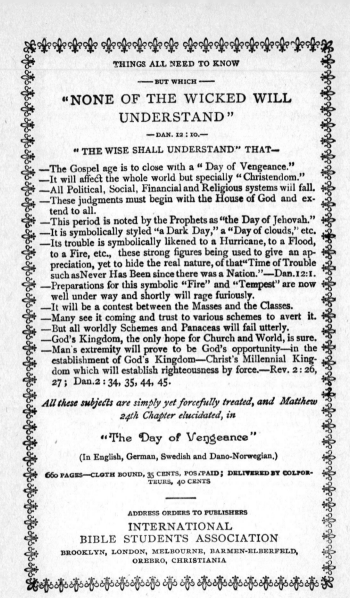

THINGS ALL NEED TO KNOW

—— BUT WHICH ——

"NONE OF THE WICKED WILL UNDERSTAND"

—DAN. 12 : 10.—

" THE WISE SHALL UNDERSTAND" THAT—

—The Gospel age is to close with a " Day of Vengeance."
—It will affect the whole world but specially "Christendom."
—All Political, Social, Financial and Religious systems will fall.
—These judgments must begin with the House of God and extend to all.
—This period is noted by the Prophets as "the Day of Jehovah."
—It is symbolically styled "a Dark Day," a "Day of clouds," etc.
—Its trouble is symbolically likened to a Hurricane, to a Flood, to a Fire, etc., these strong figures being used to give an appreciation, yet to hide the real nature, of that "Time of Trouble such as Never Has Been since there was a Nation."—Dan. 12:1.
—Preparations for this symbolic "Fire" and "Tempest" are now well under way and shortly will rage furiously.
—It will be a contest between the Masses and the Classes.
—Many see it coming and trust to various schemes to avert it.
—But all worldly Schemes and Panaceas will fail utterly.
—God's Kingdom, the only hope for Church and World, is sure.
—Man's extremity will prove to be God's opportunity—in the establishment of God's Kingdom—Christ's Millennial Kingdom which will establish righteousness by force.—Rev. 2 : 26, 27 ; Dan. 2 : 34, 35, 44, 45.

All these subjects are simply yet forcefully treated, and Matthew 24th Chapter elucidated, in

"The Day of Vengeance"

(In English, German, Swedish and Dano-Norwegian.)

660 PAGES—CLOTH BOUND, 35 CENTS, POSTPAID ; DELIVERED BY COLPORTEURS, 40 CENTS

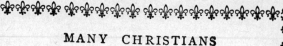

MANY CHRISTIANS

ARE

IN GREAT PERPLEXITY ON TOPICS TREATED
SCRIPTURALLY IN A VOLUME
ENTITLED

"THE NEW CREATION."

—It throws new and helpful light on the Creative Week of Genesis.

—Recognizing the true Church of Christ, begotten of the Spirit as the New Creation, it proceeds to explain Scripturally the steps of Grace Divine—Justification, Sanctification, and Deliverance in the First Resurrection.

—It takes up in order the duties and obligations of the New Creation—toward the Lord, toward each other, toward earthly friends and neighbors, toward parents, children, husbands, wives, etc.

—The Lord's Memorial Supper or Sacrament is discussed and explained: what it is and what it is not should be clearly discerned by all of God's people.

—Baptism is the topic of an entire chapter. The many mistakes of nearly all denominations are pointed out in kindly spirit, and then the true Baptism is set forth in convincing style,—indisputable, incontrovertible.

—The foes and besetments of the New Creation are carefully considered, and the Scriptural method of overcoming them; also the present and the future inheritance of the saints.

(English and German)

740 PAGES—CLEAR TYPE, CLOTH BOUND, 35 CENTS, POSTPAID; DELIVERED BY COLPORTEURS, 40 CENTS

ADDRESS ORDERS TO PUBLISHERS,

INTERNATIONAL
BIBLE STUDENTS ASSOCIATION

BROOKLYN, LONDON, MELBOURNE, BARMEN-ELBERFELD,
OREBRO, CHRISTIANIA

THE WATCH TOWER
—AND—
HERALD OF CHRIST'S PRESENCE,

This journal, edited by the author of "STUDIES IN THE SCRIPTURES," should regularly visit all who have the slightest interest in the topics discussed in this and the other volumes of the "SCRIPTURE STUDIES." It is issued twice a month, 16 pages, at one dollar (4s.) a year in advance.

That *none* of the interested may be without it, the arrangement is that those who need may have it on credit on application, while those too poor to pay may receive it regularly *free* by stating the facts and making request each May. All new tracts are sent to THE WATCH TOWER list, which it is desired shall represent all interested in present truth, the "harvest" message.

German, Swedish, Dano-Norwegian, and French editions of THE WATCH TOWER are also published regularly.

INTERNATIONAL
BIBLE STUDENTS ASSOCIATION
BROOKLYN, LONDON, MELBOURNE, BARMEN - ELBERFELD, OREBRO, CHRISTIANIA

This Society never solicits donations, but it uses voluntary contributions as wisely and economically as possible in the propagation of Christian knowledge along the lines presented in "STUDIES IN THE SCRIPTURES." It yearly circulates tons of tracts and papers free, through the mails and through voluntary agents.

It justifies that portion of its name which relates to the Bible— (not by publishing Bibles, nor by circulating them gratuitously, but) —by supplying Bibles and Bible-study helps at wholesale prices; and often below the usual wholesale rates. We mention a few of these on succeeding pages, of course ranking "STUDIES IN THE SCRIPTURES" as the most important helps or "Bible Keys," and THE WATCH TOWER, semi-monthly, their efficient supplement.

Readers who desire to cooperate in the circulation of "STUDIES IN THE SCRIPTURES" will be supplied at cost prices, and can have tracts ad libitum. Write us respecting this!

PEOPLES PULPIT TRACTS
TREATING LIVE TOPICS, SUPPLIED FREE.

Samples will be sent free to any one requesting them, and quantities for free circulation will be supplied free to all subscribers to THE WATCH TOWER, they being considered working members of the Society, whether they specially contribute to its funds or not. Send for free samples.

THE EMPHATIC DIAGLOTT.

This work, widely and favorably known, is a Greek New Testament, with a literal, word-for-word, English translation, under the Greek text. It also gives an *arranged* English translation in a side column. Furthermore, it indicates the grammatical emphasis of the Greek text, so important yet so little appreciated, and not shown at all in the common version.

This very valuable work, published under the author's copyright by the Fowler & Wells Co., New York City until now (the year 1902), has been sold by them at $4.00 in cloth and $5.00 in half-leather binding. For several years a friend, an earnest Bible student, desirous of assisting the readers of our Society's publications, has supplied them through us at a greatly reduced price; now he has purchased the copyright and plates from the Fowler & Wells Co., and presented the same to our Society as a gift, under our assurance that the gift will be used for the furthering of the Truth to the extent of our ability, by such a reduction of the price as will permit the poor of the Lord's flock to have this help in the study of the Word.

REDUCED PRICES.—These will be sold *with* THE WATCH TOWER *only*. In cloth binding $1.50 (6s. 3d.)—includes postage and one year's subscription, new or renewal, to W. T. On thin paper, in full morocco leather, divinity circuit, red under gold edges, silk sewed-leather lined, $2.50 (10s. 6d.)—includes postage and one year's subscription to W. T.

YOUNG'S ANALYTICAL CONCORDANCE.

—GREEK, HEBREW AND ENGLISH—

This work is at once a Greek and Hebrew Lexicon, giving the meaning of the original terms in English, also a Concordance, giving all the words of Scripture, and the words which they translate. The value of the work is becoming more apparent daily, as *theorists* attempt to palm off private interpretations under the guise of a better definition of the *original*."

In this superb volume every word is arranged under its own Hebrew and Greek original, exhibiting 311,000 references and 30,000 various readings. Its size is large quarto: 1094 pages. Our price is $6.00, delivered, by mail or express, and the purchaser may order any four volumes of SCRIPTURE STUDIES cloth bound, *as a premium*. This is the "Author's Edition," and the latest revision. For prices in Great Britain, apply to the British Branch.

STRONG'S EXHAUSTIVE CONCORDANCE.

—GREEK, HEBREW AND ENGLISH.—

An excellent work similar to yet differing from "Young's." Not many will have use for both. Some prefer one, some the other. In cloth, $3.00; half leather, $5.00; postage, 65 cents. For prices in Great Britain, apply to the British Branch.

INTERNATIONAL
BIBLE STUDENTS ASSOCIATION

BROOKLYN, LONDON, MELBOURNE, BARMEN-ELBERFELD,
OREBRO, CHRISTIANIA

WHAT SAY
THE SCRIPTURES
ABOUT....

Spiritism?

PROOFS THAT IT IS DEMONISM.

—ALSO—

"THE SPIRITS IN PRISON" AND WHY ARE THEY THERE?

———

THE necessity for this little brochure lies in the fact that Spiritism is showing an increased activity of late, and meeting with considerable success in entrapping Christians who are feeling dissatisfied with their present attainments and craving spiritual food and better foundation for faith.

The aim is to show the unscripturalness of Spiritism, and to point those who hunger and thirst for truth in the direction of God's Word—the counsel of the Most High. "Thou shalt guide me with thy counsel, and afterward receive me to glory."—Psa. 73:24.

———

119 pages; in paper covers, 10 cents (5d.)

———

ADDRESS :—

INTERNATIONAL
BIBLE STUDENTS ASSOCIATION
BROOKLYN, LONDON, MELBOURNE, BARMEN-ELBERFELD,
OREBRO, CHRISTIANIA

WHAT SAY THE SCRIPTURES
ABOUT HELL?

AN EXAMINATION OF EVERY TEXT OF SCRIPTURE IN WHICH THE
WORD " HELL " IS FOUND.

A CORRECT understanding of the subject of this booklet is almost a necessity to Christian steadfastness. For centuries it has been the teaching of " orthodoxy," of all shades, that God, before creating man, had created a great abyss of fire and terrors, capable of containing all the billions of the human family which he purposed to bring into being; that this abyss he had named " hell;" and that all of the promises and threatenings of the Bible were designed to deter as many as possible (a " little flock ") from such wrong-doing as would make this awful place their perpetual home.

While glad to see superstitions fall, and truer ideas of the great, and wise, and just, and loving Creator prevail, we are alarmed to notice that the *tendency* with all who abandon this long revered doctrine is toward doubt, scepticism, infidelity. Why should this be the case, when the mind is merely being delivered from an error?—do you ask? Because Christian people have so long been taught that the foundation for this awful blasphemy against God's character and government is deeplaid and firmly fixed in the Word of God— the Bible—and consequently, to whatever degree their belief in " hell " is shaken, to that extent their faith in the Bible, as the revelation of the true God, is shaken also;—so that those who have dropped their belief in a " hell," of some kind of endless torment, are often open infidels, and scoffers at God's Word.

Guided by the Lord's providence to a realization that the Bible has been slandered, as well as its divine Author, and that, rightly understood, it teaches nothing on this subject derogatory to God's character nor to an intelligent reason, we have attempted in this booklet to lay bare the Scripture teaching on this subject that thereby faith in God and his Word may be reëstablished, on a better, a reasonable foundation. Indeed, it is our opinion that whoever shall hereby find that his false view rested upon human misconceptions and misinterpretations will, at the same time, learn to trust hereafter less to his own and other men's imaginings, and, by faith, to grasp more firmly the Word of God, which is able to make wise unto salvation; and on this mission, under God's providence, it is sent forth.

PRICE 10 CENTS [5d.] PER COPY.—88 PAGES.

Special wholesale rates to colporteurs and those who desire to aid in circulating these booklets widely.

ADDRESS :—

INTERNATIONAL
BIBLE STUDENTS ASSOCIATION
BROOKLYN, LONDON, MELBOURNE, BARMEN-ELBERFELD,
OREBRO, CHRISTIANIA